£1.00 MAR

The BUMPER BOOK

of BRITISH LEFTIES

The BUMPER BOOK
of BRITISH LEFTIES

PAUL ROUTLEDGE

POLITICO'S

First published in Great Britain 2003
by Politico's Publishing, an imprint of
Methuen Publishing Limited
215 Vauxhall Bridge Road
London SW1V 1EJ

A catalogue record for this book is available from the British Library.

ISBN 1 84275 064 X
Printed and bound in Great Britain by Creative Print and Design

Contents

Introduction

The Left in Britain has for too long succumbed to fear of personality, assailed on one side by Tony Benn's insistence that politics is about policies not people, and on the other by the long shadow of the cult of Stalin. But the parties and the unions have their own heroes, mostly unsung, and villains, seldom solemnised in the annals of radicalism.

Often, the most they could ever expect was a brief mention in the obituaries section of the Labour Party annual conference report. And only then if they were acceptable to the leadership, even in death. Even that brief commemoration has gone – along with the annual report.

It is time to celebrate British Lefties, even those who have abused the country of the comrades for 'pelf and place' as the old socialist hymn has it. They, too, played a role. Some continue to do so, moving seamlessly between Old Labour and New when office beckons, and from the outside-left to comfortable berths in government.

The idea that the Left is a dour, mirthless territory is wholly false. Nobody told better jokes than Mick McGahey. And a lifetime of observing, talking to and drinking with men and women on the political Left in Britain cannot but lead to the conclusion that their sense of the absurd has been deeply underrated. This book sets out to remedy that error.

Not all of the events set down here are deliberately funny. Some, like the activities of the Cambridge school of spies, are desperately serious. But there is something comic even about Kim Philby, the philandering KGB agent. And the antics of semen-greedy Tom Driberg, the most flamboyant homosexual MP of the twentieth century, are simply damn good theatre. Not to mention the great disappearing act of Victor Grayson.

If these people were alive today, they would get an Arts Council grant for their one-man shows. Their performance politics should be applauded. It continues down to the present day, albeit in an attenuated form. They just don't make them like Jimmy Airlie, the hero of Clydeside, any more. Imagine a book entitled *Blair's Babes: The Entertainment Years*.

Amid the humour is sadness, sacrifice and grief. Many of the people in these pages gave their lives to fighting for the causes in which they believed, in some cases literally so. That, too, should be remembered with honour.

I make no apology for the eclectic nature of this collection. It is a personal, subjective list, and it makes no attempt to be definitive. For definition, go to the *Dictionary of Labour Biography* (edited by Greg Rosen and published by Politico's in 2002). For fun, praise, curiosity and blame, come here. That being my objective, I am compelled to include a number of apostates, partly to record their shameful conversion from the paths of Leftiousness, and also, where they are alive, in the hope of annoyance. They, too, contributed to the rich political heritage that Gordon Brown understands, but which leaves Tony Blair shaking his head in disbelief.

Some have been left out. The omissions are on the whole deliberate. After brief and superficial consideration, I decided that Neil Kinnock cannot yet be considered a Leftie. It is too early to make a judgement. Others disqualified themselves (rather as employers say that striking workers have dismissed themselves) on grounds of high seriousness, or pomposity. James Callaghan is the most prominent of this tribe, remembered only for his 'Crisis? What crisis?' remark, which would have been funny if he had actually said it.

There is scandal here. Labour shame has traditionally been held to be financial, rather than sexual – as if the Tories had somehow cornered the market in human frailty. But, as these pages show, there is plenty of evidence that, in matters erotic, the Left is no slouch. *Ergo*, Joe Ashton is not remembered for his time as Parliamentary Private Secretary to Tony Benn, but for the sorry fact that his political career ended in a Thai massage parlour somewhere off the M1 in Northamptonshire. Ron 'Afghan' Brown is still recollected as the man who showered with his lover at Westminster, and inspired the Sun headline 'I Never Stole Nonie's Knickers'.

There is also heroism. The courage of the early trade union pioneers. The sacrifice of socialists who went to fight Franco in the Spanish Civil War. And in our own time, the commitment of the Pentonville Five dockers who went to jail rather than submit to the diktat of Edward Heath's Industrial

Relations Court. As Jim Mortimer is wont to say: most British socialists of the present generation are very fortunate. They have never been in prison for their beliefs. I would go further. They have never been on strike, or sacked. They have never felt the hot breath of the bosses down their neck, or known what it is like to go home and tell your wife that the employer has locked you out. Or, worse still, blacklisted you. It is the suffering that defines the best.

On the other side of the coin, there is the prospect of fame and fortune. Being a Leftie can turn out to be a good business call. In the Thatcher years, many a good living was made on television by excoriating the Iron Lady. It was easier then. There were pricks to kick against. Making fun of Tony Blair and New Labour is more difficult, too much like punching a sponge. Rory Bremner does it hilariously, but since he has voted for all three main political parties he does not count as a proper Leftie. To qualify, you have to believe, or at least to have believed. Oh, well, to have put up a plausible show, anyway.

It goes without saying, but I shall say it anyway, that nothing in this book is actuated by malice. *The Bumper Book of British Lefties* is designed to show the human – all too human, sometimes – face of socialism. If it succeeds in that humble aim, then perhaps the sneerers and sceptics will have second thoughts.

I must confess that the word 'Leftiousness' is not an original coinage. It was first minted by Barrie Devney, Industrial Correspondent of the *Daily Express*, to describe the enemies of 'the forces of righteousness', which usually boiled down to the transient whim of Joe Gormley, in the National Union of Mineworkers. Thanks also to Francis Beckett, the political writer, for permission to quote from *Enemy Within: The Rise And Fall Of The Communist Party*, a highly readable account of the CPGB. Finally, I am grateful to my fellow industrial journalists and the Lefties I knew in my time as Labour Editor of *The Times* for the comradeship we enjoyed in the halcyon years of our trade. They provided the stories. Any faults of recollection are mine.

Paul Routledge, July 2003

A

DIANE ABBOTT became the first black woman MP in 1987, and this achievement obscured her strong credentials as a Leftie. But only briefly. Immediately after entering Parliament as the MP for Hackney North and Stoke Newington, a new seat, she joined the hard-Left Campaign Group, sympathising with causes such as **Tony Benn**'s Bill to ban foreign nuclear bases in the UK. **Baroness Falkender**, the former Downing Street fixer, described her 'a politically activist Eartha Kitt . . . she may purr her way to the top, but with left-wing claws like that, she is no pussy cat'. Abbott never made any secret of her politics. The daughter of a welder and a mental hospital worker, both Jamaican migrants, she was born in Paddington in 1953 and joined the Labour Party in 1971, moving directly into CND and the Campaign for Labour Party Democracy. After Newnham College, Cambridge (and a 2:2 in History), Abbott was a trainee civil servant in the Home Office, where she complained of being 'just one token black person in a fundamentally racist institution'. She also denied wearing a see-through blouse, while later confiding to *She* magazine that her finest half hour was a clothed lovemaking session with a naked man in a Cotswold field.

Abbott is often ready to defy the Labour leadership and follow her political conscience. So, she voted against renewal of the Prevention of Terrorism Act, backed abolition of the Special Branch and MI5, opposed the Gulf War and called on the government to cancel a victory parade. She backed the miners' strike in 1985, arguing that the law was used 'as it has been used in Ireland, used against the black community, used in colonial struggles since time immemorial, as a weapon of the British state against working people'.

Her rebellious nature, combined with a full-bodied sense of humour, did not endear her to the New Labour hierarchy. Early in the life of the new government, she incensed **Gordon Brown** with remarks about economic policy, and found herself no longer a member of the Treasury Select Committee. This she took in her stride, as she does most things.

JIMMY AIRLIE was a larger than life leader of men who adapted to the post-Communist era with more skill than most, largely through a showman's sense of humour that disarmed his critics. He could hold an audience in a bar, at a meeting, at a social event, in the palm of his hand, with a mixture of folksy wisdom and repartee. He had a machine-gun laugh to match a phenomenal repertoire of jokes and stories of the labour movement, often to the chagrin of 'moderates' who were the butt of his wit. It all began in the shipyards of the Clyde, the cradle of many a life on the Left. Airlie was born in Renfrew, near Glasgow, in 1935, the son of a boiler-maker. He served an apprenticeship with shipmakers Simon and Lobnitz, and became active in the engineering union as a young man.

After National Service, he also joined the Communist Party, and sprang to public prominence in the Upper Clyde Shipbuilders' 'work-in' in 1971 when the workforce of UCS refused to allow the Tory government to close down the yard with the loss of thousands of jobs. Prime Minister Edward Heath was forced to navigate a U-turn on his policy of no state money for 'lame duck' industries, supporting the UCS consortium until it could be rescued. Airlie, chairman of the UCS shop stewards' co-ordinating committee, was widely credited with being the brains of this quasi-revolutionary strategy, while fellow Communist **Jimmy Reid** was the public face of the work-in. However, he quit his role after the men at Govan Shipbuilders refused to pay a 50p a week levy to help redundant fellow-workers.

He was elected assistant divisional organiser of the AEU in 1979, and four years later became the first Communist to win election to the union's elite executive council, on which he served for the next two decades. The top post of president eluded him, but he was the union's best-known and respected figure. Airlie had a surprisingly flexible approach to industrial policy, arguing that workers did not pay him to conduct a revolution, but to get them the best possible deal. He derided 'fundamentalists' like Arthur Scargill, arguing that 'as a Communist I am well aware that long-term progress sometimes demands short-term sacrifice'. Airlie was the acknowledged leader of the Ford Motor Company's unionised workforce, which set bargaining bench-marks for the rest of industry. On one occasion, when Ford's top managers asked for a one-to-one meeting without shop stewards, he secured the backing of suspicious union militants, and when leaving the room put his head back round the door to wisecrack: 'Don't worry, lads. I'll not sell you down the river – unless it's absolutely necessary!' Airlie quit the CP as it was in the throes of disintegration in 1991, and joined the Labour Party. But his self-definition could scarcely be bettered. 'I am a Communist,' he once said. 'I have been a Communist all my life. My entire career has been devoted to advancing the cause of the working class. There is no substitute for principle. Principle is not a luxury. It is a necessity.'

Jimmy Airlie died in 1997.

BILL ALEXANDER was given the most effusive obituary that *The Times* ever awarded to a British Communist. A hero of the Spanish Civil War, he was also assistant general secretary of the CPGB in its postwar heyday. Alexander was born into a large Hampshire family, the son of a carpenter. As a chemistry student at Reading University, he met with Welsh hunger marchers *en route* to London, an encounter that changed his life. After graduating, he joined the Communist Party and was in the front line of the street battles against Oswald Mosley's blackshirts. When General Franco rose up against the Republican government in Madrid, Alexander did not hesitate. 'The people stood up to stem the tide of Fascism. I decided the natural thing for me was to go and help stop it there before it reached my home and family,' he said. Evading police controls in the UK and France designed to enforce the infamous Non-Intervention Agreement, he joined the British Battalion of the International Brigade and took part in the battles at Brunete and Teruel in 1937. Following the battalion's brilliant artillery performance at Teruel, Alexander was promoted to captain in the field and in 1938 took over as battalion commander. He was wounded in the shoulder and invalided home.

At the outbreak of the Second World War he joined the regular army, but was refused a commission. Following intervention in the Commons, the authorities relented and sent him to Sandhurst. He served with distinction in North Africa, Italy and Germany, rising once again to the rank of captain. Upon demobilisation, Alexander went to work full time for the party, in Liverpool, the Midlands and Wales, before being called to King Street as AGS in 1959. He quit party work to teach in the late sixties, but remained a Communist until his death at the age of 90 in 2000. He spent the last thirty years of his life sustaining the memory of the Spanish Civil War and the two thousand Britons who risked everything to fight Fascism: 526 of them died. A rugged, courageous man – he volunteered to help J. B. S. Haldane test a rescue diving bell after the loss of the submarine *Thetis* with all hands in the Irish Sea in 1939 – Alexander was perhaps the most outstanding example of a Communist admired as much by his opponents as his comrades.

TARIQ ALI has gone through several stages of Leftiousness, but he is still a serious troublemaker and with great good fortune will continue to be so. As he prepares to pick up his Freedom of London bus pass at the age of sixty, his rhetoric has mellowed. 'In politics, as in cooking, there can be no dogmas,' he told a recent interviewer, no doubt conscious both of the *bon mot* and the reality behind it. In the run-up to the war against Iraq, Ali found himself in strange company on the million-strong protest in London. 'I find myself walking next to a new generation – maybe not 'left' in the way we knew it, but progressive.' He believes it is no longer possible to say with absolute certainty 'as we did twenty years ago' that the working class is the agent of change. Ali was being disingenuous, knowing that historically it has most often been people like him who are the agents of change, and the working class are their troops.

Tariq Ali was born in Lahore in 1944, into a family of 'a very old, decaying feudal aristocracy' but the son of radical Communist parents. His Marxist father fought British imperialism, and his mother gave her jewels to the party. Young Ali was sent to a Catholic School, and then to Government College, part of Punjab University. He claims to have been radicalised at the age of twelve, during the 1956 Suez crisis. He was elected president of the Young Students' Union, organising demonstrations against dictatorship at home and abroad, which earned him a ban on engaging in student politics. On the advice of an uncle serving with Pakistani military intelligence, he was packed off to Oxford, where he read PPE at Exeter College, joined the University Labour Club and became president of the Oxford Union in 1965. Barred from returning to his homeland, Ali embraced the student revolution of the sixties. He supported the Vietcong freedom fighters in Vietnam, and, disgusted with the Wilson government's attitude to the war, quit Labour and joined (indeed, for a time headed) the International Marxist Group. 'We shall see workers' soviets in Europe in the seventies,' he proclaimed. We did not, and a disillusioned Ali turned to radical writing and broadcasting. He edited *New Left Review*, wrote plays and novels, worked on Channel 4's programme on the developing world, *Bandung File*, and ceaselessly attacked the West's wars against weaker countries. No public platform was complete without his shaggy-haired defiance. 'I hate the ignorance involved in waging war. It drives me crazy,' he says. 'I despise people who become apologists for the USA.' At the same time, he is hostile to religious fundamentalism, and opposes Palestinian suicide bombings. Ali expects 'more bad things' but looks forward to the emergence of a European power willing to flex its muscles. Not much to show for a lifetime on the Left, perhaps, but Intellectual Ali showed how to fight the good fight with all his might.

FRANK ALLAUN was unquestionably the most tireless campaigner for pacifism and disarmament of his generation. To the Tories, he was 'not just some kind old pacifist, but one of the Soviet Union's foremost apologists in the country.' Others would have claimed that title, and Allaun was too modest to make such claims about himself. A small, wiry man with an earnestness bordering on zealotry, he was a Communist until his early thirties, and worked as an engineer, shop assistant, and lecturer before turning to journalism. He was industrial correspondent of the *Manchester Evening News* when elected to Parliament as Labour MP for Salford East in 1955. It was nine years before he tasted government service, as a PPS to Colonial Secretary Anthony Greenwood, but only six months before he resigned to begin an unremitting campaign of hostility to right-wing Labour on the backbenches, a private war that continued until his retirement in 1983. Allaun opposed practically everything: membership of the EEC; incomes policy; Labour defence policy; trade union law reform; the Vietnam War – but most passionately, nuclear weapons. He was prominent in the formation of CND, and helped organise the first Aldermaston March for Peace. As a member of Labour's national executive, he was a constant thorn in the side of the Wilson and Callaghan governments. In later years, as an NUJ member, he campaigned for a 'right of reply' in the media, and sponsored a Media Bill in the Commons. A prolific pamphleteer and regular contributor to the *Morning Star*, he died in November 2002, aged 89, virtually the last of the journalist radicals who articulated the cause of socialism in the twentieth century.

ANONYMOUS. At the height of the Left's power in the unions in the 1960s, a gnarled veteran of the Communist Party braved rain, wind and shine to sell the *Morning Star* outside the Winter Gardens in Blackpool where party conferences were held. When the Conservatives were in town, his audacious sales pitch was: '*Morning Star*!

Morning Star! Read what the Commies are *really* up to!' He was very successful, though Tories were sometimes dismayed to find that they had actually contributed to the CP by buying his paper.

JOE ASHTON scaled the lowest heights of ministerial responsibility in the 1970s, but will always be remembered as the politician whose political career came to an abrupt end after a police raid on a Thai massage parlour somewhere off the M1 in Northamptonshire. 'All political careers end in tears,' he said. Not least his own. Ashton, a forthright ex-draughtsman and MP for the safe Labour seat of Bassetlaw, was driving home from Westminster in November 1998 when 'on a crazy impulse' he turned off the motorway into Northampton for a massage. Minutes after he prepared himself for this relaxing exercise, police wielding sledgehammers broke down the door of his private room, and recorded his presence on video. They were all dressed in 'civvies' and Ashton first thought they were a criminal gang. He was swiftly disabused by an officer, who assured him he was not committing an offence, but could he give his name all the same. In the hope of keeping his name out of the newspapers, he used his other Christian name, calling himself J. William Ashton, with his correct address at the Barbican. So as not to look like a 'bloody laughing stock' as a 65-year-old pensioner, he also knocked six months off his true age.

Police suspicions were further aroused by the discrepancy between his car registration in Sheffield and his address in London. They asked him to report to Northampton. Ashton went straight to his lawyers, assuring them that no sexual activity had taken place, nor had he paid for any. The police interviewed him in his lawyer's London office, to avoid further embarrassment, and everybody had a good laugh when he properly identified himself. It was, thought Ashton, 'a classic case of Sod's Law', and that would be the end of it.

But Ashton, of all MPs, should have known better. He had been an

award-winning columnist in the *Daily Star* during the 1980s, and under-
stood the ways of tabloid journalism. This was too good a story to keep
under wraps. It broke, inevitably, in the *News of the World*, in March 1999.
In his autobiography, *Red Rose Blues*, Ashton described it with customary
vigour: 'The news hit the family home with all the impact of a Wild West
outlaw raid.' Nor did the scandal end there. He quit as director of his
beloved football club, Sheffield Wednesday. Weeks of tabloid torment
followed, until the *Mail on Sunday* tracked down the hapless girl masseuse
who had fled to a remote village in Thailand. Friends said she had been
offered large sums of money to say she had had sex with Ashton, but she
insisted: 'I never offered him sex, and he never asked. I am so sorry for Mr
Joe. I want people to know he did not do anything wrong.' That rings true.
But it was too late to save Ashton's reputation. He confirmed his intention
to stand down at the next election.

It was a classic sad end to a political career that started in the mean
terraced streets of Attercliffe, where even in wartime Churchill was
booed when he appeared on the cinema screen. Ashton, born in 1933,
the son of a miner and a cutlery buffer, told his grandfather he wanted
to be a journalist 'and then a Labour MP'. He did both, but the other way
round, entering Parliament in a by-election in 1968. In 1974, **Tony Benn**
appointed him his PPS, and later campaign manager in his 1976 party
leadership bid. They parted company after the campaign failed
abysmally, and Ashton became a government whip under the prime
ministership of James Callaghan. He lasted only a year, though he did
stage a partial comeback as front-bench spokesman on energy in the first
year of **Michael Foot**'s leadership. Thereafter, it was the dismal grind of
select committees until he hit the headlines for what he called 'mischie-
vous devilment'. Intriguingly, he said in his autobiography: 'I can tell all
those blokes who haven't yet reached 65 that all of us are still eighteen in
the head from time to time. There is a self-destruct button just waiting
to be pressed, and sometimes the temptation to press it is irresistible …
some of us are hooked on risk.' So, what would have happened if the
police had battered down his cubicle door fifteen minutes later?

B

BERYL BAINBRIDGE, the novelist of modern life and figures from history, was known as 'Basher' at school in Liverpool because she was always in fights. Her behaviour would now be known as 'attitude', and it took her into the Young Communist League. Her father, whom she described as 'a committed socialist all his life', did not complain when she was taken under the wing of a local Communist family, who took her to meetings and concerts, and introduced her to books outside the mainstream. She told an interviewer in 2002: 'I still have their *Life of Rasputin* somewhere. I did a painting of Rasputin and then one of Stalin, and my father had it pinned in the kitchen for years.' The dénouement came when her party mentors took her to see Paul Robeson, and Bainbridge was mistakenly hit on the shoulder by a police truncheon. 'It wasn't very serious, but my father made me leave after that,' she recollected. The incident did not entirely put her off politics, either on stage or off. She was Ken Barlow's Ban the Bomb girlfriend in *Coronation Street*. On a reprise of J. B. Priestley's *English Journey*, she met up with Pat Wall, a friend from Liverpool days and a Militant Tendency member. They agreed that people were different in the 1950s, 'more committed to politics. If you came from the North you had to be, it was in your blood.' In 1988, she was a founder of Charter 88 and spoke at a rally for Ken Livingstone. But the Left has plainly lost her. 'I'll always vote Labour, but I do find most politics a bit ridiculous now.'

JOHN BALL is more often mentioned than **Wat Tyler** in **Tony Benn**'s *tours des horizons* of early British Lefties. He was one of the leaders of the fourteenth-century Peasants' Revolt, brutally put down by Richard II. Ball was executed in 1381, after the revolting peasantry had marched on London from Kent. His is most remembered for his simple, levelling quotation taken as his text for a revolutionary sermon: 'When Adam delved and Eve span, Who was then the gentleman?'

TONY BANKS once described Karl Marx as 'one of mankind's greatest intellectual forces' and was **Tony Benn**'s key vote-swinger in the unions when the Left seemed poised to capture the commanding heights of the Labour Party. But it was his irretrievably 'cheeky chappie' image that deprived him of his ultimate goal: the London mayoralty. He lost the Labour nomination to Nicky Gavron, who was as loyal to **Ken Livingstone** as the Mayor was disloyal to his old party. Despite his Cockney sparrer image, Banks was born in Belfast, the son of a retired diplomat, and attended grammar school, York University and the LSE. He was variously an Anglican verger, trade union researcher, adviser to Judith Hart, an official of the Broadcasting Union and the last chairman of the GLC before entering Parliament for Newham in 1983. He signed virtually every Leftie early day motion around, won the uncoveted palm as the MP who asks most questions, was appointed a whip and resigned. **Tony Blair** appointed him Minister for Sport, the job he wanted but in which he never looked at home. 'I don't want people to think I'm bonkers. I'm basically deadly serious … Unfortunately, I think I've diverted them too much. They think I'm just a cheeky chappie.'

ARTHUR BAX was driven out of a key role as press and publicity officer of the Labour Party on suspicion of being a Communist spy. MI5 kept him under surveillance, and claimed to have evidence of him supplying a Czech intelligence officer with material about the party's internal affairs. He was appointed the party's media chief in 1946, but not until 1962 was he was confronted with MI5's 'evidence', derived from telephone taps, photographs and bank statements. The security service did not seek a prosecution, because possession of 'confidential' party documents (usually leaked to newspapers anyway) was part of his job and not contrary to the Official Secrets Act. MI5 fed the information to George (later Lord) Brown, who was conducting a witch-hunt for crypto-Communists in the party. He persuaded Bax to resign on health grounds. Chapman Pincher, the spy writer, alleged that Bax confessed to passing on political information 'for at least four years' before quitting Transport House.

Subsequently, his wife insisted that the evidence was 'completely fabricated'. Bax had contacts with foreign press men, and was sometimes paid for articles. He also helped a Czech correspondent, Antonin Buzwk, to set up the Czech News Agency, which the authorities suspected was a front for spying activities. Mrs Bax said her husband was 'an innocent in these matters' who had no idea that the Czechs had anything to do with intelligence. She made a scene at Curzon House, and claimed an MI5 investigation cleared her husband. He later worked for the Oxford University Press, before setting up the press office for Enfield Borough Council in 1966. Three years later, he joined the *Enfield Weekly Herald*. Bax died in 1989, still stigmatised as a Soviet agent.

MARGARET BECKETT is a unique survivor of Labour's old guard, the only woman minister of the Wilson/Callaghan era still holding office. As much to the point, she is still holding the fort when New Labour is under fire. **Tony Blair** is really in trouble when Beckett is wheeled out to defend the government on the *Today* programme, a function for which she is sparingly used. She is popular in the Parliamentary Labour Party, and even more so in the unions. In an ideal world, Blair would presumably dearly love to ditch her, but she would be as formidable on the backbenches as the front. So she carries on at the conglomerate department of DEFRA, taking the flak from the country lobby, the foxhunters, the farmers and the green queens. She is up for it. As Margaret Jackson, an industrial chemist, she joined the Labour Party staff at Transport House as a research assistant in 1970, where she was a quite flighty adornment to the staff. She went on to become political adviser to Judith Hart, before capturing Lincoln from Dick Taverne in 1974 and, on the way, a husband, Leo Beckett, her election agent. She lost the seat in 1979, but came back four years later in Derby South, promptly joined the Campaign Group, and ran on a left-wing ticket for both the NEC and the Shadow Cabinet. Beckett was on and off the NEC, but stuck with the Campaign Group until 1988 when it decided to challenge Neil Kinnock's leadership. Elected deputy leader to John Smith in 1992, she picked up the gauntlet that few others dared to touch in the 1994 poll for leader, picking up 19 per cent of the vote. She also stood for deputy leader against **John Prescott**, taking 44 per cent the vote. This was a very creditable performance for the daughter of a carpenter and school-teacher from Ashton under Lyne. She was head girl of her Catholic high school, a fact that few could forget when Blair made her Leader of the House after a spell at the Department of Trade and Industry. Her brisk, non-nonsense manner at the Despatch Box had some Tories quaking at the knees, no doubting reminding them of their school matron. She has been called a working class Princess Royal, and quite apart from the physical likeness, there is something in the simile. Wise men do not seek her disfavour.

STEVE BELL, the genial man-mountain whose corrosive contempt for Tony Blair is only given full rein when he sits down with his pen and ink, has been described as 'the most popular cartoonist on the Left'. And it is true that many open the *Guardian* to look for his latest caricature of New Labour, just as they did when he was savaging the

Tories. Bell did not invent the image of John Major with his shirt tucked into his underpants (that was the work of the master, Alastair Campbell) but he brought it to perfection with his depiction of the last Conservative Prime Minister wearing his pants outside his trousers, a satirical mimic of Superman. He cheerfully admits that he flogged the motif for all it was worth, and that he does not disdain money. For Bell, a good day is to 'earn money, have a laugh and stiff a Tory'. Bell hails from Slough, and spent formative years in 1960s Birmingham in the company of 'a ragbag of dewy-eyed Trots, Anarchists and clanking Tankies.' He joined the Labour Party when the SDP Gang of Four were leaving. His first cartoon strip, *If...*, in the early 1980s, attracted an admiring audience, and his editor Peter Preston judged it right to put Bell on the leader page where his scabrous wit could have greatest impact. His portrayal of Thatcher as a swivel-eyed maniac led on to a flash of inspiration that she and Blair shared the same eye pattern: one genial and twinkling, the other gripped in a manic stare. 'With Blair, what you see is what you get, which is teeth, ears, conical head, receding hair and preachy domineering attitude ...what he really gives us is the illusion of political substance, unlike his hefty former friend next door.' Critics on the right argue that he is a dinosaur from the CND age, but he has seen off two prime ministers and will certainly leave his mark on Blair.

TONY BENN is the hell-fire preacher of the Church of the Left. He reduces his congregations to self-flagellation with sermons on the iniquity of false Leftiousness and worship of the failed gods of capitalism. People even pay good money – up to £20 a head – for these exercises in shame. The experience cleanses them. They feel better, and then, as in the real Church, they go out and commit the same sins all over again. It is a measure of his belief in his prophet status that allows Benn to keep going, at the end of his seventh decade, careless that his pearls only too often fall before swine. Anthony Neil Wedgwood Benn was born into politics, in 1925. His father and his grandfather had sat at Westminster, and the family business is continued by his son Hilary, now a middle-ranking government minister. Benn was educated at Westminster School, where his report said he 'does not work hard enough in school or out', and New College, Oxford. He trained to be an RAF pilot in the latter stages of the war, professing disgust at the drunken behaviour of his fellow servicemen, which confirmed his life-long policy of teetotalism. Intoxication enough awaited him in politics. While working for the BBC, he landed the safe seat of Bristol South East vacated by the ailing Stafford Cripps, and became the 'baby of the House' at a by-election in late 1950, just as the Attlee government was running out of steam. Benn became a protégé of Hugh Gaitskell, the right-wing Labour leader, and made himself useful in many ways: introducing his party to the virtues of television, for instance. He won a seat on the NEC, and was brought into the Shadow Cabinet by Gaitskell.

Benn was plainly destined for great things, but the sudden death of his father made him the second Viscount Stansgate, disbarring him from the Commons. He engaged in a struggle lasting nearly three years to change the law so that he could disavow the hereditary peerage, and take his place at Westminster. The campaign made him a household name, soon shortened to the more demotic Tony Benn (an example not lost on the present Prime Minister). Harold Wilson, evidently forgiving of his Gaitskellite days, made him Technology Minister, enabling Benn to emerge as champion of Concorde, partly built in his constituency. Labour's defeat in 1970 saw Benn move effortlessly to the hard Left, building up links with extra-parliamentary organisations like the Institute for Workers' Control. His popular advocacy of a referendum on membership of the then EEC triggered the resignation of Roy Jenkins as deputy leader (and gave him a new nickname: 'Referbenndum'), but when the vote was held in 1975, it was decisively in favour of Europe. Undeterred, and with Wilson's third government in power by courtesy of the striking miners, he cultivated links with the Left while in office as Trade and Industry Secretary.

Demoted to Energy after the referendum, he harboured leadership ambitions when Wilson resigned but came fourth in a field of six. In opposition after the 1979 'winter of discontent', Benn was the most high-profile promoter of radical Leftist changes in Labour's internal power structures, including an electoral college embracing the unions and the rank and file as well as MPs to choose the leader (which survives, in an attenuated form) and compulsory re-selection of MPs (which does not). He challenged **Denis Healey** for the deputy leadership, and came within a whisker of success. However, in the electoral calamity of 1983, which he had done so much to bring about with the 'suicide pact' manifesto, Benn lost his seat and was once again in the wilderness. He was never to be so influential again, though a grateful NUM sent him back to Westminster as MP for Chesterfield within months. There, he found himself on the political fringe as Labour under Neil Kinnock tacked towards the centre ground. Yet as a consistent critic of the anachronistic powers of the Prime Minister, the growing irrelevance of Parliament and the marginalisation of the voice of organised Labour, he carved out a uniquely authoritative role at Westminster. Nobody less deserved Wilson's jibe that he had 'immatured with age'. Benn's American wife, Caroline, who had played a big part in his political theatre, died of cancer in 2001 and he retired from the Commons, only half jesting that he wanted to spend more time in politics. He is still box office, quite literally, and still picks up gold nuggets from many decades in the public eye. 'I danced with the Queen in 1945,' he said in June 2003. 'I won her in a raffle.'

JOHN DESMOND BERNAL was a pioneer scientist, Marxist and political activist, known to fellow students at Cambridge as 'Sage' because he seemed to know everything about everything. At the age of two, he astounded passengers on a liner to the USA by speaking in English and French. During the Second World War, his brilliance so impressed war planners that they demanded his services 'even if he is red as the flames of hell'. Born in Nenagh, Ireland, in 1901, he was educated at Stonyhurst College and Emmanuel College, Cambridge. In 1923, he joined the nascent Communist Party, and visited the Soviet Union in 1931 with a group of British scientists. Bernal became professor of physics at Cambridge, and developed X-ray crystallography with Dorothy Hodgkin. In 1934, he left the Communist Party but continued to hold Marxist views, publishing the Social Function of Science in 1939. Bernal moved to Birkbeck College, London, as professor of crystallography.

The war brought him into government work, as scientific adviser to Lord Mountbatten. With Solly Zuckerman, he conducted research into the impact of bombing on people and buildings. He also advised on the choice of Mulberry harbours for the Normandy landings, convincing Churchill of his idea by floating paper boats in a bath on the *Queen Mary* as they travelled to the Quebec conference in 1943. In peacetime, Bernal was a founder of molecular biology. He lost none of his Leftiousness, however, becoming vice-president of the World Peace Committee. In 1951, he founded Scientists for Peace, the forerunner of CND. Bernard was awarded the US Medal of Freedom for his war work, but during the McCarthy era he was barred from the USA. Eastern bloc countries showered him with honours, including the Lenin Peace Prize, and he continued writing, unconcerned about political critics, until his death in 1971.

ANNIE BESANT made her name with one mould-breaking strike: the revolt in 1888 of the match girls in London's East End. An unlikely convert to socialism, Annie Wood was born in London in 1847 of Irish parents fleeing the potato famine, but she could point to a city MP as her great uncle and received a privileged upbringing on a Dorset estate. An unhappy marriage to Frank Besant, a clergyman much her senior, led her on to freethinker Charles Bradlaugh, who encouraged her wide-ranging journalism and social inquiry. She joined the Fabian Society, finding the case for socialism 'intellectually complete and ethically beautiful'. But it was her investigation into the lot of working women, sparking a strike by match girls at Bryant and May's factory in Bow, that established her claim to a place in the Lefties' hall of fame. The 1,400 women who struck without a union found an articulate champion in Annie Besant. Many of the women suffered with 'phossie jaw', a cancer of the face caused by over-exposure to phosphorus. After a brief struggle, the employer surrendered to demands for better pay and conditions.

Besant, a veteran of the Trafalgar Square socialist riots, held advanced views about birth control and insisted that celibacy was harmful to women and shortened their lives. But a year after her triumph with the match girls, Besant, dissatisfied with the Fabians' slow progress to social change, switched political direction completely under the influence of Madame Blavatsky, the founder of theosophy. Celibacy now became more attractive, with Besant arguing that the brute sexual instincts of man must be kept under complete control. In 1893, she left for India where ten years later she became president of the Theosophical Society until her death in 1933. Not all her political impetus disappeared. Besant was active in the Indian independence movement, but she was lost to the British left.

ANEURIN BEVAN remains an icon of the Left, fifty years after his death. But was he also a Soviet spy? **Kim Philby** told his biographer Philip Knightley that wartime parties held at the Earls Court home of Tommy Harris, a wealthy art dealer, attracted a number of what came to be known as the Cambridge spy ring. Tantalisingly, Philby recorded that 'the regulars were me, **Burgess**, **Blunt** and perhaps Aneurin Bevan'. MI5 were certainly interested in Nye's wartime exploits. His wife Jennie Lee angrily documented the interest of the security services in her memoir, *My Life With Nye*, stating that in 1940, MI5 employed members of their staff 'to worm their way into Nye's confidence, even into our home.' After Russia entered the war, the Left, from the CPGB to elements in the Liberal Party, were campaigning for a second front to take the pressure off the Red Army. Influential Jewish families in Britain were part of this crusade, none more militantly so than Rebecca Sieff, wife of Israel Sieff, the Marks & Spencer mogul, and a close friend of Lee. She recorded that over dinner at the Sieffs' home, Brook House, she and Nye discussed the conduct of the war with **Michael Foot**, Frank Owen (sympathetic editor of the *Evening Standard*) and some others. Bevan was certain that he was being spied upon, and when one member of the company who professed to share their views went to the lavatory, Nye followed him and strong-armed a confession out of him. He admitted being paid by MI5 'or some other secret service outfit' to report on Bevan's movements.

Bevan's official biographer, Michael Foot, does not relate this story in his book, though he does concede that Marxism appealed to the fiery Welsh socialist, because it explained the politics on his doorstep and he admired its 'sweeping and spacious visions'. Bevan was also a leading figure in the Unity Campaign, a broad Left movement encompassing Communists, Left-Labour, the ILP and the Socialist League, formed in the late 1930s. The campaign attracted huge audiences at public meetings before establishment Labour crushed it. By the war's end, Bevan had turned against the CP, evolving his own vision of democratic socialism.

The story of his life has been chronicled more comprehensively than is possible here, but it is worth recalling that this giant of the Left, born in the Welsh mining village of Tredegar in1897, was virtually self-taught. He went down the pit at thirteen, and simultaneously went through the local Workmen's Institute Library. He became active in the ILP, chaired the local branch of the miners' union, before going to London to study in the Central Labour College where he found Marx's *Communist Manifesto* 'an inspiration and a weapon' for all rebels like himself. Back in south Wales, he found work as a full-time union official, and was a driving force in the great strike of 1926. Elected to Parliament as MP for Ebbw Vale in 1929, he was always on the Left of the party, being briefly expelled for his pains. In 1934, he married an equally forceful socialist, Jennie Lee, and for the next quarter of a century their partnership dominated the Labour Left. In 1945, Attlee gave Bevan the task of establishing the National Health Service, his greatest (indeed, perhaps only) enduring achievement.

Shifted sideways to the Ministry of Labour in January 1951, Bevan quit the government three months later ostensibly over the imposition of NHS charges for dentistry and spectacles, but in reality over Hugh Gaitskell's Budget that massively increased arms spending. His response in 1952 was *In Place of Fear*, a manifesto for the democratic Left. Intellectually, it was unchallengeable. Practically, it had no hope because right-wing party and union leaders dominated the political landscape, and Bevan tacked towards them. He formed a working relationship with Gaitskell, who made him Shadow Foreign Secretary as he cast adrift from unilateral disarmament, warning his party conference 'not to send the Foreign Secretary naked into the conference chamber.' In fact, he knew, because Khrushchev had told him on a visit to Moscow, that the Russians did not want the UK to give up its nuclear weapons, because they could be a bargaining chip in negotiations with the USA. Bevan was briefly deputy leader before his death from cancer in 1960.

RODNEY BICKERSTAFFE was wont to tell the curious: 'I'm a bastard.' And when they demurred at his frankness, believing it to relate to his no-prisoners leadership of Britain's largest union, Unison, he would add: 'No, I mean a real bastard'. After a lifetime in the public eye as a trade union leader, he began a voyage of personal discovery, which turned up his past and an entirely unexpected present. For almost half a century, Bickerstaffe had wondered who his real father was. His mother Elizabeth worked as a nurse in an east London hospital.

During the Second World War a handsome young Irishman, Tommy Simpson walked into Casualty, complaining of stomach pains. The product of this union, as the saying goes, was Rodney, in April 1945. Tommy disappeared back to Dublin, and Elizabeth Bickerstaffe moved back to her native Doncaster, where she became matron of a day nursery. 'Bick', as he is often called, had to fight the stigma of illegitimacy – sometimes literally, in the playground – at school, but gained a place to read sociology at Newcastle Polytechnic. On graduating in 1966, he became an official with the National Union of Public Employees, the union his mother had joined as a nurse.

He moved up through the ranks to become general secretary in 1982, with two clear goals in mind: the establishment of a National Minimum Wage, and the creation of a super-union of 1.4 million members embracing NUPE, the local government union NALGO and the health union COHSE. The second required exceptional negotiating skills, because the unions are some of the most conservative bodies on earth, but it came off. The first required a Labour government, a remote prospect in the 1980s, but that reform made the statute book despite the personal hostility of **Tony Blair**. In 1998, as he prepared to retire, he asked his ailing mother to unlock the secrets of her heart. She gave him a last-known address in a Dublin suburb, and by dint of some hard detective work he found his Irish family, including three brothers. His father had died seven years earlier. The family was reunited, discovering that they were all steeped in trade unionism. This is one of those rare Leftie stories: a true one, with a happy ending. Bickerstaffe retired in 2000, and became president of the National Pensioners' Convention. He declined a peerage.

SID BIDWELL is best remembered, if he is remembered at all, as the artist whose charmless painting of the Palace of Westminster adorns a corner of the Strangers' Bar in the House of Commons. He boasted of his 'brilliant oils', but they are not collectors' items today. Yet he was a transparently honest man, of a kind now largely lost to politics. Born in Southall, Middlesex, in 1917, the son of an ILP activist, he worked as a goods guard and shunter on the Great Western Railway after an elementary education. He joined the Labour Party as a teenager, but switched to the Revolutionary Communist Party in 1939, returning to Labour a decade later. He was elected to the borough council in 1951 and as MP for Southall in 1966. By this date, the constituency had the second highest proportion of migrants from the Indian sub-continent in the country.

Bidwell, who escaped the railways to become an adult education officer, first for the National Council of Labour Colleges (NCLC) and then the TUC, he quickly espoused the interests of his Asian electors. He successfully brought in a Bill to exempt Sikhs from wearing motorcycle helmets. His championing of Asian causes did not prevent (unsuccessful) attempts by black activists to deselect him before the 1987 election. Bidwell was active in CND, and the pro-Soviet Friends of Afghanistan Society, and once described his political differences with the Communist Party as 'negligible'. He was a regular contributor to the *Morning Star*. He was never remotely considered for office, and died in 1997. The *Daily Telegraph*'s epitaph described him as an unreconstructed Marxist who managed to serve as a Labour MP for twenty-six years without anyone on either side of the Commons taking offence at his views.

REG BIRCH was the cleverest Leftie to be deprived of high trade union office by the Communist Party. He launched his own party, the CPGB (Marxist Leninist), and was the only Maoist to sit on the TUC General Council, whose proceedings he found 'an effing bore'. Birch, a newly elected full-time officer of the engineering union AUEW, was expelled from the Communist Party in 1967, ostensibly because he was in correspondence with the Chinese and Albanian parties. His expulsion, he assumed, was because he intended to stand against Hugh Scanlon, the broad Left candidate for the presidency of his union supported by the CP. His candidature would have split the Left vote, and he had to be marginalised. Until that date, Birch had risen effortlessly through the party hierarchy. Born in 1914 in Kilburn, north London, the son of a builder and decorator who introduced him to classical literature and sent him to Sunday School, he left school at fourteen to work as a tea boy in a local factory. At sixteen he became an apprentice tool maker and five years later joined the Communist Party. During the war, he was jailed at the Old Bailey for refusing to obey wartime restrictions on industrial action. He was a shop steward at de Haviland's, and a member of the union's district committee.

Birch was not happy with the revisionism of post-war years, and made his first visit to Peking in 1956, the year of Stalin's denunciation. In 1957, he was elected to the CP executive, observing: 'They looked round for a prominent trade unionist who could stomach Hungary, and they chose me.' He never became president of his union, though he did become a member of the elite executive council and chief negotiator at Ford's. On one unforgettable occasion, company executives outlining new death in service benefits heard a loud knocking under the table. It was Birch. 'It's my dead members,' he explained, with his customary deadpan manner. 'They want to know if it's retrospective.' A short, wiry man with a lean face and penetrating blue eyes, Birch was cultured company with the most thoroughgoing contempt for 'social democrats', among whom he numbered his old comrades in the CPGB. He died, aged seventy-nine, in 1994. The epitaph he gave himself: 'I'm just a British worker.'

CHERIE BLAIR looks an unlikely Leftie after six and a half years as the First Lady in an irretrievably right-wing New Labour government. But before she hosted parties for the rich and famous in Number 10, Cherie Booth had a genuine political pedigree, inherited from her outrageous father, actor **Tony Booth**. She joined the Labour

Party while still at school in snooty Crosby, Lancashire, strongly influenced by a local Quaker couple. She is remembered as 'moderately left of centre, quiet and a good listener', whereas **Tony** had little politics but much ambition. After they married, the pair settled in Hackney, supporting the local Labour MP Ron Brown (brother of the notorious George) against the Militant Tendency until he defected to the fledgling SDP. A party member who spoke to Cherie's biographer Linda McDougall said she was 'temperamentally more drawn by leftishness … equality for the working class, that sort of thing'. She made it to the Labour shortlist for the Crosby by-election of 1981 but failed to win the nomination, despite the promise of help from her father and his lover Pat Phoenix of *Coronation Street* fame. Her luck turned in 1983 when she was chosen to fight the safe Tory seat of Thanet North on the Kent coast. The two well-known Tonies – **Benn** and Booth – boosted her campaigning, while unknown husband Tony washed the dishes. Cherie fought a traditional, left-wing, *Tribune*-supporting, anti-bomb campaign, but came third behind the Tories and the SDP in the 'Falklands election'.

Had she got the safe seat instead of her husband, political history might have been different. Cherie did not abandon her own political life immediately. She was a member of the hard Left-dominated Labour Co-ordinating Committee, indeed a member of its executive committee, but she was 'not a raving left-winger', insists **Peter Hain**. Motherhood in 1984 coincided with a falling-off in her political activity, and a friend called her Lady Muck. Subsequently, she was awarded the soubriquet of Lady Macbeth, though a female *Sunday Times* columnist writing in the early 1990s thought her 'marginally to the right of Mrs Mao'. Certainly, she was ambitious for her husband, insisting that he run – if necessary against his friend and mentor **Gordon Brown** – after John Smith died. In the words of her biographer, Cherie 'put iron in Tony's soul'. He won, she became a QC, hired a fitness consultant, a fashion adviser, a spin doctor (Alastair Campbell's partner Fiona Millar) and finally had her own headed notepaper from Number 10. It was not all plain sailing. She requisitioned the Chancellor's flat in

Number 11, and her First Lady role triggered more rows in Downing Street about who pays for what – Cherie or the government – than anything else, according to a civil servant who worked there. She also set up her own chambers, Matrix, specialising in human rights cases, which frequently brings her into conflict with her husband's government.

Cherie also used the law to protect her privacy, injuncting the *Mail on Sunday* in a 2 a.m. hearing over revelations by her ex-nanny Ros Mark, who had written a mildly kiss-and-tell memoir about life with the Blairs. Since then, those who have had any contact with the first family have learned to keep their mouths shut. Not so Cherie. In the 2001 general election, she was asked to pose for the cameras with Tony on the prime ministerial plane. 'Are you trying to make us look as if we have joined the Mile High Club?' she asked. A school friend once said that Cherie Booth fancied being Britain's first female prime minister. That title was snapped up by a woman with more political staying power. And her long-range ambition to become the first female lord chancellor was scuppered in late 2002, when it was revealed that she had used the services of a convicted conman to buy two flats in Bristol. One was for her son Euan, about to study at the city's university, who had earlier distinguished himself by getting drunk in Leicester Square. Her £526,000 investment was made from the Blairs' 'blind trust', and the resulting media frenzy prompted her to make an act of public contrition. 'I am not Superwoman,' she wailed.

TONY BLAIR rates only four mentions in *Who's Left?*, the Tory Party index of Labour MP and left-wing Causes, 1985–1992. They are worth a fresh outing. He is recorded as a member of Parliamentary Party CND in 1986, and later that year signed an early day motion demanding the closure of the chemical and biological germ station at Porton Down, condemning experiments there that were 'only for finding better ways of killing members of the forces and civilians.' In 1987, he signed an EDM applauding the 'fortitude and resolve' displayed 'by the men and women on the Wapping picket lines' after twelve months of strike against News International. In February 1998, he signed another EDM, criticising the USA's 'evil campaign' against Nicaragua and 'President Reagan's state-sponsored terrorism' in Central America. Thereafter, he joined the Shadow Cabinet, became Prime Minister, and discovered the sterling virtues of Rupert Murdoch and the fine, upstanding nature of American presidents, of whatever political stripe. State-sponsored terrorism became a war against terror, and strikes were denounced as irrelevant and self-defeating. Such a loss to the Left!

DAVID BLUNKETT, the recidivist Home Secretary, rose to fame as a Leftie, and in the finest traditions of the Labour Party promptly ratted on his early convictions when fortune, in the shape of Cabinet status, beckoned. In 1985, he pledged that a Labour government would lift the penalties imposed on hard-Left Liverpool and Lambeth Labour councillors for breaking the law by failing to set a rate. The next year, he promised at the annual conference to 'take back' into public ownership British Telecom, oil, gas, industries for defence, aerospace, steel, pharmaceuticals, computers 'and our technology future', blithely ignoring that most of these had never been nationalised. In 1986, he congratulated the madcap 'Nuclear Free Zone Local Authorities', and later praised the Marxist government of Nicaragua, and claimed that apart from Poland 'it is difficult to recall which other Eastern European states owe their lack of democratic government to the USSR'. He was the very model of a modern major Leftie. Subsequently, he moved into the 'soft Left' of the Labour leadership and became a favourite pet of **Tony Blair**. In 1996, as Shadow Education Secretary, he promised reforms that the *New Statesman* described as 'authentically new Labour ... (that) will appeal to middle-England *Daily Mail* readers'. His private life, with the exception of his mysterious divorce, is too dull to rake over here. But he did once set himself a test that may be worth recollecting in a few years' time, when he will no doubt be Lord Blunkett: 'If I can look back in my dotage and genuinely believe we have made a difference, I shall be very happy,' he insisted. Unquestionably, he will judge in the affirmative. But what kind of difference?

ANTHONY BLUNT was a spy of the front rank, but not much of a socialist. While at Cambridge, he was 'vaguely surprised' to find so many of his fellow intellectuals were joining the Communist Party in the 1930s. He was attracted to the university's brilliant Marxists, **Guy Burgess**, **James Klugmann**, **John Cornford** and others, and came to the conclusion that their political approach offered a real basis for understanding his own subject, the history of art. But when asked to join the CP, he refused, offering the lame excuse that there were too many points about which he was not clear, and he did not want to commit himself until he had thought them out. A visit to Russia in 1935 did not end procrastination, but Blunt's vacillation was of some help when he was recruited by Victor Rothschild to MI5 after Dunkirk. He could – and did – claim that his flirtation with Communism had been 'purely on the intellectual side' and his explanation was accepted, freeing him to spy for the Russians throughout the war.

Between 1941 and 1945, he passed 1,771 documents to his Soviet handler, including intercepts from the Enigma code-breakers at Bletchley Park. Blunt, a devout homosexual, shared with Burgess and two women a flat in Bentinck Street in wartime London, where binge drinking and debauchery went on night after night. Their landlord was Victor Rothschild, and one of the women, Theresa Mayor, later became Lady Rothschild. Muckraking biographer Tom Bower later claimed that 'Tess', blonde, clever, rich and sociable, had 'a secret passionate relationship' with Blunt, putting him to bed when he was drunk, and occasionally sleeping with him. Clearly, this particular rampant homosexual could make exceptions to the rule. Her sporadic relationship with Blunt roused suspicions that she too was engaged in espionage, but she disdained efforts to make her talk after his exposure.

Blunt was born in 1907, the son of an Anglican priest and sometime British chaplain in Paris. His outstanding performance in mathematics and languages earned him a fellowship at Trinity College, and after volunteering as a talent spotter for the KGB (he recruited **John Cairncross**) he volunteered for military intelligence at the outbreak of war. When it was over, he became director of the Courtauld Institute and Surveyor of the King's Pictures, but kept up his spying for five more years. His last job was to hand over £5,000 to **Kim Philby** in a north London street. Blunt was investigated eleven times between 1951 and 1964, but never cracked until he was put up against Arthur Martin, MI5's most feared interrogator to whom he confessed. Between then and 1979, when he was unmasked by Margaret Thatcher, Blunt co-operated with the security services, but that did not save his knighthood. He had been offered safe passage to Moscow, where he could join the rest of the Cambridge spy ring in exile, but shuddered at the thought. 'I simply couldn't live in the Soviet Union,' the effete aesthete told his handler Yuri Modin. 'I known perfectly well how your people live, and I assure you it would be very hard, almost unbearable, for me to do likewise.' No wonder Klugmann thought he was 'hopeless'. Blunt died in 1990.

PAUL BOATENG put the wind up the Tories, until they met him. He was a black Labour activist, chairman of the GLC's confrontational Police Committee, and a Bennite. He had worked as a trainee lawyer with Birnbergs, the trade union and civil rights firm of solicitors sometimes linked to the Communist Party. On the night of his parliamentary victory in Brent South, he declared: 'We can never be free in Brent until South Africa is free too. Today Brent South! Tomorrow Soweto.' But his actions on entering the Commons in 1987 should have given them a clue. Boateng joined the hard-Left Campaign Group and the soft-Left Tribune Group. Today, he is Chief Secretary to the Treasury, the first black Cabinet minister. He sends his five children to private school, wears Savile

Row suits, is more Blairite than Blair and is credited with being the only Labour politician who could pay for his own dinner at the Ivy.

But, then, he has always been used to the good life. He was born in Hackney in 1951, but his Ghanaian father Kwaku Boateng returned to west Africa to serve as a Cabinet minister in Kwame Nkrumah's government. The young Boateng was chauffeured to Achimota School, the Ghanaian Eton. In 1966, his father was jailed after a coup, and Paul returned to England with his sister and Scots mother, Eleanor, a teacher. She worked in a school in Hemel Hempstead, and partly under her influence he joined the Labour Party Young Socialists. He studied law at Bristol University, and then trained as a barrister before becoming a **Ken Livingstone**-supporting GLC councillor in 1981. Four years later, he beat off a challenge from two other ethnic minority candidates, Sharon Atkin and Keith Vaz, to win the safe Labour seat. From there, despite dalliance with the **Benn** camp, he never looked back. Within two years, he was on the opposition front bench, and in 1991 he was nominated Class Traitor of the Year by hard-Left *London Labour Briefing*, which he had once supported. But which class? He plainly regards himself as in a class of his own. His only slip came in 1987, at celebrations to mark the demise of the GLC, when he wore a judge's wig, a leather jockstrap, suspender belt and stockings. Naturally, a *News of the World* photographer was in the audience. Boateng, a lay Methodist preacher, was not amused. The episode did not prevent him becoming Home Office Minister for Family Policy, and a staunch defender of the police despite his remark in 1984 that Tory laws gave rise to 'a tendency towards a police state'. Some observers think that if Labour went Left again, he would follow the trend. Perhaps. But he would be so o'fully upset.

MARGARET BONDFIELD, a passionate opponent of British involvement in the First World War, accused an angry crowd in 1917 in Nelson, Lancashire, of being 'howling crows' sending their menfolk to death. 'Russia has shown us the way out, and has asked the people of this country to take our stand on the side of democracy and peace,' she argued. Such a stand took nerve, but Margaret Grace Bondfield was never short of that. Born in 1873 in Chard, Somerset, she was the eleventh child of a sixty-one-year-old father well known for radicalism in the textile industry. At fourteen, she left home to become a draper's assistant in Brighton, and soon became involved in the women's movement under the influence of one of her customers, Louisa Martindale, a feminist who loaned her books and introduced her to other radicals. Moving to London in 1894, Bondfield became active in the Shop Workers' Union, and four years later was appointed assistant secretary.

She wrote widely about, and investigated, the conditions of shop workers, advancing the novel idea that men and women should both work and share housework. She persuaded a Liberal government to introduce maternity benefits. Bondfield was secretary of the Women's Labour League and active in the Adult Suffrage Society which, controversially, demanded votes for all women, not just the middle class. In 1923, she was elected Labour MP for Northampton, and in 1929 Ramsay MacDonald made her Minister of Labour, the first British woman Cabinet minister. However, in office she moved sharply to the right, backing the policy of ending unemployment benefit for married women in the financial crisis of 1931. She lost her seat in the election of that year and never returned to Westminster. A teetotaller and staunch anti-Communist, not least after serving on a TUC delegation to Russia in 1920, she never married but had 'a real romance' with Mary Macarthur, founder of the National Federation of Women Workers. Bondfield's main contribution was to encourage women to engage in mainstream trade unionism, from which they had traditionally been marginalised by men. She died in 1953.

ALBERT BOOTH cut such a low profile as to be virtually invisible, despite being **Michael Foot**'s favourite son and a member of James Callaghan's 1976 Cabinet. While Secretary of State for Employment, he was referred to in *The Times* variously as Arthur Booth, Alan Booth and by his correct name – some said within the space of a week but it was actually much longer. Booth was a devout member of CND, to the extent of leading an anti-nuclear march through his constituency of Barrow in Furness.

This was not the wisest step to take, since both Polaris and later Trident submarines were built there and many otherwise solid Labour voters took exception to this principled opposition to their jobs. He was ousted in the Falklands War election of 1983. Booth's other great claim to fame was to deprive **Tony Benn** of his ambition to become Employment Secretary, while he also entered the halls of infamy as the politician who gave **Peter Mandelson** a research job at Westminster after he had been sacked from the TUC. A former engineering draughtsman of unassuming manner, he belongs to the class of MPs who rarely, if ever, revisit the scene of their glory (real or imagined), the House of Commons.

TONY BOOTH is perhaps the most rounded of Lefties, having spent a life 'crumpeteering' and mercilessly teasing his son-in-law, Tony Blair. Twice bankrupt, married four times, and the father of seven daughters, he sleeps in his late mother Vera's bed on his occasional visits to Downing Street. It has been kept for sentimental reasons by his daughter **Cherie Blair**, the First Lady and owner of two flats in Bristol. Booth is forever famous as the Scouse git in *Till Death Us Do Part*. His long-standing friend and political compadre, the Yorkshire TV writer Ron Rose, said: 'Tony was just playing himself in that role. The politics were more or less his own.' As far back as 1964, he was filmed heckling George Brown at an election rally. In the show, Booth was the long-haired Liverpudlian Leftie, with just a bit of the Trot about him, opposed to his father-in-law, Cockney bigot Alf Garnett.

The stage roles are moving uncannily closer in real life. Booth has never really lost his deep-seated Scouse hatred of the bosses, of whom Blair is now the supreme champion. He whacked New Labour over pensions, complained that his grandchildren were 'prisoners' in Downing Street, and growled that the Prime Minister had botched reform of the Lords by stuffing it with his cronies. Blair admits that he gets 'a little bit of grief from Tony along the way.' That has the whiff of understatement about it. Booth has told his own life story many times, most notably in a second volume of autobiography, provocatively titled *What's Left?* and published in 2002. This relates the drinking years, the acting career, the brush with death in a fire, the abandonment of Cherie as a child and their subsequent reconciliation. An *Independent on Sunday* profile picked up a remark by Booth's father, assumed to be a Scouse joke, that John Wilkes Booth, assassin of Abraham Lincoln, was a distant ancestor. Tony Booth may not wish to repeat that feat, but he should get a BAFTA award for his brilliant performance as the father-in-law from hell.

BILLY BRAGG is not his real name, nor is Dougal, the name he gave himself as a child to avoid being called Big Nose. Stephen Bragg, the punk rocker who became leader of Labour's official band, Red Wedge, is an Essex boy, born in Barking in 1957. For a boy who failed his 11-plus, he did very well for himself and now lives in some splendour on the Dorset coast. Bragg's father might have voted Communist, because he was a friend from school days of George Wake, a CP shop steward. The future rock star left school with only one O level, his academic fervour dulled by a teenage love affair. His first television appearance on *That's Life*, playing 'on a shitheap', announced 'I wanna be a star in the USSR' and 'Romford Girls make love with their hair in curlers'. Incongruously, he then joined the Royal Armoured Corps, because he wanted to drive a tank (presumably against the USSR), but bought himself out after completing basic training.

His socially aware music and low cover-prices for his records made Bragg an anti-hero in the Thatcher years. He also sought, and gained, public prominence by giving soundbites on political issues, having voted Labour for the first time in 1983. His notoriety was further assisted by accepting a banana from a girl fan's fanny. Bragg was a star in the USA before he toured Eastern bloc countries, where his music was more appreciated than his punk stroppiness. He flirted briefly with the Militant Tendency, before being taken firmly under Neil Kinnock's wing as the official ambassador for 'yoof'. **Julie Burchill** derided him as 'the Saatchi and Saatchi of socialism'. The general election of 1987 rather passed him by (another love affair), and his Labour Party membership lapsed in 1991, over policy in the Gulf War. In 1992, he was belting it out for the miners facing the second wave of devastation of their industry. Bragg, though **Blair,** had a progressive agenda, not a socialist one, and sang 'Jerusalem' at a gig when the Basildon result came through. In the election of 2001, he returned to Labour's aid with a tactical voting campaign on Dorset, partly via the Internet. His verdict to an official biographer is: 'My life was a mass of contradictions rather than a shining path of political correctness.' A view difficult to contest, but rather hard on himself.

JO BRAND, the deadpan stand-up comedian, was never happier than when slagging off Tories, particularly their 'appalling' women. But the day after Tony Blair took power, she was prescient about the flaws of the Project. 'Comedy thrives on the excesses of the human personality and there is not an awful lot to say about someone who is trustworthy, does their job properly, loves their husband/wife and doesn't take bribes,' she wrote in her *Independent* column. 'Labour may look like this now, but as we all know, there are few people in politics who haven't got something seriously wrong with them.' Her suspicions soon proved well founded, as the Bernie Ecclestone cash for favours scandal engulfed Blair. She was right to observe: 'Never trust a man with testicles.' Brand was born in Clapham, south London, the daughter of a consultant engineer; she attended Benenden School (where Princess Anne was educated) when the family moved to Kent. An enthusiastic Brownie, she appeared in one of their plays before moving back to London where she later worked with psychiatric patients at the Maudsley hospital. When she married Bernie Bourke, a psychiatric nurse, at Christmas 1998, she was attacked by the deeply unpleasant Dr Adrian Rogers of the Conservative Family Campaign, confirming at least honorary Leftie status.

FENNER BROCKWAY went to interview Keir Hardie as a young journalist of Liberal convictions and returned a socialist. Thereafter, he showed more political consistency, except in the great matter of pacifism, which he embraced at some peril in the First World War but abandoned in the face of Fascism. He also demonstrated that the good do not always die young, surviving to within six months of his 100th birthday.

Born in Calcutta in November 1888, the son of a missionary, he was educated at missionary school in Blackheath where he showed an early crusading zeal, campaigning against masturbation and homosexuality. He worked for Liberal candidates in local and parliamentary elections, but also studied the works of socialist writers. He became a journalist, and when the *Daily News* sent him to interview Hardie, his life changed overnight. Initially, he joined the proto-communist Social Democratic federation, but soon quit for the ILP, of which he remained a stalwart for the next four decades. At twenty-five he was editor of the party's, *Labour Elector*, and from this platform he launched a fiercely pacifist campaign against the First World War. In 1916, Brockway was arrested for criticising conscription, and on refusing to pay a fine, got two months in Pentonville. On his release, he was re-arrested as a traitor, briefly thrown into the Tower of London and then, via the dungeons of Chester Castle, into Walton jail, Liverpool. There, he organised a prisoners' strike against the 'silence' rule, and wrote a jail newspaper on toilet paper.

Released six months after the Armistice, Brockway threw himself into the anti-war movement and work for the ILP. He also edited the TUC's general strike newspaper, the *British Worker*. He always believed that the strike failed 'because the TUC never believed in it.' In 1929, he was elected Labour

MP for East Leyton, only to lose his seat in the 1931 election that followed the formation of the national government, which he opposed. That year, he took the politically-suicidal step of backing the ILP's defection from the Labour Party, and he was in the wilderness for the next twenty years. However, he continued to work for peace until the emergence of Franco, Mussolini and Hitler. 'I could no longer justify pacifism when there was a Fascist threat,' he explained, though he did take on the role of chairman of the Central Board of Conscientious Objectors during the Second World War. Impressed by Attlee's government, Brockway rejoined the Labour Party and won Eton and Slough in the 1950 election. He remained an intransigent left-winger, and was a founder of CND. His views did not endear him to the voters, and he lost his seat in 1964, just as Labour gained power. Harold Wilson gave him a life peerage, which he intermittently used to support the government. A tireless busybody, Brockway was also chairman of the Movement for Colonial Freedom, the British Council for Peace in Vietnam and the World Disarmament Campaign. He wrote more than twenty books, including four volumes of autobiography, and innumerable pamphlets and articles. He was still scribbling away when the grim reaper intervened in Watford Hospital in April 1988. Brockway is commemorated by a stature in Red Lion Square, close by the hall of the same name where he declaimed so often.

GORDON BROWN, Chancellor of the Exchequer, began his political career as an establishment Leftie. A child prodigy at Edinburgh University in the 1960s, he unhorsed the system's choice as rector and edited a radical campus newspaper that carried long, approving reports of the UCS work-in on the Clyde, as well as scantily clad girlie pin-ups. He eased his way through the notoriously clannish tickets of Scottish Labour by enlisting the aid of hard-Left and Communist fixers who virtually controlled the supply of MPs to Westminster. A son of the manse, he was born in Glasgow in 1951, and raised in the Fife coastal town of Kircaldy, famed (if not notorious) for its noisome manufacture of linoleum. His Ph.D. thesis, on the relationship between unions and the Labour Party in Scotland, spawned a biography on his hero **James Maxton**, the charismatic Scots socialist. His ascent to the party's executive north of the border also produced *The Red Paper on Scotland*, the first intellectual attempt to map the ground for a devolved nation. Brown's introduction to this collection of essays, 'The Socialist Challenge', began the process of redefinition that was eventually to produce New Labour.

Safely elected as MP for Dunfermline East in 1983, he began to tack towards the centre ground. He joined the Tribune Group at Westminster (and dragged an uncomprehending **Tony Blair** with him) more as a tactical move than as a thoroughgoing commitment to the Left. In any case, *Tribune* was already in the process of becoming a soft-Left ally of Neil Kinnock, the new leader. Brown was loud in his support for the suffering families of the 1984 miners' strike – his constituency was in the closure-threatened Fife coalfield – but noticeably more cautious in backing the strike itself, to say nothing of the naked syndicalist ambitions of **Arthur Scargill**. John Smith appointed Brown Shadow Chancellor in 1992, and he set about axing Labour's traditional 'tax and spend' image with Presbyterian enthusiasm.

His drive for the top was decisively checked after the death of his mentor in 1994, when Blair elbowed aside his teacher, ignoring their long-standing pact that he would not stand against Brown. The rest is recent history, but one nagging question still remains: is Gordon Brown the secret socialist that the *Daily Mail* would have us believe? Or is he merely another clever Scotsman on the make? His massive increases in public spending suggest the former. His readiness to back Blair's costly wars suggests the second. On the Left, they live in hope, rather than expectation.

RON 'AFGHAN' BROWN earned his media soubriquet for the servile admiration he showed for the Soviet invasion of

Afghanistan in 1979. But he was equally famous for breaking into the flat of his mistress and appropriating her knickers, and for his screwball behaviour in the Commons from which he was suspended three times. Despite severe facial disfigurement caused by an electrical burn, he was attractive to women, wittily offering: 'I have sex weekly, very weakly.' Born in Edinburgh in 1940, he trained as an engineering fitter and became active in the old Amalgamated Engineering Union (AEU). Brown was elected to Edinburgh Town Council in 1970, and subsequently to the Lothian Regional Council four years later, where his rebellious nature earned him suspension from the Labour whip. Elected MP for Edinburgh Leith in 1979, he lost no time defending the least-defensible left-wing causes, beginning with the Soviet-installed Karmal government in Kabul. He was active in Labour Friends of Libya, and regularly visited Colonel Gadaffi's revolutionary paradise, though his intervention did occasionally free British detainees in Tripoli. He backed the Militant Tendency against Labour leaders, and **Tony Benn** against **Denis Healey**. He was fined £50 for brandishing his pay slip in Mrs Thatcher's face in 1982, but had the nerve to ask her to reopen diplomatic relations with Albania and North Korea.

He hinted at his most dangerous flirtation with controversy in 1987, calling for the nationalisation of 'fun houses' following the acquittal of madam Cynthia Payne. The following year, he was caught in a compromising situation in the Commons showers with his research assistant, Nona Longden. He tried to joke his way out of the scandal, insisting he 'may be bonkers but wasn't bonking'. Brown was suspended from the Parliamentary Labour Party for three months in May 1988 for waving the Mace round his head in a fury over not being called to speak in a debate on the poll tax, and lost the sponsorship of the AEU. Deselection followed in 1990, and though he put up a respectable showing as an Independent Labour candidate in 1992, his Westminster career was over. Brown turned to the Scottish Socialist Party, as the Militant Tendency had become north of the border, but failed to win a seat in the Holyrood parliament.

RAY BUCKTON brought a genial style to the traditionally aggressive posture of the train drivers' union ASLEF. At his desk in a Hampstead mansion once owned by Sir Joseph Beecham, the pharmaceutical magnate, Buckton would dispense whisky and bonhomie to industrial correspondents while outlining the latest strike misery for commuters. He delighted in his clichés, remarking: 'I've never seen the lads so angry! Telegrams are flooding in from every depot!' before breaking into infectious laughter. Yet there was a serious Leftie side to Buckton, He passionately opposed apartheid, and was a leading figure in the British–Soviet Friendship Society. No union was more supportive of the miners in their three national strikes, and in 1984 he told the Soviet trade union paper *Trud* that Britain was 'rapidly turning into a police state' under Thatcher. Buckton was born at Rillington, north Yorkshire, in 1922, the son of a Tory-voting estate worker, and was a boy member of the Junior Imperial League for their sausage and mash suppers. He began his railway career as a cleaner on steam engines at York automotive power depot, and progressed to fireman. He told this author he only drove a train once – a B16, 4-6-0, for the cognoscenti – and nearly took it through the buffers at Scarborough station. This may have been one of his tall tales, at which he excelled, along with playing the harmonica and growing roses.

He also claimed to have taken firing turns from York to Normanton so that he could climb over the garden wall of the author's home in Railway Terrace to service the daughter of a local ironmonger. Buckton benefited from Workers' Education Association courses, and became active in York Labour Party before becoming a full-time ASLEF official in 1960, and general secretary ten years later. Buckton played a key role in the TUC for two decades, until the right-wing conspired to evict him from the general council in 1986. He retired a year later. One embarrassment dogged Buckton to the end of his life: his friendship with crooked newspaper tycoon Robert Maxwell, who paid for private hospital treatment for cancer. Buckton's handling of the 1982 'flexible rostering' dispute was much criticised, but few realised that ASLEF was fighting for the last vestiges of joint regulation in the railway industry. He retired with his wife Barbara, a stalwart of the Unity Theatre, to Albufeira, on the Algarve coast, and died there in 1995.

JULIE BURCHILL is the daughter of an old-style Communist (known to her as a Stalinist and 'the most important man in my life *ever*') and proclaims herself a Marxist. However, she seems to have taken the fissiparous tendency of the Left to new extremes, espousing what might be called Marxist–hedonism whose political slogan is 'I want IT now!' Born in Bristol in 1959, the only child of a 'wildly anti-American' shopworkers' union official, who contradictorily admired John Wayne, she ran away from home at the age of fifteen to work in a chemist's shop in King's Cross. Two years later, she achieved her ambition to work as a journalist on *New Musical Express*, where outlandish politics were normal.

Burchill's irrepressible desire to shock took her to the heights of Fleet Street personality journalism. Her outrageous opinions brought her £130,000 a year from the *Sunday Express* alone. But was the self-styled Queen of the Groucho Club really a Leftie? In her autobiography, *I Knew I Was Right*, for which the old tabloid term 'racy' is entirely appropriate, she accepted that Communism was over, but insisted that Marxist analysis is 'logical and sensible'. Twice-married Burchill finally found love and happiness with Charlotte Raven, 'a Marxist, praise the Lord, in a sea of Miscellaneous Men'. Her political conclusion is that the present system is born to die, and 'only a hoosier of the corniest order can believe that Communism will never walk the earth again'. This is all very encouraging, but if Burchill were doing more to make it happen than a few asides in a 200-page diary of self-indulgence, then her credentials as a Leftie would be more substantial.

GUY BURGESS was such a consummate actor that he managed to convince fellow-homosexual **Tom Driberg** that he was not a Soviet spy, despite overwhelming evidence to the contrary. Burgess found his politics at Eton in the late 1920s, where a dockers' organiser speaking to the boys opened his eyes to the poverty and struggle of life in London's East End. He also learned of the coming catastrophe with Fascism in Germany from a lecture by Sir Harold Nicolson, Counsellor in the German Embassy in Berlin. At Cambridge, Burgess was recruited to the Communist Party by the historian **James Klugmann**, to whom he argued that it was futile to campaign against the war without campaigning against the causes of war. 'If you think like that, your place is in the Party,' said Klugmann. As the most brilliant student of his day, Burgess was elected to the Society of the Apostles, an outfit even more secretive than the CP. But he did not neglect his political duties, helping to organise a successful strike by waiters in Trinity College.

He did not remain long in the Communist Party. In his famous Moscow statement with **Donald Maclean** in February 1956, Burgess disclosed that the pair abandoned their political activities at Cambridge not because they disagreed with the Marxist analysis but because they thought they could put their ideas into more practical effect in the public service – in its broadest sense. In other words, they entered the British establishment in order to destroy it. Burgess tried first to join *The Times*, but a trial in the sub-editors' room flopped and he joined the BBC as a talks producer. Here, he advanced the cause as best he could, before joining Section Nine of the Secret Intelligence Service, MI6, working on wartime propaganda. To his dismay, the section was wound up and he returned to the BBC, this time, however, with an added undercover role working for MI5. In 1943, he joined the News Department of the Foreign Office, before moving to the new Labour government in 1946 as personal assistant to Hector McNeil, Minister of State in the Foreign Office. He had often used McNeil in his BBC programmes, and the two were on close (but not sexual) terms.

Burgess was appalled by the government's support for the Americans' post-war strategy, which his immediate boss was obliged to endorse. In 1947, he asked to transfer to a political department, preferably the Far East. There, he spoke up favourably for the Chinese Communist Revolution, which in his Marxist analysis was 'Socialist in content, national in form'. At the outbreak of the Korean War, Burgess was sent to the British Embassy in Washington, tasked with explaining British policy on the Far East to the State Department. The ambassador, who did not like him, soon transferred Burgess to work on America and the Middle East. From there, after a brush with the American police for being caught speeding three times in one day, he was recalled to London in disgrace.

Burgess had made up his mind to leave the FO, and sounded out work prospects on the *Daily Telegraph*. Meanwhile, he contacted Donald Maclean, who confessed that he was being 'followed by the dicks'. Maclean asked for his help to get to Moscow, and Burgess booked two tickets on the Southampton–St Malo ferry. From there, they travelled by train to Berne, where the Czech Embassy gave them visas for Maclean's onward flight to the Soviet Union. Burgess was not supposed to accompany him, but on impulse joined him on the plane from Prague. Once in Russia, the authorities sent the pair to a provincial city. Burgess was most unhappy. For him, it was 'permanently like Glasgow on a Saturday night in the nineteenth century'. He long harboured a desire to return to England, bored with a minor role writing for the Russians until he found a gay partner Tolya. He still wore his old Etonian tie, and read *The Times*. He insisted to Tom Driberg that he was not starry-eyed about the USSR, but did prefer to live in a socialist country. He died there in 1963, aged fifty-two.

JOHN BURNS became famous as 'the agitator of all work'. He immortalised the 'docker's tanner', the pay claim that brought the London docks to a standstill in August 1889. Still only thirty, black-bearded, his brawny frame bursting out of a blue reefer suit and waving his trademark straw hat, Burns electrified casual dock labourers gathered on Tower Hill with his appeal to stand shoulder to shoulder in their demand for a penny an hour increase to six pence (2½ p). The solid strike involving 100,000 men that followed was denounced in *The Times* as 'revolutionary', though the men did not have a union or other form of organisation. The *Morning Post* condemned Burns as 'a kind of pinchbeck Danton threatening London with a reign of terror'. A month after the walk-out began, the employers caved in and agreed the principle of the docker's tanner. Initially, the men could not recognise the victory for what it was, and heckled Burns when he explained the terms of the deal, which also introduced an element of joint regulation of employment. But the reputation of the washer-woman's son from Lambeth had been made. And Burns had ambition to match his conceit and oratorical sway over the mob.

He was a skilled worker, who educated himself after leaving school at the age of ten, and became an articulate spokesman for the Marxist Social Democratic Federation. His eyes were set on Westminster, and in the election of 1885 he polled almost 600 votes in Nottingham West. Two years later, he was jailed for six weeks for his part in defying a police ban on demonstrating in Trafalgar Square. However, by the time of the great dock strike, Burns was a London County Councillor, and in 1892 he was elected Independent Labour MP for Battersea, his political base. To the dismay of his acolytes, Burns allied himself with the Lib-Labs at Westminster, rather than the socialist ILP, and was openly scornful of Keir Hardie. When Sir Henry Campbell-Bannerman formed a Liberal government in 1905, Burns accepted the Cabinet post of President of the Local Government Board. Less was heard of his old socialist views in this job, or in his next post as President of the Board of Trade. Burns decried radical economic policies, and supported the Osborne judgement of 1909 that attacked trade union funding for the nascent Labour Party. He quit the government in 1914 in protest at the war, and did not stand in the 'coupon' election of 1918, which decimated the Liberals. He lived quietly, surrounded by his books, until his mid-eighties, another firebrand Leftie tamed by the system.

C

JOHN CAIRNCROSS is usually described as 'the Fifth Man' in the Cambridge ring of Communist spies, but he always denied ideological motivation and insisted that he was a loner. When the KGB files finally surfaced, he was portrayed as a 'convinced' Communist who 'at once expressed his readiness to work for us'. What is certain is that Cairncross was recruited to work for the USSR by **James Klugmann**, the influential Marxist. The extent of the damage he did to British interests is disputed. He may not have given Stalin the A-bomb, but he did deliver literally tons of top-secret Enigma intercepts on German dispositions from Bletchley Park, which helped the Red Army win the battle of Kursk, a turning point in the Second World War. Cairncross was born in 1913, the son of a Scottish ironmonger and his primary-school teacher wife. Academically gifted, especially in languages, he graduated from Glasgow University, then picked up further degrees from the Sorbonne and Cambridge, where he shared a staircase with **Anthony Blunt** at Trinity College. Blunt talent-spotted the chippy young Scot, who came top of the Foreign Office examinations and went into the diplomatic service.

Guy Burgess, already working for KGB, said in a report to his handlers that Cairncross was 'not a gentleman' and felt no respect for the FO. He was recruited in 1937, in comical circumstances in Regent's Park, and given the code-name 'Molière'. For years, Cairncross claimed to have been 'trapped' into working for the Russians, but telegrams from his Paris-based handler Arnold Deutsch ('Otto') that came to light in 1998 described him as 'very intelligent, proud and ideologically on our side…a convinced communist.' He passed on sensitive Foreign Office material, including details of the appeasement lobby within the FO. In 1940, he was promoted to the post of private secretary to Lord Hankey, Minister without Portfolio in Churchill's government with responsibility for the intelligence services and involved in Tube Alloys, the code-name for Britain's atomic bomb research. In 1941, Cairncross provided 3,449 intelligence secrets to the Russians – a figure only exceeded by **Donald Maclean**. Renamed 'Lizst', he moved on to Bletchley Park, where he passed on thousands of Enigma decrypts.

In 1944 he was posted to the counter-intelligence department of MI6, where he worked alongside fellow spy **Kim Philby**. After the war, while working for the Treasury, Cairncross continued his espionage, but came under suspicion in 1951 after Burgess and Maclean had fled to Moscow. MI5 officers found an unsigned FO note in his handwriting in Burgess's flat, and picked him up. Cairncross stood up well to interrogation, but was forced to resign. He left the country to become an academic in America, building up a reputation as an authority on French literature and even as a minor poet. He moved on to the UN Food and Agriculture Organisation in Canada, still undetected.

In 1964 MI5's redoubtable investigator Arthur Martin extracted a full confession from him, on a promise that he would not be extradited or prosecuted. He was not finally exposed until 1979, when the *Sunday Times* tracked him down to Rome and Cairncross confessed to journalist Barrie Penrose. The ensuing publicity, not to mention a year in an Italian jail on currency charges, forced him first to France and finally, a sick old man, back to England with his American opera singer girl friend half his age, Gayle Brinkerhoff, in 1995. Two years later, following the death of his estranged wife Gabriella, he married her just before he died. She completed his autobiography, *The Enigma Spy*, and commented: 'He was an amateur. We used to joke that he must have been a nightmare to the KGB, the worst spy material this century.' But he was a rare foreign holder of the Order of the Red Banner.

JAMES CAMERON cordially loathed careerist politicians, almost as much as they feared his coruscating pen. His own politics were straight from the shoulder. 'From the moment when politics were anything more than a word, I accepted socialism without any particular reasoning or argument,' he said, towards the end of his life. His socialism was intuitive, rather than rational, though he slightly envied those who could convince themselves logically. His grandfather was a minister of the kirk in Glasgow, but his father, a failed barrister, discovered a genius for story-telling of the Catherine Cookson variety. He prospered somewhat, and James was born in Battersea in 1911 during one of the family's periodic upheavals before they settled in Wendover, convenient for his alcoholic father's excursions to the Shoulder of Mutton. His mother died young, leaving Cameron 'the father to my father.' He was apprenticed to the journalism trade with D. C. Thomson, the notoriously anti-union publishers, in Dundee, where he fell in love with his landlady's daughter Elma. They married when he moved to the *Scottish Daily Express* in Glasgow, where she died in childbirth.

Cameron moved to the *Express* in London, remarried, and lived ten 'wild, violent, diverting, obsessive, exasperating' years as the paper's chief foreign reporter before falling out with Beaverbrook. He quit in 1950 after the sister paper, the *Evening Standard*, published the scare headline of the generation: 'FUCHS AND STRACHEY: A GREAT NEW CRISIS . War Minister Has Never Disavowed Communism.' Coincidentally, left-winger John Strachey had been appointed Secretary for War on the day that atom spy **Klaus Fuchs** was jailed for passing secrets to the Russians. There was no crisis, except that manufactured by the *Standard*. Cameron wrote to *The Times*, dissociating himself from the 'purge-by-Press' and resigning from the organisation that initiated the witch-hunt. He moved to the *Picture Post*, then a hard-hitting magazine under Tom Hopkinson. There, too, he came to grief, with an exposure of Allied complicity in atrocities committed by anti-Communist troops in the Korean War. The article was suppressed, but a proof was passed to the *Daily Worker,* which, to his horror' promptly splashed with it.

He quit the magazine, and worked for many more years on the liberal *News Chronicle*, leaving shortly before it merged with the illiberal *Daily*

Mail. Cameron went into television documentary work, always arguing that 'facts are less important than the truth.' As one of the few British journalists to have seen three A-bombs explode, he never wavered from hostility to nuclear weaponry and was prominent in the foundation of CND in 1958. In his autobiography, *Point of Departure*, Cameron insisted: 'I have never had the responsibilities of a formal political attitude.' *Au fond*, he was a well-intentioned anarchist, as the best journalists are. He died in January 1985.

KEN CAMERON, the Mr Punch lookalike of the labour movement, would look at the clock at mid-morning during trade union conferences and announce that it was now one p.m. in Moscow, and therefore the drinking could begin. He was, quite literally, the bagman for the NUM during the Great Strike of 1984, sometimes carrying around hundreds of thousands in cash in black bin liners. The true story has never been told, and probably never will be. He and **Arthur Scargill**'s driver once collected £200,000 from the Co-op Bank, and told the inquisitive chief teller they had been given a good tip on a horse. 'He didn't even ask the name of the horse,' Cameron related later. Yet as general secretary of the Fire Brigades Union, he also presided over the longest period of stability in the fire service after the national strike of 1978, a feat that owed much to his ability to get on with politicians of every stripe. That even included throwbacks like Lord Ferrers, the Home Office minister under Thatcher, who pretended mystification when the FBU asked for pension rights for non-married partners of firemen. 'Oh, you mean money for Fifi!' he expostulated.

Cameron was born in Fort William in 1941, the son of a GPO linesman and an Irishwoman who scrubbed floors 'in service'. He left school at fifteen to work in a grocer's shop, then, encouraged by an uncle who chaired the local Watch Committee, signed on as a police cadet. He hated every minute, and fled to the Aberdeen *Press and Journal* as a trainee reporter. His career in journalism ended after he and a rival reporter fell into a swimming pool while reporting a water polo game. After a spell labouring, Cameron headed south to Birmingham, where he became a firefighter. He was also active in the FBU, winning election to the national executive in 1978 and a full-time national officer's post three years later. He was a surprising victor in the 1980 general secretaryship election, and held the post for twenty years before retiring in 2002. Cameron, a dyed-in-the-wool Labour Leftie who was more often to be found in the company of Communists like **Mick McGahey** than the nabobs of the TUC (of which he eventually became one), has married twice and had two children. His rueful recollections of a lifetime of Labour are as entertaining as was the **Airlie** Experience.

JOHNNY CAMPBELL saw it all and divulged nothing. As the last Moscow-inclined editor of the *Daily Worker*, he agonised over the legacy of Stalin, whose actions he saw at close quarters in the 1930s, but could not bring himself to repudiate a life of Communism loyal to the USSR. Campbell first came to notice in 1924, as editor of the *Workers' Weekly*, in which he published an appeal to soldiers not to turn their guns on the workers either in a class war or a military war. He knew about war, having served in the trenches where he lost the toes of one foot, giving him a limp for life. A sharp, slender man with a most unparty sense of humour, Campbell was charged with incitement to mutiny. Labour's first government, in office only months under Ramsay MacDonald, decided to withdraw the charge, and the Tories rammed home an indictment of 'soft on Communism'. MacDonald called a general election, in which the Tories used the notorious, forged Zinoviev Letter to discredit Labour and secure a handsome victory. A year later, the authorities raided CP headquarters and carted off a dozen party leaders and officials. They were jailed for up to a year on the original charge, plus an extra offence of seditious libel.

Campbell became the British party representative on the Comintern in Moscow in the bleak 1930s, a role more important in form than reality, but one that allowed a unique vantage-point on Stalin's regime. After the Stalin–Hitler pact, Campbell opposed the Comintern line of rejecting the war against Fascism, and was forced to recant but was then rehabilitated when the Nazis invaded the USSR. He was appointed editor of the *Daily Worker* in 1949, and was popular with the staff. He took a more flexible line than Bill Rust, his predecessor, but struggled with de-Stalinisation in the Soviet Union and his own historic loyalties. After Khrushchev's denunciation of Stalin and the Hungarian uprising of 1956, the *Worker* lost a third of its journalists. Campbell bent to the wind of change, but never divulged what he learned in the dark days of the thirties. **Phil Piratin**, one of the party's MPs, once asked him what went on in Moscow at that time. Campbell spoke indistinctly of being there to represent the CP, and was plainly in such torment that Piratin halted his questions. Campbell stepped down from the editorship in 1959, and also quit the party's national executive.

DENNIS CANAVAN graduated from teaching mathematics to adding up the lies and treachery of the Blair Revolution, a process of enlightenment that forced him out of the Labour Party. A slight, red-bearded figure with a rasping voice, he was caricatured as the Scottish Dennis Skinner, but proved to have more nerve than the ultimately loyal 'Beast of Bolsover'. Born in Cowdenbeath, Fife, in 1942, the son of an electrician, he boycotted a Coronation pageant at school when he was only nine. Canavan joined the Labour Party in 1965, and via Stirling District Council became MP for what is now Falkirk West in 1974. From the start at Westminster he was agin: agin anything that smelt of the establishment, from the Falklands war to the Royal Family.

A passionate nuclear disarmer, he also supported a United Ireland (briefly Labour Party policy) and opposed the Terrorism Laws. He rebelled against Wilson, Healey and Callaghan, and in due course against Tony Blair, whom he attacked as the product of an elite school who rejected state education for his children and 'pontificated' against teaching methods in comprehensives. Blair could not wait to get rid of him, and did so when Canavan was rejected as a Labour candidate for the Scottish Parliament and then stood as an Independent. He was a runaway winner, with 55 per cent of the vote. Life for 'Mr Angry' was not always so trouble-free. He and his first wife Elnor were divorced in 1990 after twenty-five years of marriage. Three years later, he married a childhood sweetheart, natural help therapist Brigid Gallagher, in the garden of his cottage in Bannockburn. In 1997 they split up.

In the May 2003 Scottish elections, he held Falkirk West with the largest majority in the Scottish Parliament.

BARBARA CASTLE had an enduring public reputation as a Labour Leftie, but this should not be allowed to overshadow her private notoriety as a woman of considerable passion. In her twenties, when still Barbara Betts, she embarked on a ten-year affair with William Mellor, a married man twenty-two years her senior then editing *Tribune*. The relationship ended in with his death in 1942, and Barbara married Ted Castle, production editor of the *Daily Mirror*, two years later. Neither was faithful to the other, though she always claimed: 'I am a puritan, a sensuous puritan.'

At the age of nineteen, she decided to find out about sex, but was disappointed with the fumble in a fellow Oxford undergraduate's rooms. Rumours of other lovers abounded. Even **Michael Foot** was roped into the erotic pantomime, after hinting of an affair on holiday during Chamberlain's Munich débâcle in 1938. 'Peace in our time,' Foot told a television interviewer, 'meant coming home after a week with Barbara.'

Barbara Betts was born in 1910, the daughter of a self-taught assistant tax inspector who placed a premium on learning – he could write Greek verse – and politics. He edited the ILP paper, *Bradford Pioneer*, and also had a long affair, though the marriage survived. Young Barbara attended Bradford Grammar School, and gained a third at St Hugh's, Oxford. She set her sights on becoming a politician, or at least a political journalist, and joined **Stafford Cripps**'s short-lived Socialist League. She and Foot contributed a column on trade union affairs to *Tribune*, and in 1943 a bravura performance at the Labour Party conference condemning the government's tardiness in implementing the Beveridge Report put her on the front page of the *Daily Mirror* and in Ted Castle's arms.

Against the odds, she took Blackburn in 1945 and held the seat for thirty years, before 'retiring' to become an MEP, and subsequently a peeress. Castle is known for many things: for introducing the breathalyser, seat-belts in cars and speed limits on the roads; for the Equal Pay Act that improved the lot of working women; for redirecting child benefit to the mother and for her fatal error in pressing prematurely for trade union reform. *In Place of Strife* robbed her of any further political advancement, allowing Callaghan to take his revenge with her dismissal from Cabinet. Castle was never really at home with the **Blair-Brown** axis, and delighted in the tremendous applause she got for attacking New Labour at the conference lectern. Towards her death in 2002, she said: 'Political careers don't end in tears. They end in fury.' Hers certainly did. If only the present generation had inherited some of her indomitable rage.

CHRISTOPHER CAUDWELL was the *nom de plume* of Christopher St John Sprigg, poet, journalist and critic, under which he wrote the classic work *Illusion and Reality*, advancing a Marxist theory of understanding the human struggle with nature. He died aged twenty-nine, fighting in the battle for Jarama in the Spanish civil war.

The son of a journalist, he was born in Putney in 1915, and while still a teenager he worked on the *Yorkshire Observer*. Back in London, he branched out, writing on the nascent science of aeronautics, turning out detective fiction and writing books on aircraft. He was introduced to Marxism in 1934, joined the Communist Party a year later, and became a committed propagandist for the cause. At the outbreak of the Spanish Civil War, Caudwell volunteered for the International Brigade, and found himself as a rifleman on the front line at the terrifying battle of Jarama in February 1937, where republican troops were overwhelmed by Fascist forces including Moors and the Spanish Foreign Legion. The British battalion put up a historic resistance, but casualties were high, Caudwell among them. Bill Alexander, historian of the war, described him as 'the outstanding Marxist intellectual and Communist who insisted on going to Spain'. Ironically, the CP had called battalion head-quarters at Albacete to insist on Caudwell's return to London, in recognition of his 'unique qualities'. The message arrived too late.

Considering his premature death, his literary output was prodigious. *Illusion and Reality* was published posthumously in 1937, and *Studies in a Dying Culture* followed in 1938, followed by a further volume in the same vein a year later. He also wrote *The Crisis in Physics* and his poems were published twice, once in 1938 and as *Collected Poems* in 1986. *The Cambridge Guide to Literature in English* praises his verse for its plain language, simple forms and unsentimental realism and urgency, while noting an 'occasional stilted earnestness'. There was nothing stilted about his life.

KEN COATES has one claim to fame, and a secret infamy. He popularised the ideas of workers' control when the Labour Party was still wedded to old-style, top-down nationalisation of industry. And in 1965 he gave this author his first break in Leftie journalism, on *The Week*, a remarkably professional printed news briefing produced above a shop in Castle Boulevard in Nottingham where I was a university student. The work consisted mostly of turning reports from shop stewards and other activists into something like prose. Naturally it was unpaid, and in those pre-desktop days, I wondered how it could keep on coming out without any visible means of support. But appear it did, and *The Week* had an impressive list of sponsors, including academics and Labour MPs.

Coates is one of those people whom Labour leaders could perfectly well do without. He was born in 1930, and became a miner in his native Nottinghamshire. He won a scholarship to the university, and was an adult-education lecturer there for twenty years from 1960. A short man with thick curly black hair and a ready smile, which he took to be knowing, Coates was associated with a number of Trotskyist groups and the International Marxist Group, but that did not prevent him rising to the presidency of the Nottingham Labour Party. He broke with the ultra-Left in 1967, and helped set up Spokesman Books, which spread the good news of the Institute for Workers' Control, though it was never as influential as it professed. To the surprise of many, Coates was elected Labour MEP for Nottingham in 1989, but the arrival of New Labour was not to his taste. He opposed the abolition of Clause IV, and Labour's candidate-rigging introduced for elections to the European Parliament. For this, he and his fellow dissident Hugh Kerr were expelled from the party. He failed to secure a return to Strasbourg in the Alternative Labour List in 1999, but happily even that reverse did not shut him up.

FRANK CHAPPLE learned the tricks of the Leftie trade in the Communist Party, and then put them to brilliant use to oust his old comrades. Born in east London in 1921, Chapple left school at fourteen and was apprenticed in electrical contracting. He joined the electricians' union when he was sixteen, and the CP three years later, subsequently describing his recruitment as 'the sort of disease you sometimes picked up on a building site'. Nonetheless, he prospered under the party's wing, as a shop steward and branch official before quitting about the time of the Hungarian rising in 1956. He was deeply involved in the 1959 High Court action that eventually forced out a corrupt Communist regime in the Electrical Trades Union, and became general secretary in 1966. Thereafter, he was uncompromising in his *jihad* against the Left, in his own union and in the TUC and Labour Party where he became a prominent figure. A small, dark, jaunty figure with a sardonic sense of humour, he called his old comrades 'slugs in the garden' and taunted an ex-colleague who suffered from arthritis: 'It's all that time you spent on your knees to employers.' He delighted in the discomfiture of the Left, and found an unconventional admirer in Norman Tebbit, the right-wing Tory Cabinet minister who described his contributions to the National Economic Development Council as 'rare but pithy'. The political distance he travelled may be gained from Tebbit's disclosure that on a private visit to his house during the 1980s water strike, Chapple told him 'more about the causes of the dispute and the roles of the union leaders involved than anyone else before or since'. He was made a life peer in 1985, but rarely attended the Lords, preferring the company of his racing pigeons. In the words of Alan Clark, the Tory diarist, Frank was a professional rough diamond.

KENNETH CLARKE, the former Chancellor, wins the

prize for the inclusion of a Tory in this collection by a short head over Iain Gilmour, famously described as 'so wet you could shoot snipe off him' and whose friendship with **Michael Foot** is well documented, not least by a joint portrait in that haunt of Old Labour, the Gay Hussar restaurant in Soho. There were other candidates. Peter Temple-Morris, the genial, silver-haired Conservative MP for Leominster, crossed the floor to join New Labour (in the process depriving traditional Labour MP John McWilliam of a rare parliamentary 'pair'). Ambitious Alan Howarth did the same and is now a middle-ranking minister in Blair's administration. But both ratted because they felt New Labour was now right-wing enough to encompass their views. Neither of them drinks beer in copious quantities, or sits next to Peter Mandelson during parliamentary debates (presumably in order to proselytise for the Left) as Clarke does. But the clincher is a quotation from Margaret Thatcher, recorded by Woodrow Wyatt: 'Those dreadful Hush Puppy shoes Kenneth Clarke wears everywhere. He's really a socialist at heart.' No greater condemnation is imaginable.

TONY CLIFF was a founder member and charismatic leader of the Trotskyist Socialist Workers' Party that emerged from the International Socialists in 1977. In keeping with the fissiparous tendency of the Left, the IS had itself sprung from the Socialist Review Group that he had formed in the 1950s. Cliff was born Ygael Gluckstein in Palestine in 1917, the son of a Zionist building contractor. His teachers identified him as a Communist because he sympathised with the plight of Arab children, and he was impatient to live up to the charge. At seventeen, he was active in Haifa Trades Council, and joined the Communist Party while still a teenager. Disillusioned with Communism, he turned to revolutionary socialist politics and moved to England with his South African wife Chanie. They were hounded out by Special Branch and lived in Ireland for five years before being permitted re-entry. His various groups and parties failed to prosper until the spectacular implosion of the CPGB, which left his SWP as the only serious political organisation ranged on the left of, and against, Kinnock's modernising Labour Party. Cliff was an unprepossessing man to observe: short and shabby, with the appearance to **Paul Foot** of a rag doll. Yet he had a penetrating mind and a sharp tongue. His critique of the Soviet Union as 'state capitalism' in character and imperialist in strategy influenced a generation of young socialists, and his ideas continue to do so. No Saturday morning in a busy high street is complete without sellers of the *Socialist Worker*. Cliff died in 2000, penniless and possession-free. His legacy was: 'Don't mourn, organise!'

BRIAN CLOUGH wears his politics like a soccer shirt, never disguising his support for the Labour Party. The footballer/club manager had 'no problem' about having money in the bank, a large house and a Mercedes while still being a socialist. Given his origins, his outlook is not a mystery.

'Cloughie' was born, one of eight, in a council house in Middlesbrough in 1935, the son of a sugar boiler at the local sweet factory. He confessed to being academically 'thick' and failed his 11-plus, but became head boy of Marton Grove Secondary Modern. His footballing talent took him out of a dead-end job in ICI's Teesside plant to stardom in the beautiful game. He could have become a political legend instead, somewhat on the lines of **Dennis Skinner**. He certainly equalled him in the gift of the gab. Clough canvassed for Labour candidates, particularly Philip Whitehead, and marched with striking miners. He even joined them on the picket lines.

When Harold Wilson was leader, Clough was offered the Labour candidacy at Richmond, Surrey, where the Tories had an impregnable majority. He was promised 'other things' if he fought a hopeless seat, but wasn't tempted. The second time he was approached, Clough almost said, 'Yes.' He was offered the chance to fight Winston Churchill in Moss Side, Manchester, where the Conservative majority was only 4,000. The bait of becoming Minister of Sport was held out in front of him, and Clough admitted later that the prospect of taking on Young Winston appealed to him 'no end – as did the prospect of ruffling a few feathers in the House of Commons'. He boasted that he could have taken his pick of any marginal seat in the country, which was probably true. Labour was just learning the value of celebrity endorsement, long established in the USA.

Clough eventually decided to stick to what he knew best: picking football teams. Politics got by without him, but he would unquestionably have been a great adornment to Westminster, particularly the bars.

MAUREEN COLQUHOUN was the first MP to be publicly identified as a lesbian, and paid the price for being different in more orthodox times. She was MP for Northampton North from 1974 to 1979, and scandalised the Labour Party by leaving her husband to live with Barbara Todd, founder of a lesbian magazine. Born in 1931, Colquhoun was a Hackney borough councillor and official of Gingerbread, the one-parent pressure group, before entering Parliament. She survived a number of attempts by the Labour Party to deselect her, before the voters saved them the trouble with an eight per cent swing to the Tories in Thatcher's first election, letting in the dreadful Tony Marlow, whose private life was at least as exotic as Ms Colquhoun's.

JAMES CONNOLLY is immortalised as the great Irish rebel. However, he also qualifies as a British Leftie: not solely on the grounds that the Irish were also British citizens at the time, but because he was born in Edinburgh and raised in the Scots tradition of socialist radicalism. He was the last of the 1916 Easter Rising heroes to be executed on 12 May 1916, shot by British soldiers while tied to a chair. He could not stand because of his wounds. This shameful end came to a life that started in 1868, when he was born into poverty as the son of Irish immigrants. At the age of eleven, he began work as a printer's devil. Three years later he joined the British Army, and was posted to Cork. Seven years in Ireland sharpened his political and nationalist instincts. He married, and returned to his native city where he fell under the spell of John Leslie, a Scots socialist, who recruited him to the ranks of Marxism.

In 1896, he accepted an invitation to become paid organiser for the Dublin Socialist Society. He swiftly founded the Irish Socialist Republican Party, and a newspaper, the *Workers' Republic*. Neither met with much success, and in 1903 he emigrated to the United States, returning in 1910 to become organiser for the Belfast branch of James Larkins's Irish Transport and General Workers' Union. The Dublin Lockout of 1913 brought him south, and he became general secretary of the ITGWU the following year. He also espoused the cause of women, arguing: 'The worker is the slave of capitalist society, the female worker is the slave of that slave.' Simultaneously, Connolly was deeply engaged in the formation of the Irish Citizens' Army, of which he was commander-general of the Dublin Brigade. As the First World War gripped the attention of the government, Connolly perceived that Britain's hour of peril was Ireland's opportunity.

His citizen army was pitifully small, numbering few more than two hundred members, and ill-equipped, but the socialist-turned-comman-dant joined forces with the Irish Republican Brotherhood Military Council to foment an insurrection against the British. Appointed, rather prematurely, vice-president of the Irish Republic on the day before the rising, he led the storming of the General Post Office and conducted military operations there for a week before surrendering to superior British firepower. Badly wounded in the fighting, he was court-martialled in a hospital bed on 9 May 1916, defiant to the end, and executed by firing squad three days later.

ARTHUR JAMES COOK was the miners' leader during the 1926 General Strike upon whom **Arthur Scargill** modelled himself half a century later, with much the same result. Cook was by some way the more pragmatic of the two, seeking to persuade the miners to return to work when a pusillanimous TUC backed down after nine days of national stoppage. He led his men to defeat only when they made clear that that was their preferred destination. Scargill compares himself favourably with his hero, arguing that 'in those days it was very amateurish. Cook was battered, not only psychologically from the desertion of colleagues and friends, but also physically. Apart from one or two hiccups, I have a very strong constitution and an amazing power of recuperation.' Scargill lived to retire, not without means.

'AJ' Cook, as he was invariably called, was born in Wookey, Somerset, in 1883, and began life as a farm labourer. In 1901 he migrated to the South Wales coalfield, where he married his landlord's daughter, became active in the miners' union and joined the ILP. Ten years later, he went to the Central Labour College in London, and used his education to good effect with part-authorship of *The Miners' Next Step*, a seminal labour movement document. On his return to South Wales, Cook was a forthright exponent of the ILP policy of pacifism in the First World War. Elected as full-time miners' agent in the Rhondda with the support of the infant CPGB, he worked closely with the Communists. Francis Beckett describes him as 'an extraordinary man, slight and unimpressive to look at, with a high squeaky voice, his speeches broke all the rules of oratory and had little logical structure'. Yet he became the most effective speaker in the country, and his slogan 'Not a penny off the pay, not an hour on the day' the rallying cry of the miners. He endured jail and sieges of his house before becoming secretary of the Miners' Federation of Great Britain in 1924, pledged to nationalisation of the industry.

The failure of the 1926 strike, when the men were beaten back after six months – and many activists never worked again – put Cook in a political limbo. Even the Communists distrusted him. Willie Gallacher wrote that 'Cook is as cunning as they make them and unscrupulous.' AJ put his trust in the election of a Labour government, but MacDonald's administration of 1929 failed to deliver for the MFGB and Cook turned in desperation to Oswald Mosley's protectionist manifesto for industry, though he rejected the latter conversion to Fascism. A leg injury sustained in the long strike forced Cook to undergo amputation in 1931, and he died of cancer, a broken man, in November that year.

By contrast, Scargill had it rather easy, retiring 'early' in his sixties with a handsome pension and his own political party to play with.

ROBIN COOK retrieved his left-wing credentials by resigning from the Blair government in March 2003 over the illegal war against Iraq, but shrank from taking the natural next step of leading the Left in Parliament. Cook-watchers were not unduly surprised. He was always willing to wound, but afraid to strike. He dithered briefly in the 1994 Labour leadership election, when his wannabe campaign manager Peter Hain rang round the Sunday papers with the message 'Don't rule out Robin.' The next day, he ruled himself out.

There has always been that fatal air of hesitation. Even when faced, in August 1997, with imminent exposure of his extra-marital relationship with his secretary Gaynor Regan in the *News of the World*, Cook vacillated. Alastair Campbell bounced him into plumping for Gaynor, in the cause of good news management. Cook denies that, claiming the he always knew he would rather be with Gaynor, but could not bring himself to confront the choice between wife and mistress. It amounts to the same thing. Irresolution. When he urged that British troops be withdrawn from Iraq, he immediately qualified his tough stance, positioning himself as the Grand Old Duke of York, only in reverse. Yet he remains a force for the politics of integrity, set alongside duplicitous New Labour, with which he has never really seemed at home.

Robert Finlayson Cook was born in 1946, in Bellshill, Lanarkshire. His father, son of a miner blacklisted after the General Strike, was a science teacher who met his mother when they both worked in a wartime munitions factory. Robin, as he was nicknamed at school, was intellectually precocious, reading most of Dickens by the age of ten and making his speaking debut at Aberdeen Grammar School a year later. Cook admitted to his biographer John Kampfner that he was an unpopular swot at Edinburgh High School, 'rather singlemindedly intellectual in my image and pursuits'. Both the nickname and the image stuck. Graduating from Edinburgh University, he went into teaching, but more urgently politics.

He fought Edinburgh North in 1970 and won Edinburgh Central in the pit strike poll of February 1974, making him **Gordon Brown**'s parliamentary senior by almost a decade. Once friends – or allies, at least – these two 'primitively competitive' titans fell out spectacularly and permanently after being on different sides in the Scottish devolution campaign. Cook rose quickly to Labour's front bench, taking Treasury, Euro and Health portfolios. He was kingmaker to both Neil Kinnock and John Smith, and might have been a genuine candidate against **Blair** had not the New Labour machine been revving up since Smith's first heart-attack.

His finest hour in opposition was the Commons debate on the 'Arms to Iraq' Scott Report, whose five volumes he mastered so swiftly and to such devastating effect that John Major's government survived by a single vote. In government as Foreign Secretary, his 'ethical foreign policy' was much derided, and he proved unexpectedly gaffe-prone. His survival after the 2001 election as Leader of the House confounded his many enemies, but he proved to be a radical (if not always successful – the Commons is a deeply conservative place) reformer. Cook and his Cabinet colleague **Clare Short** wrestled with their consciences over Blair's determination to go to war in Iraq without explicit United Nations backing. In Cook's case, conscience won.

JEREMY CORBYN MP can always be relied on to turn up and say (or parrot) the correct Leftie things. In the Tories' index of Labour Lefties published in 1992, his entry is the longest, taking up five pages. An unstoppable public speaker and semi-professional backbench rebel, he joined the Labour Party while still at grammar school in Shropshire. Corbyn flunked North London Poly and worked as a union researcher before joining National Union of Public Employees (NUPE) as a full-time official. Elected MP for Islington North in 1983, he immediately plunged into controversy, inviting Sinn Fein leader Gerry Adams to the Commons and hiring republican Ronan Bennett, as his researcher. Irate Commons authorities withdrew his staffer's security pass. Undeterred, Corbyn sponsored or signed a forest of early day motions on Nicaragua, CND, the SAS shooting of IRA bombers in Gibraltar, the great coal strike, and every other Leftist cause. Slight, bearded and scruffy, he is the nearest thing at Westminster to a student revolutionary: contemptuous of office, happiest when protesting. Should he ever grow up, it would be a great loss to the theatre of politics.

JOHN CORNFORD, the promising Cambridge poet, died on a Spanish civil war battlefield outside Cordoba in December 1936, the day after his twenty-first birthday. His comrade, the historian Ralph Fox, had been cut down by fascist Francoist forces while making a forward reconnaissance ahead of his International Brigade unit, and Cornford was shot trying to retrieve his body. Thus was cut short a life that offered so much.

Born in 1915, he was the son of the writer Frances Cornford. Under her influence, he began writing poetry as a child. Educated at Stowe School, Trinity College, Cambridge, and the London School of Economics, he joined the Communist Party in 1933. While still an undergraduate, he wrote in *Cambridge Left* in 1934: 'There can be no doubt that the future is with the revolutionary participator, not the impartial observer nor the romantic Utopian idealist.'

He put his theory into action at the outbreak of the Spanish civil war, going out to fight as one of the first British volunteers in August 1936. He expected to be 'staying a few days, firing a few shots and then coming home'. Ironically, in the light of the bloody internecine strife between the anarchist POUM and the Communists, initially, he joined the POUM. He did return home later that month, and took back six recruits and transferred to become a machine-gunner with the International Brigade. He took part in the defence of Madrid, fighting on one occasion behind barricades of books in the university. Cornford was regarded as one of intellectuals of the best type, unlike the 'Bloomsbury odds and sods' who exasperated the largely working-class field commanders. Sixty per cent of the International Brigaders were Communists. Cornford's verse, inevitably meagre in production, owes more to the modernism of Eliot and Auden than his mother's style. His *Poems from Spain 1936* and some love poems are the best survivors. Cornford's lover, the Cambridge historian Margo Heinemann, never quite got over his death, and remained a Communist for the rest of her life.

MICK COSTELLO emerged from the most unlikely background to become industrial organiser of the Communist Party, and industrial correspondent of the *Morning Star*. An engaging and cultured man, he used a natural sociability to great political effect during the seventies, when the CP was strong enough in the trade unions to be feared by the secret state and employers.

Costello was born in London in 1937, the son of a New Zealand classics scholar and an English mother. His father was a divisional intelligence officer in the Second World War, fighting his way through Greece, Western desert and Italy. In 1944, he joined the staff of the New Zealand legation in Moscow, where the young Mick was brought up amid the post-war privation of Soviet Russia and attended a Russian school. Despatched to Lindisfarne College in North Wales in 1950, he became a medical student at Manchester University in the 1980s where he beat pin-up girl **Anna Ford**, the future newscaster, to become president of the students' union – the first Communist to hold such office since the Attlee government.

Costello loved the atmosphere of the party, and cut a mildly roguish figure: slim, dark, with a ready sense of humour, fluent in several languages (including Russian), hard-drinking and attractive to women, he seemed the apotheosis of a new kind of Commie – intellectual but practical. He worked for the party in Kent, and King Street headquarters, and in 1969 was appointed industrial correspondent of the *Morning Star*. Costello changed the job from journalism to campaigning. He worked on the story, and the people who made the story, as a loosely attached representative of **Bert Ramelson** from whom he inherited the post of industrial organiser – 'the most exciting job I have ever had' – in 1978. Costello continued the Ramelson strategy of influencing labour movement policy from within the unions, but his range of manoeuvre soon came under pressure, internal and external.

STAFFORD CRIPPS was so Olympian that Winston Churchill was moved to remark: 'There, but for the grace of God, goes God.' His imperturbable self-assurance may be traced to his origins. Cripps was born in 1889, the son of a Conservative MP married to one of the remarkable Potter sisters who included **Beatrice**, wife of the pioneer Fabian **Sidney Webb**. His father, a wealthy lawyer, was at this stage 'totally opposed to socialism'. Young Staffie was a child prodigy, diagnosed as having 'too great a brain development' at the age of fifteen months. After Winchester, Cripps read chemistry at University College, London, but switched to the law and married Isobel Swithenhurst, the daughter of a prominent Tory and heiress to the Eno's Fruit Salts fortune.

Unfit for service in the First World War, he suffered a physical and mental breakdown managing an explosives factory in Scotland. Cripps, a devout Christian, was attracted to the Labour strand of pacifism. His father was also on the move, accepting a Liberal peerage as Lord Parmoor and then joined Labour's first government as Lord President in 1924. The young lawyer Cripps, making a name in commercial law, was hesitant. He thought the general strike of 1926 'revolutionary', and it was not until 1930, when legal work took him to the London slums where he 'discovered' the appallingly bad conditions of workers and their families, that Herbert Morrison was able to persuade him to join the Labour Party. Astonishingly, he was knighted and appointed Solicitor General before becoming an MP, which he duly did at a by-election in Bristol South-East in January 1931.

The pious Cripps refused to serve in the National Government formed that year 'from the point of view of a Socialist future', and moved sharply to the Left. 'We are not here to do hospital work for the Juggernaut of capitalism,' he told the party conference, urging a takeover of the banks and the City, and nationalisation of industry and the land. The gentleman revolutionary now helped to found the Socialist League, which sought a popular front with other parties of the Left against Fascism (including the Communists), and set up (and funded) the left-wing journal *Tribune*. For his pains, he was expelled from the Labour Party, and promptly set off on a trip to Russia. In 1940, Churchill recognised his peculiar qualities and sent Cripps as first envoy and then ambassador to Moscow, where he could be 'a lunatic in a country of lunatics'. He only just made it. His plane from Sofia was struck by lightning, and only the ingenuity of the pilot, flying upside-down saved the day.

Cripps was by turns fascinated and appalled by life in the USSR. He thought Revolutionary Day was not as good as the Durham Miners' Gala, but conceded that the workers – even in wartime – were better fed and clothed than they would have been in a Lancashire industrial town. He returned in 1942, a powerful advocate for the Russian fighting spirit, as Leader of the House and a member of the War Cabinet. He was even spoken of as an alternative to Churchill, but the wartime premier sidelined Cripps by sending him to India to scout a settlement in the tense sub-continent. Readmitted to the Labour Party in 1945, he celebrated by announcing 'Capitalism must go,' but took no steps to ensure that it would after Attlee appointed him President of the Board of Trade. Indeed, he assured the Americans that Labour was not inaugurating socialism, but attempting to prove that it could run state capitalism better than the Tories.

He again acted as midwife to Indian independence, and in 1947 succeeded Hugh Dalton as Chancellor of the Exchequer after Dalton's gaffe in telling a reporter details of the Budget on his way into the Chamber. But Cripps, a chainsmoking teetotaller, was unwell, and was compelled to retire in 1950, dying two years later. Cripps is chiefly remembered as the austere, ascetic model for a 'reliable' Labour

Chancellor. His biographer, Chris Bryant MP, prefers to remember him as the man who did more than any other to bring the USSR into the war, with the exception of Hitler.

BOB CROW took over from **Arthur Scargill** as the trade union movement's most prominent baseball-hat wearer, and did so with infinitely more menace than the miners' leader. As leader of the railwaymen's union, his intimidating scowl was a favourite of *Evening Standard* picture editors, for whom it was a gift. Crow struck terror into the hearts of commuters, and for once an up-and-coming militant trade union leader lived up to his advance billing. Strikes increased after his election in 2002 in succession to the much-loved **Jimmy Knapp**. Crow was born in 1961 in Shadwell, east London, the son of a docker who was a devout member of the TGWU. Not bookish, he left school at sixteen and worked in various manual jobs on the London Underground. He joined the Communist Party in his early twenties, and simultaneously became active in what was then the National Union of Railwaymen.

He was soon involved in strikes and emerged as a hard-man of the union Left in the Thatcherite 1980s when the railways were targeted for privatisation. In 1985, after learning militancy at Scargill's knee during the great pit strike, he became a full-time officer of the union, moving on rapidly to the LU's seat and the assistant general secretaryship in 1994. He formed a political alliance with the equally-ambitious Mick Rix, campaigning to become leader of the train drivers' union ASLEF. They both joined Scargill's Socialist Labour Party. Later they both quit, but Crow continued to breathe defiance against New Labour. In the 2003 Assembly elections in Wales, his union supported Plaid Cymru, on the grounds that it was more socialist than Blair's party – a plausible pitch. Crow supports the death penalty (though not for crossing picket lines) and Millwall Football Club, whose motto 'No one likes us, we don't care' might be regarded as his political credo.

BOB CRYER ought to be remembered as the man who saved the Keighley and Worth Valley Railway for future generations, but he would probably settle for a Leftie footnote in history. He also fought for the retention of the unique Settle–Carlisle line, the highest in England. That both are still going concerns is a testament to his Yorkshire terrier nature. Cryer was born in 1934 in Shipley, north of Bradford, and read economics at Hull University before embarking on a career in teaching. He was an early convert to left-wing causes, joining CND in 1958. He entered the Commons in 1974 for the barometer seat of Keighley, and immediately established himself as an axis of heckling with **Dennis Skinner.** He also mastered the black arts of parliamentary procedure to great effect. Unexpectedly given ministerial office at the DTI by Callaghan, he chafed at government secrecy and finally resigned in 1978 in protest at the government's refusal to fund the Kirkby industrial co-operative. Ousted from his seat in the khaki election of 1983, Cryer became anti-Europe MEP for Sheffield but returned to his first love, the Commons, in 1987 for Bradford South. At Strasbourg, his chief achievement was to get a Dutch cabbage reclassified Red Danish rather than Niggerhead. Cryer opposed the 1991 Gulf War, and when the Danes rejected Maastricht, led backbenchers in a chorus of 'Wonderful, Wonderful Copenhagen.'

A tall, austere man who sometimes exhibited a sense of humour failure, he was a teetotaller and rejected what he saw as the spurious cross-party comradeship of the House. He died in April 1994, when his car overturned on the M1. His wife Anne received minor injuries, and went on to succeed him as MP for Keighley from 1997. John Major inadvertently paid Cryer the best tribute, once dismissing him as 'one of the foremost conspiracy theorists in the House and an acknowledged expert at muckraking'.

D

LAWRENCE DALY was incontestably the most brilliant trade union leader of his generation, doomed by his loss of faith in Communism and a fondness for drink that took him to addiction and life in the gutter. As general secretary of the National Union of Mineworkers in the yo-yo years from 1968 to 1984, he brought a powerful intellectual edge to union power. Despite his short, bald, bull-like appearance, he was also deeply attractive to women, not a few of whom found his personal magnetism irresistible. He could hold a pub audience spellbound with his tales of the Scots mining communities, rounding off with an emotional rendition of Burns's love poems. On one occasion, **Mick McGahey** asked Daly's latest girlfriend what she did 'for your worrk.' In an absurd mid-Atlantic accent, she replied dreamily: 'Ah lurve!' 'And what kind of work is that?' asked McGahey, to giggles from Daly.

Lawrence Daly was a self-taught intellectual, who only found any purpose after he left school, went down the pit in Fife and joined the Young Communist League. His father, also a collier, had been a founding member of the CP in 1922. Daly was a firebrand, refusing to bow the knee to management. He became NUM branch secretary at his pit at the age of twenty-one, and moved swiftly into the troubled heart of Scottish mining politics. But in 1956, the year of the Hungarian uprising, he rejected the 'voluntary mental servitude' of the Communist Party, and struck out with allies to form the Fife Socialist League. It won two council seats and Daly garnered a respectable 5,000 votes in the parliamentary election of 1959. He beat a Communist to become secretary of the Scottish miners.

Four years later, on a militant ticket of opposition to pit closures, he was elected general secretary of the national union. 'All our troubles started when that Scottish bastard came down the M1,' said a senior National Coal Board manager, forgetting that the M1 does not go to Scotland, and Daly did not drive. Otherwise, his analysis was correct. The miners' national strike of 1972 – the first since 1926 – began after Daly persuaded the NUM executive to defy the advice of president Joe Gormley and go with the wishes of the men. Daly organised the dispute, brilliantly articulated the men's case before the Wilberforce Inquiry and drank Number 10 dry while negotiating the final settlement. 1974 was a repeat version, except that it brought down Edward Heath's Tory government and installed Harold Wilson for the third time.

Daly, by now Labour, was remarkably loyal to his government, even though its incomes policy was anathema to his old comrades on the Left. He became an increasingly isolated figure, in and out of clinics for the drink. As the Great Strike of 1984 loomed, Arthur Scargill, the new NUM president, eased him out with an early retirement package. Bereft of a political meaning in life, Daly rapidly went downhill, and ended up on the streets round Euston where the NUM headquarters used to be. He was last heard of in a nursing home in West London. But his has been a glorious life, lived to the full, and perhaps too much beyond.

TAM DALYELL is Father of the House of Commons, but behaves like an unruly distant cousin from an aristocratic branch of the family. An old Etonian with unimpeachable left-wing credentials, he defies establishment logic. His forebear General Tam Dalyell was the only man to escape from the Tower of London, but the craggy, shock-haired ex-teacher who harries governments whatever their stripe often seems determined to be sent there. Repeatedly suspended from the Commons for calling Mrs Thatcher a liar, he branded his own leader, **Tony Blair**, a war criminal over the invasion of Iraq and called on him to go. Superficially, Dalyell is a mass of contradictions. A baronet who passionately believes in the virtues of democracy. A former president of the Cambridge University Conservative Association who opposed Empire. A non-pacifist ex-soldier who opposed every British war from Suez onwards. Yet there is a strand of consistency in the Dalyell paradox. He opposes the concept that might is right, arguing that international relations must be conducted through the law. In an age of American super-power, aided and abetted by a supine Labour government, this is not an easy doctrine to espouse. It is even harder to sell, though few do it better than this soft-spoken Scot.

Tam Dalyell was born in England in 1932, of an upper-class Scots family resident in the ancestral seat of The Binns since the seventeenth century. His father, Lt Col. Gordon Dalyell, was a soldier and Resident of Bahrain. Like her husband, his mother Eleanor, through whom the baronetcy descended, spoke Arabic, and in the manner of the day his parents went off to Kuwait on imperial business, returning when he was five. After Eton, he did National Service in the Royal Scots Greys, as a tank crewman, then read history at King's College, Cambridge. He returned to his native Scotland to teach, and became fascinated with ship schools, taking groups of children round the Mediterranean. On the SS *Dunera*, he heard from a local NUM boss that the safe mining seat of West Lothian was suddenly vacant, and he should return to claim it. He did so, and entered Parliament in 1962.

When Labour came to power, Dalyell was appointed PPS to Richard Crossman. He also fought Wilson's plans to transfer secretly Britain's Indian Ocean territories to the Americans, and succeeded in saving Aldabra with its giant tortoises and pink-footed boobies. 'I was an absolute pain in the arse,' he admitted. And so he continued to be, first with devolution in Scotland (which he opposed) and later with Thatcher and the sinking of the *Belgrano*. As with most of his campaigns, he never quite won – but his sheer persistence convinces the people that government is shifty and probably wrong, a formidable achievement for a backbencher. Dalyell supported **Michael Foot** against **Denis Healey**, and was rewarded with front-bench responsibility for science. Little more than a year later, he was sacked for voting against

the Falklands war, instead of abstaining. He is not a natural absten-
tionist, as Blair found to his cost during his various military adventures.
He accused the Prime Minister of being 'the appeaser', to George Bush.
'Blair is a man who has disdain for both the House of Commons and
international law,' he wrote in *Red Pepper*. Only Tam could get away
with it. Only he would dare.

JACK DASH was an astute, charismatic leader of the London
dockers in the post-war years, right through to the 1980s, whose
trademark salutation was 'Good morning, brothers!' A lifelong
Communist, he achieved many of the reforms for which he fought so
long, but lived long enough to see their dismemberment at the hands of
the Thatcher government.

He was born in 1906, and raised in the poverty-stricken neighbour-
hood of Elephant and Castle. Unusually, his mother, Rose Johns, was a
middle-class girl, an actress whose family owned tenements in Hoxton.
She fell in love with a jobbing stage hand, and when they married, her
family disowned her. Jack was orphaned when she died of tuberculosis
aged forty, and his father later succumbed to a lung complaint picked up
in the First World War. He never forgot the simple charity of the
working-class families in Rockingham Street who welcomed him to their
kitchen table.

Dash's introduction to politics came in the London street protests that
raged during the general strike of 1926, but was temporarily put aside
while he served two years in the Royal Army Service Corps. He even rode
in the Royal Tournament at Olympia before returning to Civvy Street,
working as a hod-carrier. He became an active trade unionist, married,
and briefly joined the Labour Party before moving to Stepney where the
Communist Party held regular street meetings. He joined the CP in
1936, after a meeting called to condemn non-intervention in the Spanish
Civil War. Dash took part in the pitched battles between Mosley's

Blackshirts in the East End, under the civil war slogan *No Pasaran!* They Shall Not Pass!' And they did not pass, though many heads were broken by police truncheons, and fines and jail terms were handed down for breach of the peace.

Dash led his first strike on the building site of the Odeon cinema in Bow Road in 1938, winning danger money for the hod-carriers – at the price of his own job. When war was declared, he volunteered for the Navy and was turned down so went instead into the Auxiliary Fire Service. 'When the blitz was at its heaviest,' he recalled in a memoir, 'when our city was alight with the second Fire of London, the toll of dead and wounded was higher than that of any single British regiment in that period.'

In 1945, he joined the TGWU and became a docker on sixteen shillings (80p) a day, and was immediately plunged into a work-to-rule that became an employers' lock-out. Strikes were still banned under the infamous Wartime Regulation 1305. Work stoppages were perforce unofficial and not supported by the union. In the Royal Docks, Dash was a member of 'a sort of industrial Socrates discussion group' where the men talked about social change. The Communists were expected ('or thought we ought') to offer the right answers, but they were sometimes bested by the non-party 'lads'. After a sympathy stoppage in support of Canadian seamen in 1949, Dash was banned from holding office in the TGWU even if elected. That year the union changed its rules to ban all Communists from office, and Dash moved seamlessly into the dockers' unofficial movement. He was influential there for thirty years more, always at the forefront of struggles over job security, wages, the Dock Labour Scheme and the ultimate dream – nationalisation of the industry. He became a much sought-after speaker at student meetings, with a brilliant demotic turn of phrase. On Harold Wilson: 'He may not be any good at putting up space rockets, but he's second to none at putting up prices!' On Ray Gunter, the right-wing Minister of Labour: 'I should hate to think of Gunter, every time he goes to bed, looking underneath to see if I'm there. I'd much prefer he found a little darling!'

The dockers' fortunes waxed through the great strikes of the 1960s and then waned mightily. By the time of his death aged eighty-three in 1989, the scheme had been abolished, tens of thousands of dockers had been made redundant and the ports sold off to private owners.

Dash once said that his only epitaph should be:

Here lies Jack Dash
All he wanted was
To separate them from their cash.

DENZIL DAVIES famously resigned as Labour's defence spokesman in 1988 in a late-night telephone call to Chris Moncrieff, political editor of the Press Association, complaining that Neil Kinnock never consulted him. 'I am fed up with being humiliated,' he said, on the record. Suspecting that a tincture had been taken, Moncrieff gave him every opportunity to withdraw, but the volatile Welshman stood his ground and the opposition was the poorer for his departure. Davies was rated a brilliant Treasury minister in the Wilson and Callaghan governments, but overplayed his hand by offering himself as a candidate for the party leadership when John Smith died. 'The others are talking rubbish,' he said loftily. He had earlier sought the deputy leadership in 1983, and did no better on this occasion, failing to secure the number of MP nominations required to stand. Davies remained on the backbenches, a maverick, occasionally rebellious figure.

Born in 1938, he was educated at Carmarthen Grammar School and Oxford. A barrister, he also lectured at Leeds and Chicago universities, and has been the Member for Llanelli since 1970. In 1998, he was questioned by police about an incident at his legal chambers involving a junior woman barrister. She was said to be 'shaken, shocked and tearful' after a row over a ballot to decide on the future of the chambers' clerk. He denied physical assault, and the issue was resolved through Bar

Council mediation, though Davies resigned as the head of chambers. 'There was no violence. I just terminated the meeting. I was quite flabbergasted when the police were called in,' he said.

In 1994, Davies was identified as a possible stalking horse to force **Tony Blair**'s leadership to the test. On this occasion, a sense of reality supervened. 'The idea is absurd, both personally for me and as an idea.' Davies is married to the equally lively Labour MP Ann Carlton, who denounced Blair as paranoid. His first marriage, in 1963, to Mary Ann Finlay, an American, was dissolved in 1988.

RON DAVIES staged the most spectacular fall from grace of Tony Blair's two governments, easily outpacing the more pedestrian folly of Peter Mandelson. A left-winger by inclination, he rose to the Cabinet as Welsh Secretary and was on track to become the first First Minister of his native Wales. But was compelled to resign in November 1998, after a famous 'moment of madness' on Clapham Common when his homosexual impulses got the better of his political judgement. Late one autumn evening, he went for a walk at the end of the common where gay men gather for casual sex. He got into conversation with a 'middle-aged Rastafarian', who asked Davies to accompany him and two of his friends to a nearby flat for a meal. Naturally, the four of them ended up in a cul-de-sac in Brixton, where one of the men produced a knife and held it at the minister's throat while he was relieved of his wallet, mobile phone, Filofax and his car. The men dumped him by the roadside, shaking, and an hour later he walked into Brixton nick to report his experiences. Initially, he claimed to have been carjacked, but police were suspicious of his account, as they cruised around with him for several hours without seeing his ministerial limo. Back at the station, they invited him to compose his thoughts, but he was unable to give them a credible sequence of events. **Tony Blair** did not fare any better the next day, despite asking him five times.

Davies resigned as Welsh Secretary and, as the scandal widened, as leader of the Welsh Labour Party, forgoing his ambition to become First Minister. A number of men were arrested, but only one homeless thirty-eight-year-old was charged. Three weeks after the incident, he was released when the Crown Prosecution Service offered no evidence. Davies continued to protest that he had done nothing improper, and begged the Commons to understand that 'I am what I am.' What he was, it finally emerged, is bisexual. He admitted seeking out 'high-risk situations' in locations frequented by gay men. His marriage collapsed, and he quit his safe parliamentary seat of Caerphilly. His moment of madness cost him his political career, which began when Davies, born in 1946, the son of a fitter and a primary-school teacher, became active in the murky world of South Wales municipal politics in his early twenties.

He entered Parliament in 1983, and quickly established a CND-supporting Left persona, backing the Wapping strikers against Rupert Murdoch, congratulating Cuba, the Sandinista regime in Nicaragua and the Communist *Morning Star*. But some found him 'nasty, brutish and short', with an eye for the main chance. Blair reluctantly inherited him as Welsh spokesman, and on hearing that a former Labour Prime Minister had invented the post of Welsh Secretary, observed: 'So I've got Harold Wilson to thank for Ron Davies.' Yet despite his sensational fall from grace, the world had not heard the last of Ron the Fixer. Davies became a member of the Welsh Assembly for his old constituency, and in 2002 had married Lynne Hughes, twenty years his junior, whom he met on a Welsh language course. She thought he was 'a sweetheart'. Davies announced that he had been 'cured' after seeking psychiatric help at a top clinic, and was starting to 're-emerge' in politics. Extraordinarily, there is even talk of putting up a statue to him, in recognition of his contribution to devolution – despite his opposition to home rule in 1979. Which all goes to show, there's nowt so queer as politics. In February 2003, At the age of fifty-six, he became a father for the first time.

FRANK DOBSON once told an interviewer: 'I don't swear at anybody. That would be terrible.' But he must rank as having the second-foulest mouth in the House of Commons, a short head behind John Prescott. On the day after ambitious Tory MP Stephen Milligan killed himself in an auto-erotic performance that included a bin liner, an amyl nitrate-soaked orange in his mouth and a noose round his neck, Dobson stopped this author in the arched passage of New Palace Yard with this observation: 'If he is the brightest and the best, and he wanked himself to death, what does that tell us about the rest of them?'

Born in 1940, Dobson comes from respectable working-class stock: railwaymen. His father was a shunter in York, his grandfather a railwayman who was run over by a train. Only a council grant enabled the young Dobson to continue at Archbishop Holgate's School when his father died from kidney failure aged fifty-six. He took a lower second in economics at the LSE, where he eschewed the student movement ('It was politics about politics about politics').

Dobson identified with London, and became a Camden councillor while working for the CEGB and the Electricity Council before becoming MP for Holborn in succession to Lena Jeger in 1979. Swiftly appointed to the front bench, he ran virtually the whole gamut of Shadow jobs from education to environment, and Blair made him his first Health Secretary. After 'resigning', he was Labour's candidate for the London mayoralty, with the hopeless task of halting **Ken Livingstone**'s bandwagon. Dobbo was then able to edge back towards his old Labour leftiness, condemning foundation hospitals and other manifestations of Blairism. He always refused to shave off his trademark white beard, and is not afraid to call a spade an effing shovel.

TOM DRIBERG exhibited brilliance and recklessness in about equal measure during a political and journalistic career that spanned half a century. He was also, variously, an alleged agent for MI5, a prolific seducer of men (including, by repute, **Aneurin Bevan**), a confidant of **Guy Burgess** and an infatuated admirer of High Church ritual. The self-confessed 'odd boy' recounted his first experience at the age of two or three, putting his fingers into the split crotch of his elder brother's trousers. From there, there was no looking back: only down, at the source of his erotic joy. Born in 1905, the son of a retired career officer in the Indian civil service, he was educated at a gruesome prep school in his native town of Crowborough. There, he discovered the joys of the boys' lavatories, a ravishment that never left him. At Lancing College, where he was befriended by Evelyn Waugh, he patrolled the local WCs and churches, and became a member of the Brighton branch of the Communist Party. At Christ Church, Oxford, he was a 'close (though chaste)' friend of W. H. Auden, and in his dressing-gown presided over meetings of the university CP in his rooms.

In the 1926 General Strike, the undergraduate Driberg was briefly held at Scotland Yard for possessing 'subversive' leaflets, and he tried his hand at journalism in the *Sunday Worker*. The following year, without a degree, he left the dreaming spires for the Street of Broken Dreams – Fleet Street. Aided by Edith Sitwell and other society friends, he proved a brilliant success first as a gossip writer, then as the William Hickey columnist on Beaverbrook's *Daily Express*. His career was almost wrecked by a prosecution for indecent assault of two coalminers whom he gave a bed for the night, but he was acquitted. He twice visited Spain during the Civil War, the second time on a lorry with two Communist printers. When the Second World War broke out, Driberg disagreed with Moscow-imposed party policy on the war. He attributed his expulsion from the CP to this act of defiance, but the espionage writer Nigel West (on information from **Anthony Blunt**) claims that Driberg was exposed as an agent of MI5 spying on his Communist pals. Neither version is proven, and Driberg campaigned for the lifting of the coalition government's ban on the *Daily Worker*.

In 1942, however, as 'a man of no party' he was elected MP for Maldon,

Essex, and even before making his maiden speech was shown round the Members' lavatories at Westminster by the rich, homosexual Tory MP Chips Channon. Sacked by Beaverbrook, he joined the leftish *Reynolds News*, for whom he reported the Allied invasion of Europe, later claiming that he had 'personally liberated' Liège and the discovery of Buchenwald concentration camp. The 1945 general election found him, reluctantly, the official Labour candidate, but still a loner in the Commons, where his disdain for run-of-the-mill parliamentary work irritated colleagues. Yet, probably on the strength of his *Reynolds News* celebrity, he was elected to the party's NEC in 1949, keeping his seat until 1972. To everyone's astonishment, Driberg married Ena Binfield, whom he had met on the Westminster circuit. Winston Churchill hooted: 'Oh, well, buggers can't be choosers.' On their wedding night in Brighton, Driberg discovered that Ena had booked a double room, and accused her of breaking her marriage vows. 'She tried to sleep with me!' he spluttered.

But the marriage of convenience was useful in other ways. Ena kept house at Tom's country mansion, Bradwell Lodge, while he dabbled at Westminster and wrote, including a biography of Beaverbrook, which enraged the peevish old peer. In 1954, fearing defeat at the next election, Driberg gave notice of quitting. He saw financial salvation at hand in the rise of commercial television. But his next real coup was an exclusive interview with Guy Burgess, the first since his flight to Moscow. The article was turned into a book, prompting fresh claims from the imaginative spy writer Chapman Pincher that Driberg was working simultaneously for MI5 and the KGB – each with the knowledge of the other. Less hysterically, he was the inspiration for the founding of the Christian Socialist Movement in 1960, by which time he was back in parliament as MP for the safe Labour seat Barking, east London.

The 'Swinging Sixties' found him drinking with Mick Jagger ('What a big basket you have!') and Marianne Faithfull – not to mention the Kray twins – rather than bidding for ministerial office when Harold Wilson ended the thirteen Tory years in 1964. He was too left-wing, too hostile to a wide range of government policy, and probably too old. Driberg's privately canvassed idea of a new party of the Left, to be called Logos, or Left Auxiliary, came to nothing and on the eve of the 1970 general election he asked Wilson to appoint him British ambassador to the Vatican. Wilson gratefully fell back on the diplomatic service rule of retirement at sixty – Driberg was almost sixty-five – hoping that this would not be 'too great a disappointment'. The glory years were over. His bank made him sell his beloved Bradwell, and his wife left him. Yet his sexual drive was virtually undiminished. In the words of his biographer Francis Wheen, 'He believed that the frequent consumption of semen kept one young.' The younger the donor, the more effective the sperm.

Driberg reluctantly gave up his safe berth at Barking before the 1974 election, and suffered a series of heart-attacks. He survived to become Lord Driberg of Bradwell in the 1975 Christmas honours list, but never lived to show the bishops how to do the job. He died in August 1976 in a cab on the way home from Paddington station. His Oxford comrade A. J. P. Taylor said: 'Tom Driberg was a good man.' His autobiography, *Ruling Passions*, published posthumously, was sexually explicit but not quite as frank as his many conquests feared. His friend Mervyn Stockwood, Bishop of Southwark, claimed some responsibility for this otherwise unaccountable act of reticence.

JACK DROMEY moved back and forth across the political spectrum with surprising skill from the 1960s when he was the hard-Left trade union hero of the Grunwick strike, to a position within New Labour's slipstream after Blair became leader. He re-ratted when it proved that Blairism was unpopular with trade unionists, because his heart and soul's desire was to be general secretary of the TGWU. He was also infuriated at Blair's casual dismissal of his wife, Harriet Harman, from her Cabinet post of Social Security Secretary in 1998, though she was later rehabilitated as Solicitor General. He ran against Bill Morris for the union's top job as 'a moderniser with a sense of history' in 1995, advertising himself as the son of a labourer from Cork who had come to Britain to dig roads.

He supported the abolition of Clause IV, and shaved off his loud ginger beard. But by mid-2002, when it was clear that the union top job would be coming up again (for his second bid), Dromey was once again praising the 'best reporting traditions of the *Morning Star* and the *Daily Worker* before it'. As national secretary for public service workers, he clashed with the government on a number of occasions. Distancing himself from New Labour proved to be insufficient, however. In the election of May 2003 he was soundly beaten by the 'real Leftie' candidate, Tony Woodley, by a clear majority exceeding 20,000. Insiders suggested that, since the contest had been without rancour, Dromey might stage another comeback as deputy general secretary, for which he immediately announced himself a candidate.

RAJANI PALME DUTT lasted virtually as long as Soviet Communism itself. He was the austere godfather of the British Communist Party for half a century, from the early Leninist years almost to its post-*glasnost* dissolution. His bleak, highbrow style combined with a mechanical narrowness of political thought to produce an unappealing but commanding figure. CP defector **Douglas Hyde** called him 'utterly inhuman' and a fellow party figure said Dutt was 'the only man Moscow trusts'. He was born in Cambridge in 1896, the son of an Indian doctor Upendra Krishna Dutt, born into poverty in Calcutta, and a Swedish writer, Anna Palme, a cousin of the future prime minister Olof Palme. He was soon in trouble at Balliol College, Oxford, serving a six-month jail sentence in 1916 for refusing conscription, and suffering expulsion from Oxford for protesting in favour of the Bolshevik revolution.

He returned to take the best first of his year, and was among the triumvirate charged by the Comintern with taking over the infant

CPGB. Dutt became the first editor of the party's theoretical journal, *Labour Monthly*, which rigidly followed the Soviet line. He married Salme Murrik, a Bolshevik agent working underground in London. In 1924, the Dutts decamped to Brussels, where they stayed for the next twelve years. He was the British representative on the Comintern, and also aroused suspicions that he was an international spy. Dutt pleaded illness, specifically tuberculosis of the spine, though these were his most productive writing years and strongly influenced a generation of young intellectuals. He also continued to direct the ideological course of the CP through lengthy tirades by letter, often highly personal in their attacks on highly placed comrades. When the Hitler–Stalin Pact was signed in August 1939, Dutt moved swiftly to back the Moscow line, in contrast to the party's general secretary, **Harry Pollitt**, and he took over the leadership. When the Nazis invaded Russia, Dutt, nothing if not politically agile, stood on his head and followed the new Comintern line supporting the war. His beloved Comintern was abolished in 1943, beaching the sectarian Dutt. He lost his deposit standing for Birmingham Sparkbrook in the 1945 election, and finally came round to the majority view that British Communists had to find a home-grown, non-violent political path to power. He even had to submit to racing tips in the *Daily Worker*, whose content he supervised. He passed over the denunciation of Stalin as 'spots on the sun' and had to withdraw.

Dutt was finally eased out of the CPGB executive committee in 1965, but continued to edit *Labour Monthly*, and backed the Soviet invasion of Prague in 1968. His position was roundly rejected by a party congress, and Dutt later turned his fire on the Common Market. He died in December 1974, and from beyond the grave a month later came his posthumously published *Labour Monthly* survey of world politics, in which he promised an 'accelerating advance in the strength and constructive role of socialism represented by the Soviet Union . . . immune from the crisis of the capitalist world'. He would revolve in his urn at the thought of the Coca-Colaisation of the former USSR.

E

TERRY EAGLETON has for so long been the token Marxist revolutionary academic that even a *Daily Mail* writer was moved to praise his memoir, *The Gatekeeper*. His regular appearances in the *London Review of Books* keep alive a vital strand of literary and social criticism that might have died without him. Raised as a strong Catholic, he has observed that it is possible to move freely from Catholicism to Marxism without having to pass through liberalism. Eagleton's origins marked him out for a life on the Left. He was born in Salford in 1943, a third-generation Irish immigrant whose father won a scholarship to grammar school but was too poor to take it up. He was an altar server in the local Carmelite convent, and educated at a 'sadistic' De La Salle Brotherhood grammar school before taking a starred first at Trinity College, Cambridge. He retained his faith, even starting a leftist Catholic journal, *Slant*, before completing his odyssey from Christ to Karl after 1970.

Eagleton's politics often got in the way of academic promotion, but sheer intellect propelled him to become Wharton Professor of English at Oxford. His links with the Left grew, and he rediscovered a joy in Irish culture and music, organising Irish evenings in a local pub. He also moved from the SWP to the Workers' Socialist League, an ultra-Left fraction with a small following in the Cowley motor plants. His literary output was prolific, with *Criticism and Ideology* (1976) and *Literary Theory* (1983) placing him at the forefront of his chosen ideological position. He moved to Dublin with his second wife in 1997, turning increasingly to creative writing. He wrote in the preface of his play *Saint Oscar* (about Wilde) that critics who turn to 'so-called' creative writing should choose drama 'because, like bingo or bowling, it gets you out of the house'. He never seemed to have much trouble getting out of the house before.

BEN ELTON, the motormouth Leftie scourge of Conservative governments of the 1980s, is not so noisy about his political affiliation these days, being less fond of New Labour than the party of Neil Kinnock ('the bravest, proudest, most dignified man'). He finds **Tony Blair** a turn-off. 'I wouldn't join the Labour Party now,' he told the *Sunday Telegraph* in 2002. 'But nor am I going to give up my membership because it would make too big an issue out of it.' For whom? Elton was born into a comfortable background, but with overtones of hell. His father, Lewis, was born Ludwig Ehrenburg, a German Jew who fled with his family first to Prague and then to England in 1939.

Elton was born in Catford, south London, in 1959, but when he was ten the family moved to Guildford, where his father became Professor of Physics at Surrey University. 'I never wanted for anything, but we never in any sense felt wealthy,' he recalled. His mother, a teacher who had been active in amateur dramatics, encouraged him to take an interest in the stage, and after grammar school he studied drama at Manchester University. Most of the rest is history: the brilliant debut as a BBC script writer at the age of twenty-one, alternative comedian, novelist, play-wright, presenter of his own TV show, and celebrity father of twins through IVF treatment with his Australian wife Sophie Gare. And millionaire owner of houses in London and Sussex, plus a hundred acre 'eco-block' of bush near Perth, Western Australia. No wonder he is 'fed up' when interviewers get round to the subject of politics, proclaiming: 'I'm an entertainer, not a political activist.'

MOSS EVANS was effectively ignored by **Jack Jones** after the Great Man concluded his high-profile reign as general secretary of the Transport and General Workers' Union. But Evans deserves a mention in the *BBBL* because he predicted the 'winter of discontent' in 1978–9 and was as good as his word in delivering it, even though the dirty jobs' strike was instrumental in ending a Labour government. James Callaghan invited the TUC's top leaders to his Sussex farm in September 1978 to sound out the prospects of trade union acceptance of his 5 per cent pay rise policy. There was none, yet Sunny Jim went to the TUC conference in Brighton three days later and did his famous 'waiting at the church' speech, teasing the brothers about the date of the forthcoming general election. They were not impressed, and strikes by tanker drivers, water workers, ambulance staff, health and sewerage workers, and even gravediggers (prompting the famous *Daily Mail* headline 'Now They Won't Let Us Bury Our Dead') followed. Evans said he could not hold them back, and he did not really wish to. But he later rued the day, which ushered in Thatcherism and the virtual demise of trade union power.

Arthur Mostyn Evans was one of twelve children born into a mining family in Cefn Coed, South Wales. Poverty drove them to booming Birmingham, where he worked in various local factories before being appointed a full-time district officer for the TGWU in the west Midlands in 1956. A protégé of Jones and **Harry Urwin** he moved to Transport House in 1996, taking over the national motor industry group. In that role, he negotiated high-profile deals with Ford Motors and in the 1978 election for a successor to Jones he easily beat John Cousins, son of the previous TGWU general secretary and former Labour Cabinet minister Frank Cousins. His victory owed much to the formidable Left machine in the union, which also controlled the executive council. He even deferred at times to Alex Kitson, his number three, leading people to believe his own remark that 'I've been a tough bastard at times, but underneath it all I'm an old softie really.' Nonetheless, he beat cancer and overcame the death of a son before retiring from the much-attenuated TGWU in 1985. He settled in Heacham, and became Labour leader of the local council ('Leader of Her Majesty's official opposition,' he quipped). At this point he also confessed that had he known the outcome of the winter of discontent, he would not have endorsed it. His tragedy was that he really did think he was leading it. Moss Evans died in 2002.

F

LADY FALKENDER, as Marcia Williams became, sprang to public notoriety in the 1960s when she was queen of Harold Wilson's kitchen cabinet in Downing Street. Her fame peaked with the publication of her 'lavender list' of dodgy resignation honours in 1976, which favoured right-wing businessmen, cronies and outright fraudsters. Never mind that the list was not hers and was not even written on lavender notepaper: the mythic power of the story is such that it is endlessly raked over. But more scandal continues to emerge. Almost thirty years after the Wilson era, Lady Falkender provides headlines in the Sunday tabloid press. It had always been rumoured that Williams had slept with the Prime Minister when she was his political secretary, but the reports were dismissed. But in late 2002, Wilson's former press secretary Joe Haines finally disclosed that Marcia had had sex with the Labour PM. He claimed that Williams summoned Wilson's wife to her London home and announced: 'I went to bed with your husband six times in 1956, and it wasn't satisfactory.'

The date sounds about right. Marcia Williams, was a striking, twenty-four-year-old blonde secretary at Transport House when she first met Wilson at a dinner with Khrushchev and Bulganin at Labour's HQ in April 1956. Wilson was then forty, and she became his secretary at the company importing Russian timber where he was a consultant. When he succeeded Gaitskell in 1963, Marcia moved into his inner orbit. By then, she had already divorced her engineer husband.

The sensational upshot of Marcia's bold-as-brass scene with Mary Wilson was a plot to murder Marcia, according to Haines. He wrote in his memoir *Glimmers of Twilight* that the Prime Minister's personal physician, Dr Joe Stone, wanted to 'take the weight of Marcia off the

Prime Minister'. He discussed 'disposing of her' on at least two occasions, once in front of Bernard (now Lord) Donoughue, who confirmed the story. Lady Falkender, by then aged seventy, denied the allegations of sex with the premier as 'nonsense, ridiculous' and dismissed the murder plot as 'outrageous, something beyond belief'. So much of what happened in Downing Street during the Wilson years is beyond belief that virtually anything is credible. But a murder plot? It is certainly true that Marcia Williams had a long-running affair with a Fleet Street political editor while working in Number 10, and that she bore him two sons. Politics can be a forgiving trade, and she was rewarded with a life peerage by her long-suffering protégé, the Labour premier. Not bad for a lass from Northamptonshire, who got a history degree at London University and pursued her political instincts into the Labour Party.

SIR ALEX FERGUSON, the manager of Manchester United, is still rated a bit of a Leftie on the basis of his early years as a toolmaker and union organiser in the Govan shipyard, but his vast wealth from football and horse-racing makes his political credentials look decidedly shaky. A *Sunday Telegraph* profiler said that Fergie (as he has now become, displacing Duchess Fergie) 'could no more bring himself to vote Tory than to support the England football team.' Yet he is a welcome visitor to New Labour's Downing Street, and a personal friend of Alastair Campbell, the erstwhile hand in **Tony Blair**'s glove. His brand of success is a perfect match for theirs: winning is what counts, and the wise do not get in the way. On balance, it would probably be better for the socialism that he learned in the yards in Glasgow if he did vote Conservative.

TERRY FIELDS was the only Labour MP to go to prison for refusing to pay the Tories' poll tax. He once declared: 'I will never be a moderate as long as I have breath in my body. I will always be a Militant.' He did not always acknowledge that he was a member of the Militant Tendency, for which he was thrown out of the Labour Party with fellow Trotskyist MP **Dave Nellist** in 1991. Fields, born in 1937, the son of Liverpool docker, was a firefighter. He was recruited to 'the Millies' during the 1977 FBU national strike, and his parliamentary candidature for Liverpool Broadgreen was endorsed by the Labour Party national executive in 1982 while the Left still had control. He fought the 1983 election on the slogan of 'a worker's MP on a worker's wage', the classic giveaway line of Militant, and won by 3,800 votes. The *Guardian* gave him 'the Jimmy Porter award for best angry young speeches', and despite moves within the party to oust him, returned in 1987 with a majority of more than 6,000.

Thereafter, the Labour hierarchy got serious, putting hit-man Peter Kilfoyle on the case. Kilfoyle, party organiser for the north-west, regarded Fields as 'not very bright nor a decent sort … with a vicious and vindictive streak directed towards his political enemies', Fields was more at home on the picket line than in Parliament, and he was no match for Kilfoyle's slick, investigative style. In 1990, he appeared before Sefton magistrates on a charge of non-payment of the poll tax, and was duly expelled from the party for being a member of Militant. He contested the 1992 election as Socialist Labour, and won a respectable 6,000 votes, but was trounced by the official Labour candidate who polled more than three time his tally. Fields became a publican, but that lasted only six months, and when the *Independent on Sunday* caught up with him three years later he was unemployed, in ill health and out of politics. 'The ideas are still there,' he said. 'But I've done enough.'

KEITH FLETT is the self-appointed epistolary custodian of the Left. On the whole, it is a sound appointment. Everybody has read him, but few have seen him. His constant stream of letters to the press, and to literary and political journals, endeavours to keep socialists on the straight and narrow. Flett is the letters editor's dream. His epistles are short, pithy, and designed to correct contributors' errors, patiently but with edge. Born in north London in 1956, Dr Flett flirted with the Labour Party in the early 1960s, but quit on the grounds (echoing Marx) that 'it should be the job of socialists to try to change the world rather than the internal structures of Labour'.

He admitted in the *London Review of Books* to being 'a lifelong member of the SWP'. Flett is president of Haringey Trades Council, which must be one of the few still functioning, and a socialist historian. Flett, London region secretary of the communications union Connect, backs the Socialist Alliance, for which he has unsuccessfully stood as a council candidate in the capital. Even more disappointing is the performance of his Beard Liberation Front, which campaigns against New Labour 'beardism'. Indifferent to Flett's propaganda, most senior Labour politicians (Hoon, **Mandelson**, Darling, Monks) have abandoned hirsutity. Perhaps he should write a letter to *Tribune* about it.

BERNARD FLOUD is largely forgotten today so his memory should be resurrected. Floud, a Labour MP who committed suicide under the pressure of exposure, was part of MI5's supposed 'Oxford Comintern', a contemporaneous but pale rival to the 'Cambridge Spy Ring'. The security services began to take an interest in Oxford students after the Union voted in 1933 not to fight for King and country. Clearly, subversion was at work. Floud, at Wadham College, had been at Gresham's School, Holt, with **Donald Maclean**. He was a member of the communist October Club, set up at the end of 1933, which merged with the broadly-based Labour Club two years later. **Denis Healey**, then a CP member, was its chairman. Floud helped establish the World Student Committee against War and Fascism, in co-operation with KGB recruiter **James Klugmann**. During the war, Floud served in the Intelligence Corps.

In peacetime, he joined the Labour Party, became a rural district councillor in Ongar, Essex (he also farmed), in 1952, and stood for hopeless Chelmsford in 1955. That year, he also joined the nascent Granada Television as an executive at the invitation of Sidney Bernstein, a favourite of Harold Wilson, but at that time well to the left of him. Granada's pioneering investigative journalism infuriated the establishment, and in the sixties, MI5 began trawling through the Oxford Comintern with greater thoroughness, and a Somerville college graduate, Jennifer Williams (later Hart), said she had become a secret member of the CP when she went into the civil service. According to spy writer Chapman Pincher, Mrs Hart named Floud as her 'first mentor', Meanwhile, after contesting Hemel Hempstead in 1959, Floud finally entered Parliament in 1964. MI5 grew even more alarmed, and sought to question the new MP. They could not, because Harold Wilson had ruled that MPs and peers were exempt from such investigation without his permission, which he would not give.

But in 1967, when Wilson proposed making Floud a junior minister, the security services seized their opportunity to demand 'positive vetting', Over two weeks of MI5 interrogation, according to Pincher, Floud admitted his Communism but denied any links with the KGB. The security services were not convinced, and gave him an ultimatum: confess and convince us that you have broken off with Soviet intelligence, and we might let you take up the ministerial appointment. The interrogation dragged on, MI5 being clearly unimpressed by Floud's state of health. He had become increasingly depressed since his wife's death in January 1967. From June, he had been receiving psychiatric treatment, including electro-convulsive therapy. On the night of 9 October, he went home and killed himself. He was fifty-two.

MICHAEL FOOT is the only serious contender for the title of Official Saint of Leftiousness against George Orwell. Ironically, considering that Foot has spent so long in the grubby world of party politics, he emerges as the more naïve of the two. He found the revelation that Orwell had informed on fellow-Lefties to the British government at the height of the Cold War in 1949 'amazing'. Foot could never have figured on such as list of untrustworthy Commies and fellow-travellers. His socialism has always been of the high-minded variety, rooted in William Hazlitt rather than Marx. Yet it has always been tinged with the vanity of a true politician. He could not resist the offer of the Labour leadership put before him by a self-appointed soviet of trade union general secretaries after Callaghan's disastrous failure in the 1979 election. His agile brain, had he but allowed it, would have told him that **Denis Healey** would have been a more electable leader. But he wrestled his conscience to the ground, conceding the specious argument that only he could unite the Labour Party.

In truth, it was not susceptible to unity, and vigorously demonstrated its various fissiparous tendencies under Foot for three years until the withering humiliation of the 1983 election. Yet he retained the magic sparkle of the conscience of the Left, most amusingly exhibited by the description of 'genius' offered by the *Dictionary of Labour Biography*. Excellent writer though Foot still is, at the age of ninety, even he might feel shy of such an accolade.

His life is the subject of several biographies. Briefly stated, he was born into a radical Liberal family in Plymouth in 1913, the son of a Liberal MP, and educated at a Quaker School before Oxford, where he was president of the Union in 1933. On graduating, he worked in Liverpool for the Blue Funnel Line. His conversion from Liberalism to socialism, variously ascribed to reading Hazlitt and seeing poverty at close quarters, took place at this time. Foot fought Monmouth for Labour in 1935, anticipating by half a century Gordon Brown's rhetoric about government for the many, not the few. He became a journalist, working his passage from the *New Statesman* via *Tribune* to the *Evening Standard* as Beaverbrook's protégé, rising to editor in 1942.

The 1945 election found him as MP for Devonport in his native city. While Attlee built the welfare state, Foot harried him from the vantage-point of the Keep Left group of MPs, mostly in the columns of *Tribune*. In 1955 and again in 1959, he was defeated at Devonport and considered abandoning politics for writing. The death of his hero **Aneurin Bevan** in 1960 gave him a plausible reason for returning to Westminster, and he held the seat until 1992. He paid due tribute to Bevan with a masterly two-volume biography. He rejected office in Wilson's first administrations, but accepted the Employment portfolio after the miners' strike election of February 1974, and in post scrapped most – but not all – of the Tory anti-union laws. He was on the losing side in the 1975 Euro-referendum, and won another second prize in the leadership election that followed Wilson's resignation in 1976, which he lost to Callaghan by thirty-nine votes. He was elected deputy leader on his fourth attempt over a time-span of almost a decade.

Once talked into being leader in 1980 – by a margin of ten votes – he presided over three years of confusion that saw leading figures quit to form the SDP, the rise and rise of the Militant Tendency and the famous 'suicide note' manifesto of 1983. Even his admiring *DLB* biographer admitted that this was 'not the happiest time for Foot'. He retired after the 1992 election, lost by his protégé Neil Kinnock. His wife Jill Craigie, the film-maker and feminist who was once raped by Arthur Koestler, pre-deceased him in 1999, but Foot continued his writing, interspersed with occasional visits to Old Labour's favourite restaurant, the Gay Hussar in Soho.

PAUL FOOT, the astringent columnist and prize exhibit of the Socialist Workers' Party, might have been tempted to send back his Orwell Prize for journalism after the full extent of the iconic author's collaboration with the security services was revealed. Foot has enjoyed a lifelong paranoia about the secret state, almost always justified by results. Yet he came from the bosom of the establishment himself. His father, Sir Hugh Foot, was governor of Jamaica, and he went from exclusive prep school to Shrewsbury where he met fellow iconoclasts Richard Ingrams and Willie Rushton. He did National Service as an officer (in Jamaica, where else?) in the King's Shropshire Light Infantry, and at Oxford was President of the Union and editor of *Isis*. There, the 'instinctive Red' came to the fore, though initially he was a member of the Labour Party. After all, his uncle **Michael** was a future leader.

He quit in 1962, after working on the *Daily Record* in Glasgow, the *Sun* and the *Sunday Telegraph*. He wrote Footnotes for *Private Eye* for five years, wrote a column, reported and briefly edited *Socialist Worker* in the 1960s, before joining the *Daily Mirror* as a columnist where he probably did his best work for thirteen years. Geoffrey Goodman, the paper's wise old Leftie industrial editor, thought him 'one of the outstanding reporters of his generation' motivated by fearless honesty, exceptional persistence and integrity. Some of the persistence found expression in political candidacy, of which he was a tireless and invariably unsuccessful enthusiast (even running for mayor of Hackney in 2002, securing more than 4,000 votes for the Socialist Alliance).

His integrity was given full rein in 1993, when the *Mirror*'s management sacked staff and crushed the National Union of Journalists. Foot walked out, returning to *Private Eye*. He survived a life-threatening illness, which confined him to a wheelchair for a long time, to resume the Footnotes column. If Foot's journalism is among the best, his books have had more mixed fortunes. *Who Framed Colin Wallace?* (1989) is a classic exposé of the British secret state's duplicity in Northern Ireland, but *Who Killed Hanratty?* about the A1 murder (1971) was overtaken by DNA evidence. He has won many prizes from the journalistic establishment, but the ultimate prize of persuading the working class of the need for revolution has eluded him.

ANNA FORD, the newsreader, was denounced as a closet Leftie by Tory chief spinner Charles Lewington (known as the Wine Waiter to his former lobby colleagues) in 1997. Her crime was to refer to the 'sensible' i.e. Europhile wing of the Conservative Party, suggesting that the staring-eyed Eurosceptics were not sensible. This was denounced in the *Sunday Telegraph* as 'a serious lapse of on-air judgement.' There are other items on the charge sheet, but not hugely convincing. Ford was 'targeted' with threats of violence at her home by thugs of the neo-Fascist Combat Eighteen group, on the grounds of being 'a Jewish sympathiser'. She also threw a glass of wine over Tory hardcase Jonathan Aitken, but that was because he sacked her from GMTV. Ford was more accurately described (by profile writer Decca Aitkenhead in the *Independent on Sunday*) as 'more class act than class warrior: her politics were leftish but hardly radical'. In the mid-sixties, the vicar's daughter from Cumbria lost an election for the presidency of the Manchester Students' Union to **Mick Costello**, the broad-Left candidate. But she is pally with some on the Tory right, sends her children to public schools, and crossed the NUJ picket line during a BBC strike in 1994. So, not much of a Leftie.

EDMUND FROW was an inveterate hoarder whose passion for collecting socialist books, pamphlets and trivia led to the formation of the Working Class Movement Library and Museum in Salford, Lancashire. Frow, an engineering worker, and his wife Ruth, a school-teacher, spent their holidays touring the country looking for labour movement memorabilia, which eventually filled their modest semi in Old Trafford. Ruth remembered their 1937 camping excursion in a Morris van: 'In the morning, when we were fresh and full of energy, we combed the shelves of unsuspecting booksellers. In the afternoon, we sat in the summer sun, reading and gloating over our purchases. In the evening, we walked or possibly moved on to another bookshop. And when all our money had gone, or when the van was full, we returned to Manchester.' Life was not all pastoral idyll. Frow was born in 1906, the son of a tenant farmer in Lincolnshire. Leaving school at fourteen, he became a drawing office apprentice and then a turner, reputedly with the best set of tools in the country. Frow joined the Communist Party in 1924, and was sacked for joining the General Strike two years later, even though his union was not involved. In 1931, he was injured in a police baton charge on an unemployment protest in front of Salford Town Hall, and served five months in jail for his part in what became known as 'the Battle of Bexley Square.' Frow became well-known locally, and featured as a character in Walter Greenwood's novel of working-class life, *Love on the Dole*. He worked as an engineer in many factories, invariably serving as a shop steward for the AEU. He and his wife produced many publications on socialist themes, and in 1987 Salford City Council took over their collection and rehoused it. The library received a £200,000 lottery grant to expand the Frows' work. Frow died in 1997.

KLAUS FUCHS, the atomic scientist, had been passing secrets to the USSR for eight years before being brought to trial in 1950. At the Old Bailey Sir Percy Sillitoe, director-general of MI5, found Fuchs an unassuming, unimpressive figure, a 'single foolish individual [who] had, by a curious trick of fate, found himself in a position to alter the whole balance of world power'. That he failed to do so did not save him from the maximum punishment for espionage. Fuchs was indeed a curious figure, born in Germany, the son of a Lutheran pastor who converted to Quakerism and instilled into his children that conscience had priority over all other considerations.

With the rise of Nazism, his father was jailed, his mother and a sister committed suicide. Klaus, already a Communist while studying at Kiel University, was assaulted and thrown into the river by the Brownshirts. He eventually fled to England in 1933, where German consular officials denounced him, but he was granted citizenship in 1942 after two years of particularly unpleasant internment on the Isle of Man and in Canada.

Dr Fuchs was wanted for British research on the atomic bomb, working under Professor Peierls in Birmingham. He proved an invaluable member of the scientific team, who did not realise he was handing over carbon copies of his research to the Russians. Fuchs went with the British contingent to New Mexico, and after watching the detonation of the first nuclear bomb in July 1945, gave his Soviet handlers details of its size, contents and construction.

After the war, he became head of the Theoretical Physics Division at Harwell, but MI5 suspicions of a traitor finally closed in on him. Apart from one payment of £100, which he did not want, Dr Fuchs gained nothing from spying save the salving of his Quaker conscience. When this began to give way in 1949 he was an easy target for the subtle interrogation skills of William Skardon (who failed to break **Kim Philby**). He confessed, and named others in the USA spy ring. He was convicted of espionage, and jailed for fourteen years. Fuchs was probably the most important of the ideologically motivated scientist spies.

G

WILLIE GALLACHER was one of the original Clydeside Reds, whose revolutionary instincts were guided by Lenin himself. In 1920, accompanied by the redoubtable **Sylvia Pankhurst**, he went to Moscow for the second congress of the Comintern. There, he met the Soviet leader, who persuaded him that the nascent British CP should affiliate to the Labour Party. It did so at its founding conference. Gallacher was dazzled by 'the genius of Lenin', and wholeheartedly backed his new party's primary aim, the defence of the Soviet Union and the propagation of its way of life. Willie Gallacher was born in Glasgow in 1882, the son of a drunkard, an experience that made him a lifelong teetotaller.

His was the classic worker's build: short, stocky and burly. Gallacher's university was seafaring and the engineering industry of Clydeside, where he was a formidable union organiser. He chaired the unofficial Clyde Workers' Committee, and fomented unrest during the First World War which convinced Lloyd George that revolution was imminent in Glasgow. In 1919, a massive strike, involving 100,000 workers, ostensibly over shorter working hours but infused with Bolshevism, paralysed – and electrified – the Clyde. It culminated in the battle of George Square in central Glasgow, when Gallacher was knocked unconscious by a police. He was jailed for five months for incitement to riot. He was to become familiar with prison. In 1925, he was in King Street when police raided the party's HQ, carting off virtually the entire leadership. They were jailed for up to a year, this time for incitement to mutiny. Gallacher and fellow Scot **Johnny Campbell** were the party's representatives on the Comintern, but that did not stop him standing for Parliament.

He was duly elected (at his third attempt) for the West Fife constituency, a mining stronghold of the CP, in 1935. He held the seat for fifteen years, building a reputation for fierce integrity that brought respect across the political spectrum. Gallacher had a surprisingly open mind for a Moscow loyalist. He was an authority on the Bible, wrote poems in prison and urged university students attracted to the party to become good teachers, scientists and historians, and not 'run away to the factories'. When war came, he sided with **Harry Pollitt**, the CP general secretary, in opposition to the Stalin-Hitler pact; events justified their stand. Gallacher lost his seat in the election of 1950, ignominiously coming third after the Tory, but he lived into his eighties, still an unwavering Communist. He died in 1966.

GEORGE GALLOWAY could never resist going one step too far, and paid the price of a promising political career. Voted by the right-wing *Spectator* as backbencher of the year, 'Gorgeous' George, so named for his permanent sun-tan and attraction to the ladies, is a rock solid Leftie in the classic Scots mould. He once told a drinking companion that he would have been 'a high-ranking official' in the USSR. Sharp suits and fine cigars apart, he was increasingly out of place in the New Labour party, whose leaders would never have given him a job in government despite his talents. Besides, there was always a tinge of scandal clinging to Galloway from a colourful personal and political past. He was born in 1954, in a slum Irish area of Dundee known as Tipperary, the son of an engineering worker. Educated at local primary and academy schools, he followed his father into industry, including a spell at the jute mill where his grandfather had worked. Galloway joined the Labour Party 'under age' at fifteen, and within three years was a party secretary.

With like-minded militants, he staged a left-wing takeover of the constituency. He tried to become the city's youngest councillor in 1977, but his bid backfired when he was discovered to be 'living in sin' with the woman who became his wife, civil servant Elaine Fyffe. However, his enthusiasm was rewarded with appointment as the party's youngest district organiser, then youngest chairman of the Scottish Labour Party in 1980. Galloway was plainly destined for greater things, boasting, 'I am a populariser, young, successful and hard-nosed.' He was also unquestionably on the Left, urging the admission of Communists to the Labour Party and supporting **Tony Benn**. Firmly established on Dundee Council, he twinned with Nablus and flew the Palestinian flag over the city hall. In 1983, he became general secretary of War on Want, a charity long associated with the Left, gaining a further opportunity to pursue his political agenda.

However, his globetrotting lifestyle soon made enemies who contrasted his taste for expensive hotels with the extreme poverty that reigned in many of the countries he visited. Galloway denied wrongdoing, and in 1987 an independent auditor cleared him of any misuse of funds, though he did repay £1,720 in contested expenses. He separated from his wife that year, and also entered Parliament as MP for Glasgow Hillhead, ousting SDP leader Roy Jenkins and hastening the demise of the breakaway party.

His past was still catching up with him. At a press conference on leaving War and Want, he confessed to having sex with at least two delegates during a conference on the Greek island of Mykonos in 1985. When he became an MP, the *Daily Mirror* then found him in an east London 'love-nest' with a former school friend, Lilian Beattie. The disclosures prompted moves in his constituency to deselect him, but they came to nothing. A keen footballer and member of the Commons team, Galloway cut a dashing figure at Westminster, though his slavish support for Saddam Hussein grated even with fellow left-wingers. In 1994, he became known as 'Member for Baghdad Central' after praising the 'courage, strength and indefatigability' of the Iraqi dictator on local television. In 2000, he married Dr Amineh Abu-Zayyad, a strikingly beautiful biologist working at Glasgow University, having lived with her since 1991.

When the war against Iraq loomed, Galloway's rhetoric became even more extreme. He called on British troops to refuse to obey 'illegal' orders, excoriated Blair as a traitor who sold his country to a foreign power, and described coalition soldiers as 'wolves'. It was this last charge that enabled Labour Party bosses to move against him in April 2003, after the *Daily Telegraph* sensationally claimed to have uncovered Iraqi intelligence documents showing that he received £375,000 a year from oil earnings via Saddam Hussein's regime. The *Christian Science Monitor* went further, alleging that he had been paid more than £6 million by Saddam. Reporters tracked him down to his holiday home in Portugal (he also has properties in London and Glasgow, as do most MPs in his position) where he was working on a book about Iraq, and Galloway described the *Telegraph* allegation as 'a lie of fantastic proportions'. He promised a libel action, and his wife Amineh insisted: 'Any idiot can see this is a disgraceful smear campaign and we will fight it. My husband is an honourable man.'

Nonetheless, Labour chiefs suspended Galloway, making it virtually impossible for him to bid for a seat in the contracting pool of constituencies in Glasgow. His own seat of Hillhead will dissapear in the reduction of MPs in Scotland following the establishment of the Holyrood Parliament – ironically, Galloway's key demand in his maiden speech sixteen years previously. Without party, with a dwindling band of supporters and directly in the sights of the media, the rise and rise of Gorgeous George was plainly over. The CSM eventually admitted that its allegations were based on forged documents, and backed down. The *Telegraph*, sued for libel by Galloway in June 2003, stood by its allegations, and a long legal battle was anticipated.

JOHN GOLLAN joined the Communist Party in 1927 after hearing his hero **Willie Gallacher** speak, and went on to become general secretary in the turbulent year of 1956. It would be difficult to imagine a greater contrast with his predecessor, **Harry Pollitt**, the square, convivial boilermaker. Gollan was slim, diffident and severe, a worker-intellectual from Edinburgh. But he shared the prison experience of his elders. In the thirties, he was jailed for six months for circulating a 'subversive' publication to soldiers, and there was nothing flabby about his Communism. He was a true democratic centralist. The year after he took over, according to CP historian Francis Beckett, he took 'the most important decision any CP leader ever took': the revival of direct Soviet subsidies to the party that had been discontinued in the 1930s.

For twenty years from 1957, the CP was in receipt of 'Moscow Gold' to the tune of about £100,000, although the cash tailed off sharply towards the end of the seventies. Apologists for this turn of events cite the collapse of party membership after the Hungarian uprising, but it was also dictated by the withdrawal of rich – mainly Jewish – sympathisers following the denunciation of Stalin and the exposure of his anti-Semitism. Gollan would nowadays be called a 'moderniser', if reluctantly so. He made a party political broadcast on television, urging voters to support the 'new British people's party' that would merely take Britain 'a step on the road' to socialism. He even criticised the Soviet Union, which would have been unthinkable in Pollitt's day. Gollan, a chain-smoker, was diagnosed with lung cancer, and retired in 1975. Such good offices as he retained in retirement he used to avert the terminal struggle between 'Stalinists' and 'EuroCommunists' in the CP, to no avail. He died in 1976.

VICTOR GOLLANCZ was the driving force behind the influential Left Book Club in the 1930s, which was as much an expression of his own compelling personality as it was 'a struggle for world peace and a better social and economic order and against Fascism', as its advertisements proclaimed. In 1927, Ernest Benn, the publisher who recruited him to build up his family business, noted ruefully in his diary that 'Gollancz must be "boss", he is a natural leader and in his own

interest he should set up for himself.' He immediately did so, taking under his wing rising stars like George Orwell.

It was not until 1936 that he joined forces with **John Strachey** and **Harold Laski** to form the Left Book Club, and subsequently the magazine *Tribune*. As a publisher with an eye to the educated market, he had no equal, but his beginnings showed no hint of the influence he would later wield. Born in London in 1893, the son of a well-to-do wholesale jeweller, he was educated at St Paul's School and New College, Oxford, before joining the teaching staff of Repton College. Gollancz became involved in vaguely radical politics, with William Wedgewood Benn's Radical Research Group.

Through him, Gollancz was brought into the publishing firm of Ernest Benn Brothers, where his marketing brilliance multiplied turnover a hundredfold within seven years. But he moved to the Left, and had sharp political and managerial disagreements with Benn, before the break that allowed Gollancz to go it alone. In the 1930s, when he confessed that he was 'as close as one hair is to another' with the Communist Party, Gollancz published Emile Burns', *A Handbook of Marxism*, memorably described as 'a bulging Marxist Bible for the masses'. He was keen that local groups of the 50,000-strong club should have 'one or two good Party members'. His ideal was a Popular Front, a concept that never took off in Britain, and the CP's strategic somersaults over the Hitler–Stalin pacts severely undermined public faith in the club. Membership dwindled away, and it died in 1948. By then, however, many of its themes – such as full employment – had become the common currency of British politics, and prepared the nation intellectually for what Richard Crossman called the 'psychological landslide to the Left' in 1945.

Gollancz notoriously failed to publish Orwell's *Animal Farm* and *Nineteen Eighty-four*, but his knack of spotting winners was confirmed with Kingsley Amis's *Lucky Jim* and other best-sellers. Gollancz never abandoned his old passionate attachment to the Left. In 1958, he was active in the formation of CND. He died in 1967, and the publishing tradition he created followed him into the grave in 2001 with an anthology of Left Book Club titles.

CUNNINGHAME GRAHAM was one of the few

Victorian adventurers who fell into the arms of the nascent Socialist movement at the end of the nineteenth century. Born in London in 1852, the son of a Scots lair and long-time Whig who could trace his ancestry to Robert the Bruce, he went to South America to make his fortune, and endured many privations before returning home in 1883 to take over the family estate of Major William Graham of Gartmore. He soon began attending Socialist meetings in Scotland and London to listen to H. M. **Hyndman, Keir Hardie, John Burns** and **George Bernard Shaw**. Graham proved to be a seductive speaker, and won election to Parliament in 1886 as a Liberal at the age of thirty-four. Once in the Commons, he declared himself a socialist. With his wild hair, Spanish beard and exotic clothes, he quickly became a figure of hate for the establishment, calling for the nationalisation of the mines 'for the benefit of the country and not the selfish interests of the capitalists'. He was suspended in 1887 for saying 'damn' in the chamber. Amid the widespread suppression of socialist meetings, Graham warned that England 'is not going to be a free country to hold meetings in'.

Months later, in November 1887, he was involved in a mass protest in Trafalgar Square that had been banned by the Metropolitan Police. A riot ensued, many were injured, including Graham. *The Times* said he should be relieved of his magistracy in Scotland. The turbulent MP was sentenced to two months' imprisonment for his part in the demonstration. On his release the Prime Minister, Lord Salisbury, asked: 'Well, Mr Graham, are you thinking where to put your guillotine?' Graham shot back: 'In Trafalgar Square, of course.'

Graham went on to co-found, with Keir Hardie, the Scottish Home Rule Association, forerunner of the Scottish National Party, and to support many progressive causes, including the matchgirls' strike. His final judgement on his career was that he had been 'ploughing sand.' He died in 1936 in Rio de Janeiro, on a valedictory journey to the scenes of his early life. Ramsay MacDonald said: 'His socialism was based on romantic ideas of freedom and his profound feeling for the bottom dog.'

BERNIE GRANT entered Parliament in 1987 with the reputation of a hard-Left, anti-authoritarian militant, and, as is so often the way of these things, died thirteen years later virtually the darling of the House. The black Labour councillor who said the police involved in the riot at Broadwater Farm estate, in which PC Keith Blakelock was beaten to death, had been given a 'good hiding', was on good terms with Tory MPs and strongly supported the Royal Family. And despite being named after commanders of the British desert army of the Second World War, Bernard Alexander Montgomery Grant had a genuine Leftie streak that never deserted him.

He was born in 1944 in British Guyana, the grandson of an African slave transported to the sugar plantations to work for a Scots planter named Grant. His mother was descended from another Scots landowner, named Blair. After Roman Catholic schools in Georgetown, and experience of radical youth politics in the Guyanese bauxite industry, he came to Britain with his mother in 1963. He studied at Tottenham Technical College and took a mining engineering course at Heriot-Watt University, but dropped out after two years in a row over eligibility for work experience in South Africa that was only open to whites. Grant worked in an international telephone exchange in London and joined the Socialist Labour League, selling revolutionary literature outside Tube stations at dawn.

It did not last long. He joined the Labour Party in 1974, and was elected to Haringey Council in 1978. In the mid-eighties he staged a deselection coup against the sitting left-winger Norman Atkinson, veteran treasurer of the Labour Party, to take the nomination for Tottenham. Grant entered the Commons in African robes, and swiftly became a stalwart of the Campaign Group. He opposed the privatisation of council services, and the 1991 Gulf War. However, the Metropolitan Police praised his work in improving relations with the black community, and Grant might have looked to **Tony Blair** for ministerial office, had not kidney illness and heart problems dogged him from the time of New Labour's accession to power. He became increasingly less familiar at Westminster, leaning on a smart cane, and died in 2000.

VICTOR GRAYSON must qualify as the most enigmatic British Leftie of them all. A showman socialist who married a beautiful young actress, he was an MP for only two years before enlisting as a private in the First World War. But he is most remembered for the greatest disappearing act of modern politics, to which John Stonehouse could only aspire. Grayson was born in Liverpool in 1881, the son of an army deserter and a domestic servant. He was apprenticed as an engineer, but decided to enter the Church.

While studying theology at Manchester University, he became interested in politics, standing as socialist candidate in a mock parliamentary election. The real thing came quickly, when the Colne Valley Labour League just over the Pennines chose him as the candidate in the 1907 by-election. Grayson was an electrifying speaker. 'People just went haywire, they went mad at his meetings,' one veteran recollected. His narrow win over the Liberals and Tories was greeted by the *Daily Express* as a 'revolutionary victory' for 'the menace of socialism'. His maiden speech attacked a £50,000 a year pension for Lord Cromer on his retirement from a colonial post in Egypt 'when outside the walls of the House people are dying of starvation'. He was lionised all over the country, speaking to packed meetings.

But he could not accept the discipline required to gain the Labour parliamentary whip, nor the constraints of Commons procedure. He was suspended for raising unemployment when other business was being discussed, having called fellow Labour MPs 'traitors' to their class and the whole House 'murderers'. Philip Snowden accused him of 'hypocritical acting' while Ramsay MacDonald compared him to Henry Irving. It was the beginning of his downfall. Grayson developed a penchant for high living, drink and formal evening dress that was anathema to his bewildered plain-living supporters back home. He was also dismissive of the trade unions as sectarian and inadequate socialist, though his radical views did find him a forum as co-editor of the socialist weekly *New Age* and then as political editor of Robert Blatchford's influential *Clarion*. Yet he rarely voted and almost never spoke, preferring what would now be called extra-parliamentary agitation. In the 1910 general election, called after Lloyd George's radical Budget had been rejected by the Tory-dominated Lords, Grayson lost his seat to the Liberals.

Defeat did not mean despair. Grayson continued to write and speak, and in the second election of 1910 stood as a socialist in Kennington, south London, attracting a risible share of the vote. He made a 'prodigal son' comeback tour of the north in 1914, but it ended in catastrophe in St George's Hall, Bradford, when he was too drunk to speak. There were consolations. Throughout his political life, Grayson, while no oil painting, was deeply attractive to women. One woman left her husband in Colne Valley to live in the same London lodging house, while several others were wildly in love with him. His friend Arthur Rose, an actor-manager, introduced him to actresses, and the matinée idol from Yorkshire had a string of affairs. Robert Blatchford said he should never marry because he was 'so cold towards women', and his biographer Lord David Clarke is in no doubt that Grayson was 'obviously bisexual'. However, he married a 'flighty' actress Ruth Norreys in 1912, and travelled to New Zealand when she went on tour playing Shakespeare in 1915. His lectures there were met with loud applause, but he was again in money troubles, borrowing to pay for his drink.

Grayson enlisted in the British Expeditionary Force, becoming private 45001 in the Canterbury Regiment. He was not long in the front line near Étaples before he was wounded by shrapnel during an attack in September 1917. Back in hospital in Blighty, Grayson was recognised as an epileptic and an alcoholic. He was discharged on grounds of 'neuras-thenia' and stomped the country attacking ILP leaders and strikers who 'robbed soldiers going into war of ammunition'.

When the war ended, so did his political career. His wife died, and without a party he could not get back into Parliament. Yet he continued to live in London in some style, drinking and entertaining friends to the theatre. But he also tangled with the establishment, publicly accusing Lloyd George of selling political honours for up to £40,000 apiece, and threatened to expose 'a monocled dandy with offices in Whitehall' who conducted the trade. The dandy was Maundy Gregory, an MI5 agent and aide to Lloyd George who spied on Grayson. In September 1920, Grayson was beaten up in the Strand, and soon after went missing, telling drinking companions that he had to go to Leicester Square but would be back shortly. He was never seen again, dead or alive.

The 'honours for sale' scandal continued until 1932, when Gregory was jailed and then sent into exile abroad with a Tory Party pension. Numerous sightings of Grayson were reported, some in New Zealand and Australia, continuing into the 1980s. His reputation as Labour's lost leader has diminished sharply, but interest in this strange man never died completely away.

H

PETER HAIN has been consistent in one thing during a long political odyssey: his sun-tan. 'Hain the Pain', as he was known in his youth, invariably looks as though he has just returned from a rather agreeable holiday in his native South Africa, which has left him quite satisfied with life. He has also travelled the classic route from pitch-digging rebel to Blairite opportunism, rewarded with a seat in the Cabinet and the respect shown to office.

Born in Kenya in 1950, he grew up in Pretoria, where his parents were active in the anti-apartheid Liberal Party. Jailed briefly at the age of eleven, he gave his first political speech at fifteen at the funeral of a family friend hanged for causing an explosion. The family fled London in 1966, and Hain became involved with the Young Liberals, then passionately radical. As a London University student, he created the 'Stop the Tour' movement in 1970, which did indeed stop apartheid South African cricketers touring Britain. He survived two attempts in the 1960s to lock him up on conspiracy and bank-robbery charges, and joined the Labour Party. Hain founded the Anti-Nazi League, dedicated to fighting resurgent Fascism in Britain, and became a research officer for the postmen's union, the CWU.

He fought Putney twice in the 1980s before securing the safe, rugby-mad constituency of Neath, South Wales, which returned him to the Commons in 1991. His membership of the Tribune group did not hold him back. Via the whips' office, Hain vaulted on to the front bench as Shadow Employment Minister and in 1997, **Blair** put him into the Welsh Office as a junior minister. He managed (just) to win a 'Yes' vote in the referendum on Welsh devolution, and then masterminded the election of Blair's candidate, Alun Michael, as First Minister in the Welsh

Assembly. His reign was brief and ended ingloriously, but by then Hain was well away, adorning the Foreign Office as Minister for Europe. In his 1996 book, *Ayes to the Left*, Hain slated the EU as gigantic conspiracy against socialism. Now, he was more pro-Euro than **Peter Mandelson**, labelling opponents of the single currency 'enemies of Europe'.

Hain finally entered the Cabinet as Welsh Secretary after **Ron Davies**'s moment of madness on Clapham Common, but retaining strong European interests. He still found time to acquire a new interest in life, a girlfriend, Elizabeth Howard, a headhunter and former head of the Welsh CBI, whom he married in June 2003. He had earlier separated from his wife Patricia Western after a marriage lasting twenty-four years. Otherwise (according to the ubiquitous 'friends'), he has led a blameless life, never smoking dope, never being drunk, and never putting a foot wrong in his rise to high office.

In the débâcle of Blair's botched Cabinet reshuffle in 2003 he took over as Leader of the Commons, while retaining the Welsh Office and some indeterminate pro-Europe role, a rag-bag of responsibilities (and opportunities) denounced by the Tories as a constitutional freak. He immediately made his mark by calling for higher taxes for the rich, a piece of old-Leftery he was promptly forced to disown by Blair.

JOHN BURDON HALDANE was a pioneer member

of the group of scientists at British universities drawn to Communism in the 1930s. At the height of the Cold War in 1948, when faced with dismissal from two government scientific committees, he declared in public: 'I certainly am a Communist – as good a Communist as anyone . . . If I got orders from Moscow, I would leave the Communist Party forthwith. But sometimes I wish we did get orders from Moscow. I would like to know what they are thinking.' This forthright testimony put his critics to flight. They should have known better than to take him on. Haldane was an intellectual giant, with a personality to match. Born in

Oxford, in November 1892, the son of a physiologist, he won a mathe-matical scholarship from Eton to Oxford University, where he took a first before switching into research in the infant science of genetics. He joined the army at the outbreak of the First World War, serving in the Black Watch as a bombing and trench mortar officer. Wounded and repatri-ated in 1915, he returned to his regiment in Mesopotamia where he was again wounded and evacuated to India for recuperation. His war experi-ences converted him to socialism, saying he would die happy if he could live to see England a country in which the occupation of grocer was as honourable as that of a soldier.

He moved to Cambridge after the war, lecturing in biochemistry and publishing a best-seller on natural selection, *Daedalus, or Science and The Future*. A chance interview with Charlotte Burghes of the *Daily Express* drew them into a relationship that scandalised the academic establishment of the day. Burghes spent a night with Haldane at a London hotel in order to obtain a divorce, and after a much-publicised court case, he was dismissed by the Cambridge authorities for 'gross immorality'. They married in 1926, and Haldane became the leading populariser of science and the virtue of scientific influence over the political process. In 1931, Haldane visited the Soviet Union with a group of British scientists, and subsequently joined the Communist Party, raising volunteers and finance for the International Brigade. Meanwhile he was elected to the Royal Society and became Professor of Genetics at UCL, where his research was recognised as ground-breaking. In 1941, Charlotte Haldane went to the USSR to report the war for the *Daily Sketch*. Her experiences of Stalinist Russia so disillusioned her that she quit the CP, admitting that she had 'lied, cheated, acted under false pretences' and denied her inner ethical tenets 'convincing myself that the end justified the means'. The marriage collapsed, but Haldane remained a party member and kept up his links with Soviet scientists. He did not quit until 1950, after his close comrade Nikolai Vavilov was purged and died in Siberia. In 1957, he left Britain in protest at the Suez invasion, and continued his scientific work in India. he died in 1964.

Charlotte Haldane described his face a 'an extraordinary contraction': a huge, domed head, protruding forehead, fierce bushy eyebrows, blue and blazing eyes, a bold Roman nose falling away into a weak little mouth and jaw. He had a thin, reedy, stammery voice, but there was little conversation, 'for when he talked it was like listening to a living encyclopaedia'.

JAMES KEIR HARDIE is credited with being the man who founded the Labour Party, but he began his political life as a teetotal Liberal, and first stood for Labour because the local Liberal Association turned him down. It is certain that socialism was where his nature would have taken him, but the road was not well signposted in the early 1880s when he became an active trade unionist.

Hardie was born in 1856 in Lanarkshire, the illegitimate son of a farm worker, Mary Keir, who subsequently married David Hardie, a merchant seaman, giving her son the name that now has iconic status on the Left. He went down the pit at the age of ten. His experiences there and self-education through books took him out of the mines at the age of twenty-three, when he became a full-time organiser and journalist, agitating in the *Miner*, journal of the Ayrshire Miners' Union. He stood, unsuccessfully, as Labour candidate in an election in 1888, and then formed the Scottish Labour Party. When the radicals of West Ham South looked for a candidate in the general election of 1892, Hardie did not hesitate and chalked up a comfortable majority. He was a curiosity at Westminster, the working man's champion, with a trademark deerstalker.

His political progress was rapid, however. Hardie presided over the formation of the ILP in Bradford in 1893. Two years later, he lost his seat, and concluded that socialists had to combine with the trade unions if the cause of labour was ever to prevail. Accordingly, he was a prime mover of the Labour Representation Committee, set up in 1900 as the fore-runner of the Labour Party. Later that year he re-entered Parliament as a Labour member for the steel and mining constituency of Merthyr Tydfil.

A pact with the Liberals dramatically increased Labour's numbers in the Commons in 1906, and Hardie was elected first chairman of the Parliamentary Labour Party. Failing health compelled to him to relinquish the post to Ramsay MacDonald, and Hardie directed more and more of his efforts to women's suffrage, colonial freedom and – extraordinarily, for his day – Scottish and Welsh devolution as well as home rule for Ireland.

Hardie's causes were not always popular among trade unionists, and his passionate advocacy of peace met with open derision in his constituency when the First World War broke out. He died in 1915, crushed and confounded, his seat falling to a militarist. But Hardie was instantly canonised as the first socialist saint, whose soul, proclaimed Bernard Shaw, would go marching on. **Sylvia Pankhurst**, his young woman friend, called him 'the greatest human being of our time'. And despite never holding ministerial office, he still ranks as the foremost inspirational figure of struggle on the British Left.

JEREMY HARDY, the diminutive political comedian, found his deadpan style did not impress the Israeli Army when it invaded Bethlehem to oust Palestinian fighters and civilians holed up in the Church of the Nativity. Hardy, tormentor of New Labour on the BBC radio show *The News Quiz*, was making a television documentary about the Arab–Israeli conflict when Likud government tanks occupied the town, firing on his group and trapping him in a hotel for several days in April 2002. He was not harmed, but a number of International Solidarity protesters there to act as 'human shields' were not so fortunate.

Hardy came to fame when he won the coveted Perrier award for comedy at the Edinburgh Festival at the age of twenty-seven. At the age of forty, he was fired from his job as a *Guardian* columnist for being too left-wing. Naturally the newspaper denied any such motive, claiming that his column did not have enough jokes. Hardy claims he was critical of New Labour, which is regarded as a capital offence by Downing Street spin doctors. He was one of the sceptics who greeted Blair with the verdict: 'No, this is shite as well.' His opinion five years later: 'I never trusted New Labour from the start but I'm still stunned by how appalling they are.' Hardy supported the Socialist Alliance in the last election, and has been identified as a member of the SWP.

ROY HATTERSLEY was the linchpin of Labour's right wing until he discovered Blairism. By simply standing still, the party's former deputy leader moved to the political Left as the ambitious young things of New Labour streamed past him to claim schools and hospitals for the free market. From his vantage-point as a lord, and rather more frequently as a highly paid newspaper columnist, he rails against the latest excesses of Tory Tony. He even earned the soubriquet 'Trotters'. Yet he once privately urged the merits of **Blair** against John Smith, in conversation with *Observer* editor Donald Trelford when the party was choosing a successor to **Michael Foot**. 'Better to skip a generation,' he advised. Still, even better to be a late Blairosceptic than never. His life has been told at length elsewhere, not least by himself. However, he still has some good spleen in him and it will be illuminating to see how far his moderation drives him towards the Left.

DEREK HATTON is a showman who found politics an entertaining new dimension for his vanity. He was the figurehead of the Militant Tendency in the turbulent 1980s, but never the brains. Sharp-suited, glib and only superficially based in ideology, he confounded the Labour Party leadership for a decade before finding his real métier in public relations and talk shows.

Deggsie Hatton was an unlikely militant from the start. He was a moderately successful 11-plus child of the 1980s, educated at the Liverpool Institute, who after a couple of false starts in manufacturing and commerce followed his father into the fire service. He embraced the Anglican Church (and Everton) before disillusion sent him to London on a community workers' course. On his return to Liverpool, he joined the Labour Party and became a community worker in Knowsley, a hotbed of Militant. He was recruited there by Tony Mulhearn, the real Trotskyite mastermind of Merseyside. Hatton was elected to the City Council, and became deputy leader in the Militant coup of 1983. He was expelled from the Labour Party in 1986 in the equally ruthless purge of the ultra-Left sect that once boasted it would control the party. Considering that he was in the front rank of politics for only three years, and then in a provincial city, Hatton cast a longer shadow than his real importance justified. But, then, he had the mouth for it.

When Neil Kinnock crucified Militant in his 1985 party conference speech lambasting a Labour council – a *Labour* council – for sending out redundancy notices to its workers by taxi, Hatton was in the audience shouting, 'Liar!' He was equally vocal in a debate on the situation in Liverpool, yelling, 'you're not getting your fucking job back,' while NUPE delegate Jane Kennedy (later a government minister) was speaking. When the national executive considered their expulsion in March 1986, Hatton was in a side room at Walworth Road headquarters, conducting shouted interviews to reporters in the street below. He was a brilliant impromptu exploiter of the occasion, even conducting one interview about the 'taxi notices' in the back of a cab. As his prosecutor Peter Kilfoyle noted: 'This was an irony too far. Nevertheless, it signalled that the ego had landed.'

Following his expulsion from the party, Hatton was removed from the deputy leadership, then surcharged for refusing to set a legal rate and barred from holding local government office for five years. Hatton went off to write his autobiography, *Inside Left*, and present a show on local independent radio, *Hatton and Co*.

The Merseyside police took an interest in his lifestyle – nice house, nice car, nice horses for the kids – but these are not criminal offences and Hatton was cleared of a charge of buying a horsebox knowing it was stolen. Charges of fraud were laid against him and others, but he walked away unscathed. 'In time, he was to make as many escapes as Houdini in evading the attempts of the legal system to call him to account,' wrote Peter Kilfoyle. There was even wild talk of Deggsie being 'planted by the CIA'. It all added to the Hatton Myth, which is now regarded by Merseyside Labour loyalists as a warning against sharp-suited personalities trading in soundbites, which sounds suspiciously like **Tony Blair**. Hatton is still wearing flash gear, but it's hard to spot on his radio programme.

DENIS HEALEY was the first former member of the Communist Party to become Secretary of State for Defence in the British government, a prospect that would have alarmed the Americans had they not got to know their man long beforehand. He has also been a man for the physical pleasures. You do not get a rubicund face like his hanging round in milk bars all your life. Nor is he averse to a bit of slap and tickle. In pre-war Oxford, he had a girlfriend at home in Yorkshire but was attracted to Edna Edmunds, 'a red-cheeked girl' described as the Zuleika Dobson of St Hugh's. She had other boyfriends, but he was undeterred and they became lovers (in unromantic Keighley) as the world became embroiled in conflict. After a good war, Healey returned to claim his Edna, frankly stating in his best-selling memoirs *The Time of My Life* that both had affairs during the years of separation, their love growing stronger as a result. Woodrow Wyatt, a connoisseur in these matters, noticed this aspect of their happy marriage, confiding to his diary in 1993: 'I always remember him describing how they would stop on their walks in the hills and make love at the side of a field. They have both been fairly lusty.'

Healey's life is a pretty open book, not least because he wrote the story of it so well. Raised largely in Riddlesden, which qualifies as the posh end of Keighley and from which he took his title, Healey travelled via Bradford Grammar School and Balliol College, Oxford, to membership of the Communist Party in the summer of 1937. By Healey's calculation, nearly one in twenty of the university's undergraduates were in the CP at this time: they were 'easy game' for the only party that unambiguously opposed Hitler. With the party's help, Healey became chairman of the Labour Club. Inertia, rather than disillusionment, kept Healey in the CP until the fall of France in 1940. By then, he was in the army, and he returned in 1945 as a major, determined to change Britain through the Labour Party.

He failed to get into Parliament, but so impressed the top brass that he was appointed the party's international secretary. Healey worked closely with Foreign Secretary Ernest Bevin on the Marshall Plan and the evolution of NATO, and became MP for Leeds South East in 1952. The rest of his career is well documented. A strongly anti-unilateralist Gaitskellite, he was Harold Wilson's Defence Secretary from 1964 to 1970, and then Chancellor from 1974 to 1979. He was at least partly responsible for the electoral débâcle of that year by mistakenly imposing a 5 per cent wage limit on pay rises, which led to the so-called winter of discontent. Had he proceeded by negotiation, rather than the bulldozer, Healey would almost certainly have got most of what he wanted, union leaders later confided. That mistake did not prevent him becoming deputy leader of the Labour Party, but it did have something to do with the formation of a 'Stop Denis' cabal of TUC chiefs who engineered the victory of **Michael Foot** after Callaghan stepped down in 1980.

'A man o'pairts', as the Scots would say, Healey has many interests, but particularly art, music and photography. He is best known as 'the best leader the Labour Party never had', and least known for being the undergraduate who recruited my grammar school headmaster into the Communist Party during his time at Oxford, not greatly to the latter's advantage.

GERRY HEALY has the strongest claim to be the Lothario Leftie of the century. He was still seducing impressionable women comrades in his seventies, and was eventually expelled from his political eminence for corrupting 'the youth'. Healy, a teenage member of the CP who quit in 1936 to bulldoze his way to the top of British Trotskyism, was memorably described as 'short, rotund and pugnacious, with a head too big for his body and a deep scar across his brow ... given to uncontrollable fits of rage, had a vast ego and an apparently insatiable appetite for women'. As a political thinker, he was as unthinkingly loyal to the Trotskyist First International as any Communist was to the Comintern, and he despised any rival for leadership of the revolution that he fondly imagined was just round the next corner. For a time in the 1960s, with student protest at a post-war height, Healy's Socialist Labour League enjoyed a certain holier than thou ultra-Left influence, but in 1985 the party (now renamed the Workers' Revolutionary Party) split over his sexual debauchery. He died in 1989, an unrepentant seventy-six-year-old lecher.

ERIC HEFFER became a Communist while still a teenager and revered Stalin as 'the greatest of men'. Yet his happy childhood in Hertfordshire could scarcely be described as a model of the deprivation that drove so many of his and previous generations into the CP. His father ran a shoemaker's shop, and his mother was a freelance caterer. He attended a C of E primary and the local senior school before trying various trades, ending up as a carpenter. Heffer later identified the sight of hunger marches passing through Hertford in 1936 (when he was only fourteen) as the catalyst of his conversion to socialism.

He first joined the Labour Party, then the CP, and was active in the woodworkers' union ASW. Called up in 1942, he was posted to the RAF in Fazakerley, beginning a lifelong attachment to Liverpool. He re-left the Labour Party in 1954 to join the Socialist Workers' Federation in

1954, which collapsed in 1957, allowing him to re-rejoin Labour and win a seat on Liverpool City Council. From this platform, he won the parliamentary seat of Liverpool Walton in 1964, and in 1974 Harold Wilson made him a minister of state at the DTI.

Heffer rewarded this generosity with a fierce attack on government policy towards the Common Market that cost him his ministerial post but instantly translated him into a hero of the Left. He was a founding member of the Tribune Group in 1982, and a devout unilateralist. Strengthened by his iconic status, and with characteristic vanity, he dramatically over-estimated his attraction to the party at large, which was willing to give him a seat (even the chairman's) on the national executive and a place in the Shadow Cabinet, but ridiculed his attempts to stand for leader in succession to **Michael Foot** and deputy leader against **Roy Hattersley**.

He scaled fresh heights of derision with his walk-out from the platform during Neil Kinnock's landmark speech on the Militant Tendency at the 1985 party conference, and dropped out of the party's high councils. In 1988, he announced that he would step down at the next election, and began work on his autobiography, *Never A Yes Man*, but cancer overtook him. He died in May 1991 and the book was published posthumously.

JIM HIGGINS must be the only ultra-Leftie to have been accorded a *Times* obituary headlined 'Good-natured Trotskyist Agitator'. The son of a Ministry of Transport civil servant and educated at Harrow (County School for Boys), he joined the Communist Party at the age of sixteen while working as an apprentice with the Post Office during wartime. When his gang had finished repairing telephone wires, they took their ladders to Hampstead to clean windows. During National Service with the Royal Corps of Signals, he was posted to Hong Kong where he was forbidden access to the cipher room and his sergeant major would hand his mail, complete with CP publications, with the bantering remark: ' 'Ere's your letters from the Kremlin, Corporal 'Iggins.'

Higgins quit the Communist Party in 1956, with so many others, and aligned himself with the Socialist Labour League led by **Gerry Healy**. A few years of Healy's 'insane sectarianism' sent him off to the Socialist Review Group, whose leading figures included Ken Coates and Tony Cliff. This transformed itself into the International Socialist Movement, whose professionally produced and hard-hitting weekly paper, *International Socialist*, found a ready audience in the student Left. When the movement became a party, with 10,000 members and an ambivalent attitude to union leaders, it was time for Higgins, national secretary of the Post Office Engineering Union, to move on again. He became a sought-after journalist for publications as diverse as the *New Statesman* and the *Spectator*. He never quite lost touch with the Left, even though in later life he became a successful publisher with his third wife. He died in 2002.

CHRISTOPHER HILL, the Marxist historian, was perhaps the most distinguished of the 1930s intellectuals who joined the Communist Party out of conviction that ideas moved people to action. His passion for principle made him enemies in the academic world, and even forced his exit from the CP after the Hungarian uprising.

Hill was born in York in 1912, the son of a well-off solicitor and strict Methodist. His mother was more easy-going, but the young Christopher's political views, evident as early as his days at St Peter's School, shocked both parents. A brilliant scholar at Balliol College, Oxford, he visited the USSR in the 1930s, returning with a command of Russian and a benign view of the Soviet system. In the war, he graduated from the Field Security Police to the rank of major in the Intelligence Corps, from which – despite his known political sympathies – he was seconded to the Foreign Office. He returned to lecturing at Balliol, but kept up his proselytising educational work among adult and student trade unions. While breaking new ground on seventeenth-century English history, Hill also published *Lenin and the Russian Revolution*, which he compared with his own period of interest. England in the mid-seventeenth century had undergone a revolution, a great social movement like the French revolution of 1789.

His intellectual commitment was put to the test when the Communist Party Congress met in April 1957 to determine its line on the Hungarian tragedy. The leadership wanted no change in the way the CP was run. Hill and two colleagues produced a minority report criticising the leaders and their abuse of Leninist 'democratic centralism' to crush dissent in the party. The leaders triumphed, and Hill quit, along with fellow historian E. P. Thompson and seven thousand other members – a quarter of the party membership. Hill went on to develop his ideas, still with a Marxist flavour. He was elected Master of Balliol in 1965, retiring in 1978, the year that his *Milton and the English Revolution* appeared. He continued writing until the late nineties, dying aged ninety-one in 2003. Asked late in life, 'Are you still a Marxist?', he would reply, 'I don't quite know. Does it matter?' Fortunately, it always did.

PETER HITCHENS carefully cultivates his image of right-wing tabloid reactionary. Yet he has an ultra-Left past of which he is, occasionally, mildly proud. In the late 1960s, encouraged by his big brother Christopher, he was introduced to the Trots as a teenager. It was anything but a brief encounter, lasting through his time at York University and into his first job as a graduate trainee reporter on the Swindon *Evening Times*. He once led a charge of protesters against a police line, and scattered them. He was 'a crazed Dave Spart', a rebel against the values inculcated by his Tory father, a naval officer who became the bursar of a private school.

Life on a provincial newspaper in Swindon brought him up against 'real people' – policemen, firefighters and editors who didn't care a toss about Trotskyism – that made him rethink his view of the world. As an International Socialist, he sold the *Socialist Worker* outside factories and pubs. It was a lonely, ineffectual existence. He contemplated resignation from the IS, but revolutionary headquarters urged him to stay put. 'We're sending you a female comrade, working in the public library. Just meet her at the station – and the rest is up to you.' Hitchens relented, and appeared on the down platform, *Socialist Worker* under his arm, expecting another Vanessa Redgrave to step off the train. To his horror, a warty blue-stocking alighted, obviously looking for him. He threw his paper into the bin, jumped on his bicycle and pedalled off to his squalid lodgings, where he wrote out his resignation.

Such was the end to his inglorious revolutionary phase, though the death of his mother at about this time might also have been influential. Since then he has not looked back: fame at the *Daily Express*, where he was nicknamed 'Bonkers' while working as an industrial correspondent, then fresh garlands at the *Mail on Sunday* where he praises marriage, simple Christianity, private schools, the countryside and old-fashioned respect for the law. He calls this his 'inner emigration' into the world of the personal and the family, motivated by a conviction that politics cannot really achieve anything. Except, of course, that they got him where he is today.

ERIC   HOBSBAWM   is very interested in sex and has compared political protest to the male orgasm. But he is mainly thought of as a Marxist intellectual, a historian who understands the wide sweep of history. A member of the Communist Party for most of his long life, he is quite at home in elites, whether it be the Apostles' Society at Cambridge to which he belonged in the 1930s or the Companionship of Honour, which the Queen bestowed on him sixty years later after he had come to terms with the market economy.

For the post-war generation of the Left, he was simply the great explainer of what the world was about, but he lost faith in the great explanation – Communism – that he first espoused in 1936. 'In retrospect the project was doomed to failure, though it took a long time to realise this,' he conceded. Instead, he put his faith in the Blair project, with which disillusionment was more swift. 'While I share people's disappointment in **Blair**, it's better to have a Labour government than not.'

It cannot have seemed like it at the time, but Hobsbawm was fortunate to be born in a cosmopolitan, mobile world, which made him a global citizen long before the concept was recognisable. He was born in Alexandria, Egypt, in 1917, the son of a Jewish cabinet-maker from east London whose family migrated from Russia in the 1870s. His mother was the daughter of a Viennese jeweller. Young Eric was brought up in the Austrian capital from the age of two until his parents died, then in Berlin with an uncle. As a fifteen-year-old pupil at the Prinz Heinrich Gymnasium, Hobsbawm joined the Socialist Schoolboys.

When the family moved to London in 1935, he began reading *The Communist Manifesto*, and joined the CP after going up to King's College, Cambridge. Unlike his fellow Apostle, **Anthony Blunt**, he was not recruited by the KGB, a failure he puts down to his overt politics – although the 'Cambridge spies' had been open Communists, to varying degrees. Hobsbawm was rejected for work with British intelligence during the war, probably due to his Austro-German background, and this rankled with him, as he spent the profitless war years in the Education Corps on the home front. In 1943, he married Muriel Seaman, a fellow-communist (the party encouraged members to find partners within the political family). She left him for another man in 1951, by which time Hobsbawm was well established in academia as a history lecturer at Birkbeck College, London.

Promotion to professor did not come until 1970, and his first books, on pirates, revolutionaries and the agrarian revolt of 1830, did not hint at the global scope of *The Age of Capital* (1978), *The Age of Empire* (1987) and *The Age of Extremes* (1994). Hobsbawm visited the USSR in 1954, returning 'politically unchanged if depressed' and with no desire to go back. Yet he could still say at this period: 'The party was what our life was about.' In the 1950s, when fellow Marxist historians defected, he 'recycled' himself from militant to sympathiser, and in the 1980s he found Italian EuroCommunism more to his taste than the industrially-dominated CPGB. He attacked 'extremist' trade union leaders, and from there it was but a short trip to the espousal of New Labour. His party membership lapsed as the CP disintegrated in 1991.

Hobsbawm still cannot entirely abandon his Marxist world-picture, however. In his autobiography, *Interesting Times*, he dismisses the US concept of a war against terror, asserting that there is no enemy, merely an occasion for America to assert global hegemony. Hobsbawm, who normally found his women from the party network, married again in 1962, Marlene Schwarz, born in Vienna. They divide their time between Hampstead and a cottage in Wales, in agreeable company. Hobsbawm is unrepentant, and has no regrets. But then, he has done rather well out of 'the god that failed'.

ARCHBISHOP TREVOR HUDDLESTON

was, in the view of some, the archetypal trendy vicar, never happier than when standing outside the South Africa embassy, megaphone in hand, denouncing apartheid. Reality defied the stereotype. Huddleston was a pacifist and Christian Socialist at Oxford in the 1930s, a stance that took him into a diminutive Anglican monastic order devoted to social justice, the Community of the Resurrection, based in Mirfield, west Yorkshire. From there, he went to South Africa in 1943, working as a priest in the sprawling shanty townships outside Johannesburg. He was quickly drawn into the black people's struggle, working with Nelson Mandela and Oliver Tambo. Desmond Tutu credited Huddleston with forcing apartheid on to the world agenda.

When 'separate development' was codified in law in the 1950, and the settlements where he worked were bulldozed, Huddleston wrote *Naught For Your Comfort*, a stunning indictment of the South African system. He was also the model for Father Vincent in Alan Paton's influential novel, *Cry The Beloved Country*. Harassed by the police, he was ordered home in 1955, where he flung himself into work for the Anti-Apartheid Movement, initiating the boycott of South African goods. He went back as Bishop of Masai, Tanganyika, before being appointed, successively, Bishop of Stepney and then Mauritius, and Archbishop of the Indian Ocean. Huddleston came back in 1983, taking up the cudgels against apartheid once again. Such a saintly life came from unpromising origins. His father was a naval captain, yet Huddleston took vows of poverty, chastity and obedience. He died in the Mirfield community in 1998, aged eighty-four. His bust stands prominently in the South African embassy.

DOUGLAS HYDE published *I Believed* in 1950, and the story of his defection from the Communist Party became a best-seller. In two years, he took the gospel of his conversion from Communism to Roman Catholicism to half a million people in audiences across the country. Hyde was, if not the most prominent apostate, then arguably its most influential. Attracted to the Left in the twenties by the shameful execution of Sacco and Vanzetti in the USA, he abandoned Methodism for Communism after witnessing police violence against demonstrators on the streets of his native city of Bristol. Thereafter, he worked tirelessly in Spanish Medical Aid and more discreetly for the CP in the west London factories gearing up for war. In 1940, he joined the *Daily Worker* then operating 'on the fringes of illegality' For the seller of the paper during the Blitz, life was even more uncerta.in. One familiar figure who used to stand outside Tottenham Court Road tube station was vaporised by a high-explosive bomb. He later wrote: 'You will never understand Communism and less until you understand such Communists as these.'

Hyde accommodated the twists and turns of the CP as the Ribbentrop Pact was succeeded by 'our gallant ally, the USSR' but in 1946, began his journey to conversion by reading the *Catholic Herald*. As news editor of the *Daily Worker*, he led a double life, until he could stand it no longer and resigned in 1948, citing events in Czechoslovakia as the last straw. He was lionised by the press – British and American – and won the ultimate media accolade of an appearance on British Movietone News. But his conversion did not last. A biographer of the CP found him in the 1990s alienated from the Catholic faith 'and much closer to his first faith than his second'. Despite his break, Hyde paid every year for an 'in memoriam' note in the *Morning Star* for Peter Kerrigan, **Bert Ramelson**'s predecessor as industrial organiser, also a commissar in Spain and (in the words of another flint-hearted comrade) 'not noted for a spirit of Christian tolerance towards such as Hyde'.

HENRY MAYERS HYNDMAN, the archetypal rich boy turned rebel, has a special place in the canon of the Left as the man who introduced Britain to Marxism. In 1880, he read *Capital* in a French translation while cruising in the West Indies, where his rich family had business interests. His interest had been roused by a novel based on the life of Frederick Lassalle, a wealthy German socialist who gave financial backing to Marx and died in a duel. Hyndman was strongly influenced by Marx's analysis of capitalism, and, naïvely, sought to share his insights with Lord Beaconsfield, leader of the Conservative Party. Rebuffed, he played a leading role in forming the Democratic Federation in June 1881. Initially, the new body was treated with suspicion. Hyndman was the son of a rich businessman, born in 1842, educated at home and Trinity College, Cambridge. He played cricket for Sussex and studied for the Bar before taking up journalism. The *Pall Mall Gazette* published his reports from the Austro-Italian War of 1866, and Hyndman toured the world writing up his observations.

He flirted with nomination as an independent in Marylebone in 1880, but withdrew under a hail of accusations from Gladstone that he was a Tory. The DF soon became the Social Democratic Federation, popularising the work of Marx and Engels, with both of whom Hyndman quarrelled. Many SDF members also chafed at his autocratic leadership, which allowed him to reject a vote of no confidence. Hyndman was a tall, corpulent, white-bearded figure, with the appearance of an Old Testament prophet. A contemporary observed that he spoke 'with the vehemence of a great soul and the simplicity of a child ... above all he had vision'. His authoritarianism drove William Morris, Eleanor Marx, **John Burns** and Tom Mann out of the SDF and into the ILP. The SDF was part of the formation body of the Labour Party in 1900, but left after only a year when its gradualist philosophy was confirmed. Hyndman stood for Parliament – unsuccessfully – several more times before the outbreak of the First World War, and then confounded more of his followers by supporting British involvement in the 'capitalist' war. He formed yet another party, the British Socialist Party, and after alienating its members, the National Socialist Party, which subsequently assumed the title of SDF.

In this continuous, confusing fissiparity his support dwindled to insignificance, and events rapidly overtook him in 1920 when the Communist Party was formed – substantially from the ranks of his old BSP – to translate into action the political strategy of Marx and Engels whose original (though unwanted) champion had been Hyndman himself. He died in October 1921. **Ben Tillett**'s verdict was that Hyndman while being 'our chief intellectual prize' was also an arrogant intellectual, who brooked little discussion and no opposition at all. 'He failed specifically because of this intellectual attitude.'

I

BERNARD INGHAM, the loyal apologist for Margaret Thatcher during her decade in Downing Street, was not always a choleric Tory. He drew a veil over his life as a Leftie, but it was lifted by Robert Harris in his brilliantly forensic biography, *Good and Faithful Servant*. Ingham was secretary of the Labour League of Youth in Hebden Bridge, west Yorkshire, where his father was a Labour councillor. While a reporter in Leeds for the *Yorkshire Post* (owned, at that time, by Yorkshire Conservative Newspapers), Ingham was a strong trade unionist, vice chairman of the city's large branch of the NUJ. In the 1959 general election, he was the convenor of a group of Yorkshire journalists gathered to supply campaign material for the Labour Party. He was then so dogmatically Labour that he would not notice when his false teeth flew out in ferocious mid-argument.

In 1964, while a member of West Leeds constituency party, he became a Fabian Society nominee for the Labour list of City Council hopefuls. He paraded his experience in writing political articles, speaking at weekend schools and taking classes with the mildly Marxist National Council of Labour Colleges as evidence of his party virtue. At the same time, he began a column in the *Leeds Weekly Citizen*, writing under the pseudonym 'Albion'. Perfidious Albion, as it turned out. But he was happy then to attack 'the terrible Tory tribe' for their 'feudal mentality in a potentially brave new world of social, scientific and technological revolution'. He could not plead youthful credulity. At this stage, he was thirty-two years old, yet still boasting that he had rebelled at the polling booth against Macmillan's 'Never Had It So Good' slogan. Ingham predicted that Labour would win the 1964 election with a majority of at least thirty-six seats, 'enough to lift Britain out of the feudal strife into which the country would sink with Sir Alec [Douglas-Home]'. Wilson won with a wafer-thin majority.

Ingham confided to friends that he would rather like to be a Labour MP, preferably for his home town. He began the long road to Westminster with a bid to win the safe Tory ward of Moortown, north Leeds, in the 1965 council elections. He took leave from the *Guardian*, where he was now northern labour correspondent, to 'take the so-called Tory citadel by storm'. In the event, the citadel defences proved more durable than he imagined. A nice old Tory lady took three times as many votes as him. Blaming 'stunning apathy on the part of Labour supporters', he abandoned hopes of becoming a Yorkshire MP and fled to the comforting bosom of the *Guardian* head office in London as number two labour correspondent. There, his political tune stayed the same – for a time. Still writing as Albion, he praised Harold Wilson as 'the outstanding national leader in British politics today', and any challenge to the government he regarded as treachery. The seamen's strike in 1966 was 'sabotage'. His left-wing *Guardian* colleague Richard Gott, who stood in a by-election in Hull as the Anti-Vietnam War candidate, was 'no better than the meanest Young Socialist who has been corrupted by that miserable bunch of intellectual bullies . . . which inhabits the fringes of the Labour Movement'. Ingham was on his way out, and increasingly his Albion columns were filled with anti-union diatribes. In the spring of 1967, without notice, the articles suddenly ceased to appear. Ingham had got a job working for his beloved government, as a press adviser to the ill-fated Prices and Incomes Board. His civil service post required him to quit the Labour Party, which he did with no obvious signs of pain.

In his autobiography, *Kill the Messenger*, which is twice as long as the Harris book and half as instructive, Ingham sanitised his Leftie past. Albion was 'not a secret', he insisted. Then why the pseudonym? He did not reproduce any of his articles, merely reflecting to his credit that the column was trenchant, rumbustious, fierce, irreverent, cheeky and loyal to Labour. It gave him an enormous kick and over the months was highly therapeutic, he added.

The therapy was questionable. He was praised by Sir Keith Joseph, for whom he 'had a soft spot'. By the same token he had never expected to win Moortown, but was pleased when a colleague said of him that 'I really might make a politician.' In a sense he did: a politician *manqué*, close to power in Downing Street, but never wielding it.

To employ the phrase he used about John Biffen, Tory Leader of the House, Ingham was 'semi-detached'. He just realised it too late.

J

MARTIN JACQUES was one of the tightly knit group of politically motivated men (and women, in this case) who destroyed the Communist Party of Great Britain from within. Whether their actions were deliberate or adventitious matters little. The effect was the same. Jacques was a Communist student at Manchester University in the last days there of his great rival, **Mick Costello**. In the words of Francis Beckett, biographer of the CP, Jacques was a brash, clever, self-assured undergraduate. In 1967 at the tender age of twenty-two he was propelled on to the party's executive. He later attributed his good fortune to a recognition by the old guard that 'the youth culture of the sixties could not be ignored'. Nonetheless, while doing his doctorate at Cambridge, he felt 'like a Martian' and was already having ideological doubts. The party itself was having doubts, after the Soviet invasion of Czechoslovakia in 1968. Ten years later, the CP published *The British Road to Socialism*, drafted by Jacques and George Matthews, editor of the *Morning Star*. These days, it would be called a socially inclusive document, designed to appeal to every group in society. It caused a mini-revolution. Hundreds of party members walked out and formed the New Communist Party.

Within the majority who remained, divisions grew up between the fashionable 'EuroCommunists' like Jacques, who wanted a broad alliance of the working class, women, gays and ethnic minorities, traditionalists like Costello, the industrial organiser who stressed the primacy of work in the unions and the key role of Communist shop stewards. In 1977 Jacques captured a key platform, the editorship of *Marxism Today*. He turned the magazine into a glossy brochure for EuroCommunism, and commissioned articles from hated figures such as **Frank Chapple**. In 1982, Jacques ran an article by academic Tony Lane, accusing shop stewards of 'sitting cheek by jowl' with managers in 'the expense account syndrome'. This was *Animal Farm* stuff, and it ignited the final split. Costello demanded that the party repudiate Jacques, who threatened to resign if it did. A compromise was agreed, but Costello resigned and returned to the *Morning Star* as industrial correspondent. These two publications became the rallying points for the CP's openly warring factions. In the mid-eighties, the 'Euros' proved numerically superior, but it proved a hollow victory. Jacques quit the party, and it was formally wound up in 1991 after seventy-one years on the British political scene. For Jacques, says Francis Beckett, joining the CP turned out to be a smart career move. He move effortlessly into newspaper punditry and in 1994 became deputy editor of the *Independent*.

CLIVE JENKINS was a prize example of not one but two old adages: that there is no fool like an old fool, and a fool and his money are soon parted. As the leader of a white-collar trade union that went through several transformations, he became a millionaire an decamped to Tasmania with a woman practically half his age. The venture did not work out, and Jenkins returned a chastened man. He was not easy to chasten, claiming that he was 'only wrong about my being wrong', For two decades, he alternately charmed and tricked the unions and the Labour Party, before departing like the Cheshire Cat, leaving only his trademark sneer. The boyo from Port Talbot, born in the year of the General Strike (which he claimed was a 'sentimental influence'), Jenkins left school at fourteen and worked as a laboratory technician. He was active in the Association of Scientific Workers, and also read Marx, spending four years in the Communist Party before returning to Labour. He studied metallurgy at Swansea Technical College, and could have pursued a career as an industrial chemist but opted to work in the labour movement. He joined the foremen's union Asset as a full-time officer in 1947, and was elected general secretary in 1961.

Seven years later, he engineered a merger – the first of many – with his old union the AScW, forming the Association of Scientific, Technical and Managerial Staffs. Jenkins used all the tools of modern business, including full-page advertisements in *The Times*, to reach areas of employment that had hitherto resisted organisation. His telling pitch to middle-class employees 'My problem is that I picked up a pen, not a shovel', played on their fears of redundancy and envy of strong manual unions. Within a decade, he could boast of half a million members, a seat on the TUC General Council and a say in Labour's highest councils.

He credited himself with masterminding **Michael Foot**'s victory in the 1980 leadership election, and (with greater justification) that of Neil Kinnock in 1983. Thereafter, despite a merger with the draughtsmen's union TASS to form Manufacturing Science Finance, his influence declined as the impact of Thatcherism tore through his membership. While climbing the trade union ladder, he showed considerable skill in exploiting the property market. In 1953, he bought an imposing period house in Regent's Park for £3,000, which by the time of his retirement in 1989 (with the pompous title of General Secretary Emeritus) was worth more than £500,000. He also bought a country house – four cottages knocked into one – in Old Harlow, Essex, for £5,300, which subsequently commanded a £295,000 asking price. He negotiated a personal pay-off exceeding £200,000. Even his boat was provocatively named the *Affluent Society*. Jenkins had married Moira Hilley in 1962, but the marriage ended in divorce in the year of his retirement. He then went to live in Diamond Island, Tasmania, with his new partner, Sherie Naidoo, a public relations consultant, from whom he later split. He died in 1999, virtually unnoticed.

JACK JONES embodied for a majority of the British people during the 1960s the very idea of a trade union leader: serious, thriving, left-wing and far too powerful.

One of the last-surviving veterans of the Spanish International Brigade, he was still being asked for his opinions by the *Spectator* on the eve of his ninetieth birthday in 2003.

You do not get much more of a successful Leftie than James Larkin Jones, named after an Irish rebel union man. Born in a 'poor and mean' terrace house in Liverpool's South End in 1913, he left school at fourteen, and after a false start as an engineering apprentice (the firm went bust) followed his father into the docks. As a child, his father took him to hear the TGWU leader Ernest Bevin, and young Jack was quickly initiated into the political militancy of the Union. He joined the Labour Party at fifteen, and in 1934 took part in a Merseyside-organised hunger march to London jointly organised by Communist and Labour Party activists. Jones has always denied being a member of the CP. Senior CP figures have always insisted that he was, without offering conclusive proof. He became a Labour councillor in Liverpool, but dropped everything to fight in Spain in 1937. 'I volunteered because of the frustration,' he later recalled. 'We felt we must do something.' Jones joined the British Battalion, and was seriously wounded in the shoulder during the battle of the Ebro in 1938. He and his comrades were ordered to capture the heavily fortified Hill 481 – nicknamed 'the Pimple' – from the Fascist forces, without air or artillery support. It was an 'almost impossible' task, he said. In the words of Bill Alexander, 'the British came to know, and hate, every stone and fold of the ground . . . conditions were almost beyond description. The heat was intense, the bare rocks were shell-shattered, the debris of war was everywhere, and the stench of blood and bodies nauseating.' The action failed, and Jones was invalided home. His battalion numbered four Labour councillors. Two did not were killed.

Jones returned to Liverpool and in 1939 was appointed full-time TGWU organiser in Coventry. The motor factories were turned over to aircraft production and, with wartime demand for unhindered output, he pioneered shop stewards with a role in joint production committees. After 1945, the ambitious Jones turned his sights on national office, but as an acknowledged left-winger was frustrated by the hard-Right orthodoxy of Arthur Deakin, the general secretary who ran the TGWU like a business. The election of Frank Cousins to the top job in 1957 changed all that, and Jones was plucked from the Midlands regional secretaryship to become executive officer, effectively number three. He succeeded Cousins in 1969, when the Wilson government had just been defeated over its *In Place of Strife* union reforms. Jones was powerfully instrumental in thwarting its successor, Edward Heath's ill-fated Industrial Relations Act. Behind the scenes in opposition, he crafted the Labour Party–TUC Liaison Committee. This bureaucratic-sounding body was actually the political engine for union influence over government. It eventually produced the 'social contract', a new deal for pensioners and the conciliation service ACAS. But, with the disastrous model of Frank Cousins before him, Jones rejected a seat in Wilson's third government in 1974. With a million-strong block vote at the Labour Party conference, virtual domination of the TUC (his union now had two million members) and a string of client unions, he scarcely needed such a public confirmation of his position.

Yet his power often proved illusory. He failed to persuade the nation to say 'No' to Europe in the 1975 referendum, failed to win a state pension worth 50 per cent of national average earnings, or a wealth tax, or a gift tax. When he retired in 1978, Jones was offered a peerage by Prime Minister Callaghan, but declined. The union was already in difficulties, and the advent of Margaret Thatcher a year later following the winter of discontent (in which Jones's battalions took a leading role) accelerated the decline. Jones took up work for retired TGWU members, which he still does, and set up the National Pensioners' Convention. He became a Companion of Honour, the highest civil award in the royal locker, and published his autobiography, *Union Man*, in 1986. To Norman Tebbit, his greatest tormentor, Jones was merely 'a reactionary left-wing leader'. His own avowal in the *Spectator* is more accurate. 'So many good men died [in the fight for Hill 481] believing in the end in the cause of democracy. Win or lose, the world needs sincerity.'

K

JOSEPH KAGAN wormed his way into the inner councils of the Wilson government by charm, entrepreneurial skill and large donations to the Labour Party. He was suspected of being a Soviet spy through his relationship with high-ranking KGB officer Richardas Vaygauskas, but insisted that their friendship was resticted to a mutual love of chess. MI5 panicked at the idea of a Russian mole in Downing Street – this was before its officers suspected that Wilson was one himself. Vaygauskas, a Lithuanian like Kagan, was expelled for espionage in 1971. The security services believed that the KGB was trying to get at the Labour Prime Minister through Kagan, and mounted an intensive campaign to prove his guilt. Wilson was obliged to issue a statement denying any impropriety. But MI5 could on this occasion be forgiven its paranoia. Kagan was born in Lithuania in 1915, the son of a textile manufacturer who sent him to Leeds University to study textiles and commerce. He was trapped when the Russian occupied his country, and then sent to a ghetto when the Germans invaded.

He escaped, and made his way to post-war Bucharest where the British gave him permission to return to Yorkshire. There, the young Jewish immigrant went into business, famously creating Gannex cloth, a waterproof, lightweight mixture of nylon and wool that made warm topcoats. Wilson, attracted to Kagan as he was to other Jewish migrants who had made their way against the odds, allowed him to finance his private office in opposition and he became a trusted confidant in the Downing Street 'kitchen Cabinet'. In 1967, he paid the deposit for and guaranteed a mortgage on a Westminster flat for Marcia Williams (later **Lady Falkender**).

A short, podgy man with a limp, he was still attractive to women, boasting of forty mistresses by the age of sixty. He married Margaret

Stromas in the ghetto in 1943, but claimed: 'My wife is not interested in fidelity. But no one has ever taken her place in my life.' His longest affair was with Judy Innes, fashion editor of the *Daily Mail*, whom he met at a Downing Street party. They had a son.

Kagan was knighted by Wilson, and created a life peer in 1976. But he fled the country after being indicted on charges of theft and false accounting, taking his 22-year-old mistress of the time. He was rebuffed by Israel, and settled in Spain, which had no extradition treaty with the UK. On a shopping trip to Paris, he was himself shopped to the authorities by a jealous mistress. Jailed for ten months and fined £56,000, he was stripped of his knighthood by the Queen. Deprivation of his peerage would have entailed legislation, so Kagan eked out his final years as an habitué of the Lords' Dining Room. He died in 1995.

BRUCE KENT was a classic establishment product. He would have been an adornment to any officers' mess. Indeed he was, briefly, as an officer training with the Royal Armoured Corps. He was saved from a life of respectability by his Catholic faith, which took him from Stonyhurst via the law at Oxford to the priesthood. He was ordained in 1958, and taken under Cardinal Heenan's wing as a potential high flyer. But Kent's eight years as chaplain to London University brought him into contact with Catholic radicals, and in 1979 propelled him into the post of general secretary of the Campaign for Nuclear Disarmament. This was the start of the Thatcher era, and Kent was vilified as a Communist. Through the post came a parcel bomb. The security services tapped his phone and logged his movements. Under his inspired leadership, CND recaptured some of its former glory, but at a cost. He finally quit the priesthood in 1987, and married a fellow peace worker. Kent published his well-argued autobiography, *Undiscovered Ends*, in 1992, but it was certainly not the end of the road for this turbulent priest. He ran a tactical voting campaign against the Tories in 1997, but was out on the streets again with anti-war movements in the New Labour years, particularly during the war against Iraq. Kent is a perfect example of the British ruling class being found out by one of its own, and that is why they hate him.

ALEX KITSON famously drove a milk wagon round Edinburgh in the company of a young apprentice, Sean Connery, then known as Tom but later to become something of a film star. In his last act as a public figure, as chairman of the Lothian Region Transport Board, he personally issued 'James Bond' with his pensioner's bus pass. Kitson hit the headlines in 1977, when he went to Russia for the sixtieth anniversary of the Communist Revolution, and praised the Soviet constitution. He also said: 'I am pleased to visit a country where the situation differs from that in my own, and one can see a consistent rise in the standard of living of ordinary workers.' Thereafter, he was known as 'Radio Moscow', yet he remained thankful until his death in 1997 that he had not joined the Communist Party while under the spell of the legendary Scottish miners' leader, Abe Moffat. Even so, he was thrown out of the Labour Party before he was twenty-three because of his Marxist connections.

Born in 1921 in Midlothian, Kitson left school at fourteen and worked as a driver's mate before graduating to the wheel. Rejected as unfit for the navy in the Second World War, he became active in the Scottish Commercial Motormen's Union, and in 1959 was appointed general secretary. His union merged with the TGWU in 1971, and Kitson moved to London as number three to **Jack Jones**. He was the T & G man on Labour's national executive for twelve years, firmly on the Left: so much so that when the party set up a commission to consider its future organisation in 1980, he was obliged by moderate union pressure not to take up his place on the investigative body. He could also be a man of contradictions. He was opposed to the closed shop, and he opposed **Tony**

Benn's bid for the Labour deputy leadership, openly attacking him in a letter to the press in 1981. He became deputy leader of the TGWU in 1980, effectively its leader during a year-long absence through illness of **Moss Evans**. He retired back to Edinburgh in 1986, and served variously as a JP and chairman of Hearts of Midlothian football club. Kitson liked a drink, particularly in the company of **Mick McGahey**, Moffat's successor. As part of a double-act with Hugh Wyper, Scottish secretary of the TGWU, he reshaped Labour in his own image north of the border. One of the products of that process was **Gordon Brown**.

JAMES KLUGMANN was born into a wealthy Jewish family in Hampstead, and attended Gresham's School, Holt (along with **Donald Maclean**), before taking a first-class degree in modern languages in 1933. He gave himself to 'a cause for life' while still an undergraduate, and acted as the go-between linking CP headquarters in London with the burgeoning group of Communists at Cambridge University. The fact that so many of his students were Communists worried Klugmann's right-wing tutor, who once asked him over a glass of sherry why this was so. Klugmann replied: 'Sir, you have to look for the common factor, and that is you, sir.' In the late 1930s, Klugmann organised support for the Spanish republicans, but stayed away from the war theatre. He travelled extensively for the Comintern, and on the outbreak of war volunteered for the army. Originally designated a batman, his intelligence swiftly propelled him up the promotion ladder to lieutenant-colonel. Posted to the SOE in Cairo, he used his powerful intellectual grasp of affairs to push the British war effort into supporting Tito's Communist partisans in Yugoslavia, rather than Draza Mihailovic's royalist Cetniks. This was only a valid recognition of the military facts on the ground: the partisans were killing Germans, while the royalists all too often collaborated with the occupiers. But the re-direction of Allied war materiel to Tito ensured that Yugoslavia became a Communist state after the war. Klugmann became a full-time official of the CP, and wrote the first two volumes of the party's history.

He was also the author of *From Trotsky to Tito*, described by Francis Beckett as 'a shabby little book to justify the fact that Stalin had turned against the Yugoslav leader whom Klugmann had once helped and admired'. He did not enjoy the task 'but considered it his duty'. The book was withdrawn when Tito was rehabilitated after Stalin's death. Klugmann also taught in Ghana after it became independent under the socialist Kwame Nkrumah. He claimed that students found him more interesting than staid Russian tutors, as he was happy to argue that 'Marxism covers everything, from the erection to the resurrection.' Subsequently, he became the first editor of *Marxism Today*, the CP's new theoretical journal (which would, decades later, accelerate the party's downfall). He continued in that role until his death in 1976.

JIMMY KNAPP spoke as if he had a railway signal box in his mouth, which was a natural by-product of spending so much of his early life in one in Ayrshire. He was hailed as a product of the Left when he came as 'the candidate from nowhere' in 1983 to succeed the opportunity right-winger **Sid Weighell**. Knapp turned out to be much more pragmatic than his critics suggested, but he did bring to perfection (if not invent) the concept of rolling one-day strikes to circumvent – successfully – the draconian provisions of Thatcherite trade union laws.

Tall, heavily built and sporting wild white hair on each side of his otherwise bald pate, his rueful boast was that he was the same age as the singer Cliff Richard but looked older than his grandfather. 'I will always look like this,' he joked. 'Cliff can only look older.' Knapp attended Socialist Sunday School at the behest of his parents, before leaving Kilmarnock Academy at the age of fifteen to become an apprentice signalman. He became a collector of subscriptions for his NUR branch within three years. At the age of twenty-one he was branch secretary and at thirty-one a full-time official living (reluctantly) in London. He failed the iniquitous examination set by Weighell to deter him from senior office, but the top job was open to all comers and he was the members' choice. It proved a sound one. Knapp knitted up the divided national executive and merged the NUR with the Seamen's Union to form the RMT. With the example of the miners' strike before him, he rejected industrial action as a means of preventing privatisation of the railways, preferring to work through the political process. 'I'm not interested in defeats,' he argued.

In 1990 Knapp, often described as looking like a dinosaur even if he was not one, astounded the faintly churchy councils of the TUC by leaving Sylvia, his wife of twenty-four years for a German woman, Eva Leigh. The tabloids had a field day when Sylvia tracked him down to a hospital in Ashford, Kent, where he was waiting for hernia operation. There was a stand-up row and a blaze of headlines, but the partnership endured. Knapp succumbed to cancer at the age of sixty, and was received into the Roman Catholic Church on his deathbed.

TED KNIGHT managed to spend a lifetime in left-wing politics without achieving anything very much except being talked about. This was no small accomplishment for a Labour politician who never cut his ties with the Workers' Revolutionary Party that had succoured him in his youth. After the Brixton riots, he claimed that Lambeth 'is now under an army of occupation'. He led Lambeth Borough Council in the rate-capping revolt of the 1980s, and was personally surcharged and disqualified from local government for refusing to set a legal rate. More than any other London politician, Knight qualified for the 'loony Left' tag used by the Tories to denigrate Labour councils.

He had a chequered history. In 1977, at a public inquiry into the widening of Archway Road, Highgate, he and **Ken Livingstone** chased the inspector out of the room on to an adjoining balcony with a steep drop to the ground. Counsel for the Department of Transport was Michael Howard, later and better known as a Tory politician, who recalled: 'I was more worried about Ted Knight because he had raised his fist. I interposed myself between the inspector and the two demonstrators not because I thought Ken Livingstone was going to throw him off but because I thought Ted Knight might punch him.' After his five-year suspension ran out, and with the surcharge paid off, Knight tried to return to the political fray, but Labour chiefs ruled out his council candidature. A financial report by Elizabeth Appleby QC found in 1995 that fraud, corruption and incompetent management had become endemic during the Knight years. His own business, Pebbles restaurant in Clapham, closed in 1988, 'a victim of the recession'. In his latter days, while bursar to a school teaching English to foreign students, Knight ran the Lambeth Social Club in a basement in the town hall. New Labour and the Lib Dems took the club to court and evicted him in 1996. One hallowed corner of the club was the Red Room, decorated with a piece of the flag that once flew from the town hall roof. He remained unrepentant, insisting: 'I consider "Red Ted" to be a compliment.'

L

HAROLD LASKI was not the first Leftie to be destroyed by Red-baiters and the political bias of the British judicial system, and he may not be the last, but he has a strong claim to be the most decent. An academic who inspired a generation of students, he brought practical experience of politics to bear on his teaching and intellectual rigour to the everyday brutality of politics. In 1945 he was brought low by a mean-spirited calumny in two local newspapers in Nottingham, which accused him of inciting violent revolution. Laski denied the allegation, and sued for libel the Tory councillor who made it and the papers who printed it. Under the guidance of the trial judge, who invited the jury not only to consider what he had actually said but also if these were 'the sort of words which Mr Laski would be likely to use?', the court found against him. Thereafter, his reputation suffered and he was branded a Communist during a lecture tour of the USA at the height of the Cold War in the late forties. It was a charge that might have had some validity during his years as a co-architect of the Left Book Club, which the CP ruthlessly exploited. In Moscow, in 1934, he had even tinkered with the idea of a non-violent revolution in Britain and at the LSE taught 'a modified Marxism', But by 1938 the Russians had already denounced him as 'a prop to bourgeois civilisation', and though he argued that a Labour government must come to terms with the Communist world, he never quite qualified as a fellow-traveller.

Harold Joseph Laski was born in Manchester in 1893, the son of a pros-perous Jewish cotton merchant. Educated at Manchester Grammar School and New College, Oxford, he scandalised his family by eloping to Gretna Green to marry a militant suffragette, Frida Kerry, in 1911. Originally a Liberal like his father, Laski began moving to the Left while lecturing at

Harvard University during the First World War. His support for striking policemen in Boston provoked the first claims that he was a revolutionary, but he joined the Labour Party on his return to England. Laski joined the London School of Economics as a lecturer in 1920, and was appointed Professor of Political Science six years later. He became a leading figure in the Fabian Society, and Labour's first Prime Minister Ramsay MacDonald, looked to Laski for advice. The relationship did not survive the crisis of 1931, and Laski emerged as a sharp critic of Labour policy from the Left. He was elected to the national executive in 1938, and denounced his earlier espousal of a Popular Front with the CP and other Left parties.

He retained his critical function, however, until his sudden death in 1950. The socialist Ralph Miliband reflected that his lectures taught 'more, much more than political science. They taught a faith that ideas mattered, that knowledge was important and its pursuit exciting.' Laski's political beliefs and theories were distilled in a series of books published across a quarter-century of influence, but in today's soundbite culture they are little read outside academia.

JOAN LITTLEWOOD was a great deal angrier about life than the 1950s generation of 'angry young men' whose plays and novels captivated the bourgeoisie. She was a genuine class struggle warrior, who looked to real working-class people to act in her productions, whether they had formal stage education or not. She articulated the way of life of bottom-of-the-pile London through *Fings Ain't What They Used T'Be*. Her masterpiece *Oh! What a Lovely War* brought together for the first time popular culture and political satire against the warmongering establishment. Littlewood asked Barbara Windsor, who auditioned for the first show: 'Where have you been all my life?' Life for Joan had been a great deal tougher. Born in 1914, the illegitimate daughter of a Cockney maidservant, she was brought up in Stockwell, and found inspiration at the Old Vic.

She was also attracted to Communism, and after a brief spell at RADA was even offered a scholarship to the Soviet Academy of Theatre and Cinema in Moscow. Her money ran out before the visa arrived. In the 1930s, she joined the Theatre of Action in Manchester, a company promising to perform, mainly in working-class districts, plays expressing the life and struggles of workers. 'Politics, in its fullest sense, means the affairs of the people,' said their manifesto. The group did not last long, but that was her message for the rest of her life, despite being victimised for her Leftie views. The BBC sacked her during the war, and ENSA also rejected her. After the war, her old company reformed as Theatre Workshop, but found great difficulty in attracting funds from the Arts Council even though it had the backing of influential Labour politicians like **Aneurin Bevan**. Littlewood took the company up to the Theatre Royal, Stratford, even though 'it stank', because it was cheap.

It was also in the right place, the East End, and the right time, 1953. Her first great success was Brendan Behan's *The Quare Fellow*, which got her into trouble with the censors, followed by Shelagh Delaney's *A Taste of Honey*, both of which transferred to the West End. Later productions did not fare so well, and she was not a success in films. Littlewood had been married to Jimmy Miller, the founder of Theatre in Action, but the union did not last and she took up with Gerry Raffles, who later became her company's manager. When he died in 1975, Littlewood abandoned show business and buried herself in the small French town of Vienne where he had had his final illness. She died, childless, in 2002, after producing an 800-page autobiography, *Joan's Book*, for which she showed characteristic scorn, telling interviewers: 'It's no good.'

KEN LIVINGSTONE is definitely a ladies' man, but he does not always behave like a gentleman. While leader of the defunct Greater London Council and, of course, a single man, he was once entertained by a woman at her home. She had prepared a meal but he signalled 'Bedroom', and afterwards said he could not stay for supper as he had an urgent appointment elsewhere. Inconsolable, the lady watched him leave, but her dismay turned to wrath when she noticed that his cab was still outside her door, and the meter was still running. Stories of this nature about Livingstone – women and taxis – are legion. He delights in them, or did so until he settled down with Emma Beal, twenty years his junior. Today, he prefers the image of proud, trustworthy father, a guise in which he is rivalled only by the born-again responsible Stephen 'Knobber' Norris. In the London mayoralty election of 2000, the pair were career bachelors.

How times change. Livingstone's beginnings were unpropitious, starting with school at Tulse Hill Comprehensive in south London, where he was born in 1945. He became a laboratory technician, picking up an abhorrence of mistreating animals that stayed with him for life. He was elected a Lambeth councillor in 1971, and to the GLC in 1973. In 1981, he became leader in a coup against Andrew (now Lord) McIntosh, a middle-class moderate, that propelled him to the political centre stage. Livingstone scorned the term 'leader' – 'Leader isn't a term we go along with on the Left of the Labour Party' – but proceeded to lead from the front with radical policies on transport, gays and lesbians, the police, Irish republicanism, and ethnic minorities. He was political correctness personified.

It worked. In 1982, he was Radio 4's Man of the Year. At the GLC he fought a war a gainst rate-capping but was saved from surcharge and disqualification from office by Tories and moderates on the council who ultimately gave in to Thatcher. Livingstone kept his hands clean by voting with the Left, knowing they would lose. He entered Parliament for the safe seat of Brent East in 1987, still spouting hard-Left rhetoric that hoisted him to Labour's national executive.

If there was little prospect of political advancement under John Smith, there was none under Tony Blair, who predicted that a Livingstone mayoralty for London would be 'a disaster'. It turned out to be nothing of the sort, chiefly because it was largely irrelevant. Apart from the successful congestion charge for motorists, and the long, expensive wrangle with **Gordon Brown** over financing the Tube, he had little to show for his first term in office. His entry in the *Dictionary of Labour Biography* suggests that Ken 'would have liked to have been a minister, even Prime Minister'. As a politician without a party, this now seems unlikely.

KEN LOACH brought socialist realism to the small screen with his ground-breaking dramas about working-class life and homelessness, *Up the Junction* in 1965 and *Cathy Come Home*, in 1966. Those hard-hitting classics came when he was losing faith in Harold Wilson's Labour Party to deliver socialism. He argued that, despite the existence of decent socialists in its ranks, Labour was simply 'the enemy in another guise.' Much later, against the glamorous backdrop of the 2000 Cannes Film Festival, where his film *Bread and Roses* about the exploitation of Hispanic workers in the USA was shown, Loach was excoriating about the Blair government, arguing that it had 'got to power on the back of a workers' movement which they now want to change'. Not so much change, as neuter. But his mark went home, and official British representation at the opening suddenly diminished.

Ken Loach was born, the son of a factory worker, in Nuneaton in 1936. After attending the local grammar school, and national service (he was one of the last) he went to Oxford, originally for the law but, as it turned out, chiefly for the drama. The BBC hired him in 1964 as a trainee director, when even the Beeb was open to experiment. Loach responded with what were later described as models for provocative television, and then moved into film with his adaptation of *Kes*, Barry Hines's novel about a boy and his hawk in the bleak pit country of south Yorkshire. Critics say the next two decades did not live up to expectations, complaining that TV plays like *The Price of Coal* were unduly grim and ideological. His films of the nineties, *Riff-Raff*, a parable of the building trade, *Land and Freedom*, about the Spanish Civil War and *My Name is Joe*, the story of an alcoholic trying to rebuild his life, won wider acclaim, while still attracting complaints that his films are 'petitions masquerading as movies'.

Loach himself grouses, 'I've spent as much time defending my films as I have making them.' Social realism is not to everyone's liking. It can be unattractive, and guilt-provoking (as it should be). Sometimes, a treatment like *Brassed Off* works better. But while he may have some explaining to do, Loach has nothing to apologise about.

GEORGE LOVELESS was the best known of the Tolpuddle Martyrs, six agricultural labourers in Dorset who formed a trade union to resist wage cuts and were transported to Australia for their pains in 1834. It was no longer illegal to belong to a union, so the men were sentenced under a 1797 Act designed to prevent mutiny in the navy. Their offence was to swear an oath of allegiance in secret. A public outcry greeted their seven-year transportation, one demonstration attracting 50,000 workpeople. The martyrs were allowed back in 1838 after completing less than half their sentence. In their absence, their families were denied poor relief. The courts held that 'if they have money enough for unions, they have money enough for food'. George Loveless, aged forty-one at the time of his trial, became a delegate to the Chartist Convention. He left a moving account of his experiences, recording that 'The whole proceedings were characterised by a shameful disregard of justice and decency; the most unfair means were resorted to in order to frame an indictment against us.' In the intervening years, as the flawed actions against striking miners in 1985 showed, only one thing has changed: the defendants now have lawyers.

DAVID LOW was the cartoonist the politicians feared and hated. Tory Prime Minister Stanley Baldwin said: 'Low is a genius. But he is evil and malicious.' His wit was equally cutting whether he lampooned Hitler or the TUC, which he memorably depicted as a carthorse. 'He is the Charlie Chaplin of caricature,' observed Winston Churchill. 'Tragedy and comedy are the same to him.' Yet his appearance on the metropolitan scene was almost an accident. Low was born in Dunedin, New Zealand, in 1891, and worked on the *Sydney Bulletin* during the First World War. His brilliant political cartoons prompted the Cadbury family, owners of the radical London *Evening Star* to offer him a job. He arrived in 1919, and revolutionised his trade on Fleet Street. Low's 'savage realism' attracted the attention of Beaverbrook, who lured him to the *Evening Standard* with the promise of a half-page for his wickedly accurate draughtsmanship and what his editor **Michael Foot** called his 'high political intelligence'. Low strongly opposed appeasement in the 1930s, inventing Colonel Blimp as his caricature of the muddle-headed British military establishment. After a quarter of a century with the *Standard*, Low moved to the TUC/Labour *Daily Herald*, and then to the *Guardian* as his last job. He died in 1963. His images outlive him.

EDDIE LOYDEN had an ambiguous relationship with the Trots, which infuriated the Labour leadership without quite giving unimpeachable grounds for expulsion. In 1984, he sent a message of congratulations to *Militant* on its twentieth birthday, and a year later sponsored a defence fund for the paper when it was threatened with a libel action by a Labour MP. He backed the Militant Tendency's drive for non-payment of the poll tax, and sprang to the support of Tony Mulhearn when he was appointed 'Euro-Liaison Officer' for Liverpool City Council. Labour's witchfinder-general on Merseyside, Peter Kilfoyle christened Loyden 'the patron saint of lost causes' who was living in a time warp, and accused him of posing like Trotsky at demonstrations while acting as a 'virtual quisling' facilitating the progress of Militant. But there was never enough evidence to draw him in the great Kinnockite purge of 1986.

Eddie Loyden was born in Liverpool in 1923 'in abject poverty and misery', and after a Roman Catholic elementary school education went to work in a boot factory for 6s 6d [32p] a week. At fourteen and a half, he went to sea as a deckhand. He served with the Merchant Navy throughout the war, and in 1946 became a launch driver. He joined the Labour Party in 1952, and became a TGWU shop steward, then city councillor in 1960. In the miners' strike election of 1974, Loyden took Liverpool Garston from the Tories, and proved a formidable Leftie thorn in the side of the Wilson government. He lost the seat in 1979, but stormed back against the trend in 1983 and kept up a consistently hard-Left tirade until 1997, when he stood down. In that time, he espoused every militant cause from CND to the closure of the Porton Down chemical warfare establishment. Memorably once described as 'a stern, unsmiling left-winger who could play a *sans culottes* in a film about the French Revolution without needing costume or make-up', Loyden never compromised. He died in 2003.

NED LUDD, also known as King Ludd and General Ludd, was a semi-mythical folk hero of the Industrial Revolution. He might have been an apprentice framework knitter from Anstey, Leicester, who in 1782 was rebuked by his master for being 'averse to work' and promptly took a hammer to the hated frame. This is the earliest recorded evidence of machine-breaking by workpeople forced to abandon their skilled handicraft for factory methods. 'Luddism' took hold in the textile industry areas, notably Yorkshire, Lancashire and the east Midlands, but also in Somerset where, in 1797, several hundred men smashed up a factory making mechanical shears. On such occasions, local people said in hushed tones: 'Ned Ludd passed that way.' A popular song, 'General Ludd's Triumph', celebrated the 'grand executioner' who sentenced to die 'the engines of mischief'.

The motive of the Luddites was not revolutionary sympathy for the French Revolution, but a keen desire to get back to the old craft ways –

and the old prices for work. In the early nineteenth century, strikes and machine-breaking became widespread, and a riot in Nottingham in 1811 had to be put down by the military. The Prince Regent, no less, offered a fifty-guinea reward for information leading to 'General Ludd' whose orders were obeyed 'as if they came from a monarch'. Hosiery makers added £600 to the price on his head, but the conspirators tripled that with an offer of £2,300 for information on the informers.

In 1812, the government made machine-breaking a capital offence. Government spies infiltrated the Luddite movement, and the hangings began. Within a year, the main conspirators had gone to the gallows, the chief among them, William Mellors, shouting 'Three cheers for General Ludd' at his arrest. The Luddite rebellion swiftly faded, though the term is still in use. Appropriately, a King Lud pub stood at the bottom of Fleet Street until recent times. It was not favoured by print workers.

M

EWEN MacCOLL was the faux-Scots stage name of Jimmie Miller, the bearded folk singer whose folk song double act with Peggy Seeger captured the spirit of the 1980s. He was also a playwright of some accomplishment and an original songwriter of hits such as 'Dirty Old Town' and 'The First Time Ever I Saw Your Face'. He was born in Salford, Lancashire, in 1915, the son of a Communist iron-moulder who had moved south from his native Stirlingshire. His Scots mother shared her husband's political passions, and MacColl grew up in a home atmosphere of debate and song. He received only an elementary education, and took any job he could during the Depression of the 1930s: site labourer, factory worker, motor mechanic. He also sang in the streets for money, and started what would now be called an agit-prop street performance group, the Red Megaphones.

MacColl wrote for factory newspapers, and even local restaurants, in a political tirade that took him on hunger marches and unemployment protests. In 1934, he married **Joan Littlewood**, an unknown RADA actor, and they founded a workers' company Theatre of Action. It went through various guises and re-formed at the end of the Second World War as Theatre Workshop, dedicated to bringing working-class men and women on to the stage, most effectively in MacColl's own highly politicised plays. The marriage ended, and MacColl changed his name in the early 1950s, under the influence of the Lallans movement in Scotland.

At this time he also initiated a folksong revival in Britain, in concert with Peggy Seeger whom he met in 1956. For the next quarter-century, they performed, recorded, collected and brought to a mass audience the rich folk song culture of Britain. MacColl wrote an autobiography,

Journeyman, but his real artistic testimony is to be found in *The Essential Ewan MacColl Songbook*. He died in 1989, and was the unwitting recipient of a posthumous honorary degree from the University of Salford in 1991.

GUS MACDONALD travelled virtually the full political spectrum from ultra-Left organiser for the International Socialists to multi-millionaire capitalist with a peerage, and ministerial office in **Tony Blair**'s government. An only child born in wartime Glasgow to 'progressive' *Tribune*-reading parents, he went to Scotland Street School (now a museum), and as a scholarship boy to Allan Glen's fee-paying academy before leaving at fourteen to become a marine engineering apprentice in Alexander Stephen's shipyard in Govan. Macdonald came to prominence in the apprentices' strike of the late 1950s, which took him into the Labour Party Young Socialists as chairman of the country's biggest branch, with more than seventy members. From there it was a short ideological hop to the CND marches and the road south to London, where he arrived in 1962 as a house guest of **Tony Cliff**, the Trotskyist icon. He stuck with the International Socialists for two years, before abdicating for the comfier climes of *Tribune*, where he was circulation manager before moving to Granada Television as presenter then manager.

He moved to the top of the pile as managing director of Scottish Television in 1990, and hammer of the broadcasting unions. Half the workforce went. Five years later, he bought the *Glasgow Herald* and *Evening Times*, consolidating the premier role of Scottish Media Group. Jobs went there, too. Then 'the political opportunity came up'. Not through the Commons, but in the Upper House as Lord Macdonald of Tradeston. He did not hesitate. Via junior office in the DTI he took Winston Churchill's old job as Chancellor of the Duchy of Lancaster, reporting (if that is the right word: it is hard to imagine Macdonald being subservient to anyone) to **John Prescott**. The *Guardian* rated him highly in the Turncoat of Turncoats League. Such criticism appeared to flow off him like water from a duck's back. Yet he announced in May 2003 that he wanted to leave the government at the next reshuffle, without giving any clear explanation, and was duly granted his wish.

MICK McGAHEY combined a steely Communist charisma with an auld Scots gentlemanly manner in private, which made him even more dangerous in the eyes of the establishment. A lean, craggy-faced man with a disarming sense of humour, he was deprived of the post for which history nurtured him, the presidency of the National Union of Mineworkers, by a cheap stratagem on the part of his old rival Joe Gormley, but never complained. He took to the grave the secrets of the Great Strike of 1984–5 rather than compromise **Arthur Scargill**, an act of understandable but misplaced loyalty.

Michael McGahey (I could never bring myself to call him Mick) was the son of a Lanarkshire checkweighman (a job reserved for miners blacklisted for trade union activity) and a founder member of the Communist Party. The outbreak of war in 1939 found him a fourteen-year-old pit boy, already a member of the YCL. Four years later, he was sacked for leading an unofficial strike. McGahey was pit delegate at Cambuslang colliery, and elected to the NUM's Scottish executive in 1958. In 1966, he got on to the NUM national executive and the following year was elected president of the Scottish miners, despite the fulmination of Catholic priests from their pulpits in the coalfields. In 1967, he ran as the Left candidate for the NUM presidency, but was beaten in a secret pithead ballot by Gormley. The NUM was not yet ready to entrust its fortunes to a Communist leader. However, his emergence into the national arena brought a new rigour to the strong, but minority, presence in the NUM leadership, a position further strengthened in 1973 when he was chosen as the union's vice-president, beating off a moderate challenger from Nottinghamshire. At the same time, he moved up the CP hierarchy, joining the party's national executive and its 'inner circle', the political committee (modelled on the Soviet politburo).

During the second national pit strike of 1974, which precipitated the downfall of Edward Heath's Tory government, McGahey called for a general election 'the quicker the better' but rejected the charge of mobilising a pay claim for 'purely political purposes'. He did, nonetheless, believe passionately that raising political consciousness through wage militancy could help create, in the party's language, 'the concrete conditions' for a transition to socialism. He also took seriously Rule 3 in the NUM rule book, which laid down one of the union's objectives 'to join with other organisations for the purpose and with a view to, the complete abolition of capitalism'. McGahey caused a storm of (largely synthetic) protest in the media during the 1974 dispute when he appeared to call on soldiers to disobey orders if they were drafted in to mitigate the impact of the strike, which had forced widespread power cuts and a three-day week in industry. He later corrected himself, saying he merely wished to 'inform' the troops of the miners' position, but the damage was done. He was demonised for the rest of his life.

Yet McGahey was a wise, pragmatic negotiator. Had he been president of the NUM, the Great Strike would almost certainly have taken place, but he would have found a principled agreement that would have allowed the men to return to work with a united union, instead of a split union and crushing defeat under the artless Scargill. McGahey, who was proud of never having committed adultery, yet had an endless repertoire of jokes that brought off the unlikely yoking of sex and Communism. His favourite involved President Richard Nixon taking Nikita Khrushchev on a tour of New York bars, ending in a strip club. The Soviet leader was so impressed that on his return he demanded a strip club in Moscow, nothing being too good for the workers. A Politburo Strip Club Sub-Committee was set up, and pretty soon the attraction opened. On the first night, there were fights to get in. After a week, it flopped. Khrushchev was furious, and arraigned the chairman of the Strip Club Committee.

What had gone wrong? Was the hall big enough? 'The Palace of Congresses, comrade. Largest hall in Moscow,' replied the trembling apparatchik. Was it properly advertised? 'Certainly, comrade. On television, radio, in the newspapers – even on factory notice boards.' And how much did you charge? 'One rouble, comrade. Every worker could afford a ticket.' And how about the stripper? Beaming with relief, the chairman of the Strip Club Committee replied: 'Don't worry, comrade. Absolutely reliable! A founding member of the Party!' At this point, he would grip his fellow drinker's knee like a vice, and growl laughter from subterranean depths. Mick McGahey died in 1999, still refusing to disavow Scargill.

DONALD MACLEAN was a quintessential product of the British establishment who turned to Soviet Communism while a student at Cambridge University and never deviated from his chosen path. His father, Sir Donald Maclean, was a successful, God-fearing lawyer and Liberal MP who rose to become Education Minister with a seat in the Cabinet of the National Government of 1931. He sent Donald junior, born in 1913, to Gresham's School, Holt, a mildly-progressive establishment (compared to the rest of the public school system), where he met **James Klugmann**, 'Kluggers', a slightly older Jewish boy who was to become a pillar of the CPGB and talent-spotter for Soviet intelligence, and others later prominent on the Left. An exhibition took him to Trinity Hall, to read modern languages where he soon came into contact with the burgeoning group of Cambridge Communists, including **Burgess** and **Blunt** who also introduced him to the rival delights of homosexuality.

Maclean was a striking figure: six foot four in height, with blond hair swept back from a high forehead, he could have played Rupert Brooke in a Hollywood film. He was active in undergraduate politics, even taking part in a demonstration that clashed with police. But it was as an intellectual force that Maclean attracted attention, and the interest of the NKVD. He was recruited by 'Teddy' (real name Theodore Maly) a Hungarian agent who directed his attention to the Diplomatic Service. Maclean swiftly 'dropped' his left-wing views, and joined the prestigious League of Nations and Western Department of the Foreign Office in 1935. Dismayed by the West's attitude to the Spanish Civil War, and widespread fear that Britain might do a deal with Hitler and leave the USSR to fight Fascism alone, he passed on what he knew to his handler.

In 1938, he was promoted to the Paris Embassy, where the outbreak of war found him in the cockpit of diplomatic intrigue. He still found time to marry Melinda Marling, daughter of a well-off American family, just as the Germans were advancing on Paris. The couple fled to London, where Maclean kept up his espionage with a new controller, 'Henry', a Soviet embassy official who followed the Macleans when Donald went to Washington in 1944 as First Secretary, with vital responsibility on development of the nuclear weapons and the formation of NATO. The information on these and other issues, such as strategy for the Korean War, was of the highest grade. An American military intelligence analysis later reported that 'all information' on transatlantic planning 'undoubtedly reached Soviet hands'. This grandiose assessment is almost certainly exaggerated, but the Russians were unquestionably pleased with 'Homer', as Maclean was known. In 1948, Maclean was posted to Cairo, where his drinking bouts – probably the result of the strain of living two lives – grew worse. He was also in danger: code-breakers had discovered the existence of 'Homer' and were narrowing down the field of possible suspects. After a particularly gruesome bender, Maclean was recalled to London in 1950 for medical treatment.

But the FO, always disposed to cover up internal 'difficulties', compounded the affair by appointing Maclean head of the American Department in London where he had wide access to international diplomatic traffic just as the Korean War was beginning. On 25 May 1951, Maclean's thirty-eighth birthday, Foreign Secretary Herbert Morrison gave permission for the security services to interrogate the 'Homer' suspect. Too late. That night, tipped off by one or more of the so-called Cambridge Comintern, Maclean fled to Moscow, taking Guy Burgess with him, opening up the avenue of suspicion that led by a tortuous route to the eventual unmasking of **Kim Philby** and Anthony Blunt. Melinda joined him in 1953. Maclean, after a long sojourn in the grim city of Kuibyshev, where he thought of suicide, was eventually given work in a Russian think-tank on international relations. He did not relent in his Communist beliefs, not even when his wife had an affair with Philby (whom he called 'a real shit'), and wrote a book, *British Foreign Policy Since Suez*, predicting the break-up of western alliances. He died in 1983, in Moscow, but his ashes are interred in the burial ground of Trinity Church, Penn, under the family gravestone, a Celtic cross.

HARRY McLEVY was a sociable man in the classic Scots mould, who liked to drink, and yarn, and sing, his favourite being 'Passing Strangers'. He rose through the ranks to become Scottish secretary of the engineering union AEEU, before dying suddenly of a heart attack on Christmas Eve 1996. A serious, and sometimes questioning, member of the Communist Party, he finally broke with the comrades in the early 1980s and joined the Labour Party. But not before he had been despatched as fraternal CP delegate to the Mongolian People's Party Congress in Ulan Bator. In his innocence, McLevy believed that prostitution was a scourge only of capitalist societies. He was astonished and dismayed to be accosted by a hooker in what passed for a supermarket in the Mongolian capital. These things did not happen in the 'society of the future'.

Harry McLevy was born in Dundee in 1936, described by **Harry Pollitt** as 'that most proletarian of cities'. He followed his father into the shipyards, but moved to Clydeside and was a leader of the apprentices' strike in 1959 that brought **Jimmy Reid** and **Gus** [now Lord] **Macdonald** to prominence. He joined the CP in 1961, and returned to his native city to build up the shop stewards' organisation there. McLevy was elected a city councillor, and also stood as CP parliamentary candidate, but mainstream politics were never quite his métier. When first approached to stand for the council, he protested his ignorance of local authorities, only to be told by his party minder: 'We ken that. If we thought you had any chance of winning, you wouldn't be the candidate.' He was a lively and intelligent contributor to the engineering union's lay policy-making body, before becoming a full-time official. McLevy, president of the Scottish TUC in 1994, was praised by another Clydeside icon, **Jimmy Airlie**, for his 'puckish sense of humour that contained a humanity and intelligence that few in my experience have had'. I can say 'Amen' to that.

ALICE MAHON predictably, does not appear in the *Dictionary of Labour Biography*, voluminous though it is. She is too stroppy, too much of an old-fashioned class warrior, too left-wing, too disrespectful of **Tony Blair**. In fact, just too much. Yet she has proved an able, indefatigable critic of New Labour's failings, particularly on the NHS, women's issues and Blair's military adventures. MP for Halifax since 1987, she decided not to stand at the next election to forestall the imposition of a Blairite short-list on her constituency party. As a constructive irritant, she is in the **Tam Dalyell** league, and will be sorely missed.

'Red Alice' was born in Yorkshire in 1937 of Labour parents (father a bus mechanic, mother a textile worker) and joined the party in 1958. She spent most of her working life in low-paid jobs: machine operator, weaver, engineer, shop assistant, and domestic. She became an auxiliary nurse in 1967, and soon became involved in union activity with NUPE. Ten years later, Mahon took a mature degree in Social Policy and Administration at Bradford University, and became a lecturer in trade union studies at the city's community college. She became a district councillor in Calderdale, and after championing the cause of striking miners won the nomination at marginal Halifax against a phalanx of men. She unseated the sitting Tory, also male.

Entering Westminster, Mahon immediately joined the hard-Left Campaign Group, and supported **Tony Benn**'s various initiatives, including withdrawal from Ulster. She dismissed Neil Kinnock as 'a no talent man who is being eaten for breakfast by Mrs Thatcher', and then apologised. Mahon was not afraid to defy the whip, on issues like defence and the Prevention of Terrorism Act. She survived in 1992 with a majority more than halved, but won by more than 11,000 at the next election before falling back to little more than half that figure in 2001 when turnout slumped below the national average of 59 per cent. Blair allowed her to become a PPS – the lowest, unpaid rung of government – but it was never likely to last. She quit within months over the issue of benefits for single parents, of whom she was once one. To Mahon's anger and distress, Halifax has been targeted by the BNP, which won a council seat in the town. She is not likely to give them an easy time.

PETER MANDELSON began his long march to fame and fortune in the Young Socialists, before progressing via the Young Communist League and the delights of Cuba to American State Department front organisations, which held greater promise of political power. At school in Hendon in the late 1960s Mandelson joined a YS-inspired campaign to end selection in the north London borough, and in 1970 was elected chairman of a re-formed YS branch comprising twenty-sometime members. According to his official biographer, Donald Macintyre, Mandelson was evicted from Hendon Town Hall during the 1970 general election for 'over-enthusiastic heckling' of the Tory candidate. He reacted with characteristic self-importance, demanding angrily of the stewards: 'Don't you know who my grandfather was?' Mandelson marched in a protest to 'Kill the Bill' – the 1970 Industrial Relations Bill introduced by Edward Heath to shackle the unions. In

school he quit as a prefect (the precursor of more high-profile resigna-
tions) over wider access to the prefects' room, before, in a fresh bout of
self-importance, quitting the YS for the YCL in January 1971 to 'broaden
his interest' in politics, as he expressed himself to the constituency party
secretary. He later played down his party past, insisting that it was short
lived and he felt 'no identification.'

So why did he do it? Some reports suggest that he was strongly
attracted to a young man in the YCL, but if so, that did not stop him from
behaving like a good Young Communist: selling the *Morning Star* outside
pubs, and *Challenge*, the YCL newspaper, and *Soviet Weekly* in a Kilburn
shopping centre. Indeed, David Shayler, the renegade MI5 officer, claimed
in 1997 that he had seen photographic evidence that Mandelson had held
an adult CPGB membership card. He 'cannot remember' but his bosom
political pal Steve Howell says he did. Mandelson spent his gap year in
Tanzania, where his experience of President Julius Nyerere's 'village
socialism' was later pleaded for his disillusion with the Left. He returned
from Africa 'more moral than Marxist'.

Political disenchantment did not, however, prevent him from going to
Cuba in July 1978 as part of a large British Youth Council delegation. But
his behaviour there, ignoring the socialising jamboree in favour of
arguments in smoke-filled rooms to water down the text of political
statements, marked out his true role. His friend Trevor Phillips, who was
in Cuba with him, insists that Mandelson 'made a mess of Soviet hopes
that the festival would end with a paean of praise to East European
Socialism'. Had he become an MI6 plant? Espionage expert Stephen
Dorrill points out that Mandelson could have been recruited as 'agent of
influence' for SIS/MI6. By the mid-1960s, the British Youth Council was
said to be financed by the Foreign Office, the usual cover for the security
services in this context.

Certainly, Mandelson went on to embrace US-financed bodies such as
the British American Project for a Successor Generation and the Trade
Union Committee for European and Transatlantic Understanding. He
left behind the 'headbangers' he once admired, and headed for Cabinet

office under his new hero, **Tony Blair**. Money, not his Leftie past, was to be his undoing. His secret £373,000 home loan from Treasury minister Geoffrey Robinson prompted his resignation in 1998 and holed him below the water line. Yet the man who so interested MI5 for so many years today has a two-man, round-the-clock armed police bodyguard following his brief spell as Northern Ireland secretary, despite his second resignation. His flirtation with the Left seems to have done him no financial or political harm. His faults lay in himself, not in the *Morning Star*.

BOB MARSHALL-ANDREWS   is the kind of newcomer to Parliament that Lefties usually only dream about: clever, articulate, rich and vastly contemptuous of New Labour. Within six months of being elected MP for Medway, 'BMA' as he quickly became known, was identified as a leading member of Labour's awkward squad on the backbenches. He rebelled against cuts in legal aid, the Dome, curbs on jury trials, and a range of other issues. When told that **Tony Blair** had climbed to 93 per cent approval in an opinion poll, he is said to have declared: 'This is a seven per cent base. We can build on that!' Naturally, he denies the story, with the kind of cheeky grin that makes you believe it is correct.

His origins were not auspicious for the forces of Leftiousness. BMA was born in Willesden, north London, in 1944. His mother was a teacher, and his father loaded Spitfires. Both voted Tory. A scholarship boy at Mill Hill School, he carried off most of the prizes but took only a third in Law at Bristol University where he wore long hair and kaftans, and met his wife Gill. Reputedly, she turned him leftwards. BMA stood for hopeless Richmond in 1974, then went through a fallow period as the ultra-Left virtually destroyed the London Labour Party. He got on with his legal career, taking silk and appearing in some of the most high-profile commercial cases, including Johnson Matthey and Barlow

Clowes. He became wealthy on the proceeds, and diversified into an array of other interests, including a game park in Tanzania and the Geffrye Furniture Museum. He also built himself an extraordinary subterranean house in west Wales, overlooking the sea.

BMA failed to unseat Dame Peggy Fenner at Medway in 1992, but turned a Tory majority of 8,000 into 5,000 for Labour in the 1997. He did not reject ministerial office, but conceded that his chances of being offered a government job were 'infinitesimal', which is exceptionally good news for those who like to see Blair on the rack of an infinitely sharper QC's brain. He has written two successful novels, the second of which, *A Man Without Guilt*, was dedicated to Tony Bevins, the equally awkward political journalist who died suddenly. Soon after entering the Commons, BMA stated his philosophy simply: 'Every time I hear **Barbara Castle** speak I get this wonderful feeling that I did the right thing when I became a socialist thirty years ago.'

JAMES MAXTON was **Gordon Brown**'s hero figure, and in the privacy of his vast Treasury office may still be. The Chancellor wrote his entry for the *Dictionary of Labour Biography* in 2001, having already written a full-length life some years before. However, unlike the calculating Brown, Maxton was a romantic figure, prey to extravagant gestures such as calling the Conservatives 'murderers' in Parliament. But, then, he came from the 'Red Clyde', where lefties were lionised.

Born in Glasgow in 1885, the son of schoolteachers, he was educated at Hutcheson's Grammar School and Glasgow University. By the age of nineteen he was active in the ILP, and also in the struggle to set up a Scottish teachers' union. A striking figure, with long dark hair and dazzling speaking skills, he was a key figure in the pre-war group of Glasgow socialists that made Clydeside a byword for industrial and political militancy. Maxton himself, a pacifist and ardent advocate of the ILP's opposition to the First World War, was jailed for a year in 1916 on charges of sedition after urging munitions workers to strike. Maxton was sacked as a teacher, and found work in the shipyards. In prison, he gave 'socialism' as his religion.

It was not until 1922 – the year his wife Sissy died after giving birth to a son – that he was elected to Westminster as Labour MP for Glasgow Bridgeton, travelling to London on a train with fellow left-wing victors. Maxton proved almost as sharp a critic of Ramsay MacDonald as he was of the Tories, urging a radical programme of reform, *Socialism in Our Time*, published in 1925. It had little success, however, beyond helping Maxton win the leadership of the ILP, which he took out of the Labour Party (and ultimately into the wilderness) following MacDonald's betrayal of 1931 with the formation of the National Government. Maxton fiercely opposed rearmament in the thirties, and preached pacificism to an unhearing Commons. He died in 1946. Brown insists that Maxton was the original moderniser, believing in 'a third way between communism and gradualism'. But to his fellow Clydesider David Kirkwood, he was 'a prophet' who spoke 'with tongues of fire'.

JOAN MAYNARD did not care that she was cruelly nicknamed 'Stalin's Granny' and 'Sheffield's Answer to Rosa Luxemburg', because her unshakeable socialism and formidable presence left her virtually immune to carping. Besides, she said, Stalin's grandmother was probably a pillar of the Russian Orthodox Church in Georgia, 'which might be a bit difficult for me'. She had many enemies, chiefly in the Labour Party, but never flinched from espousing left-wing causes. Vera Joan Maynard was born in 1921, the daughter of a smallholder in Easingwold, Yorkshire. Educated at the village school in Ampleforth (the home of a rather larger, exclusive Catholic public school), she became a sub-postmistress, but her rural background took her into the National Union of Agricultural Workers, of which she became county secretary in 1954. Maynard joined the Labour Party in 1946, and was the party's agent in Thirsk for twenty years before finally landing a parliamentary seat at Sheffield Brightside in 1974, ousting a right-wing Labour drunk, Eddie Griffiths. She had long been a star turn at the annual conference, 'a striking jet black-haired Yorkshire lass' at the rostrum urging nationalisation of the land, to the discomfiture of Labour leaders, some of whom owned farms.

At Westminster she threw herself into every Leftie lobby available from Troops Out, CND and Anti-EEC to lifting her party's ban on contacts with foreign Communist parties. Maynard was one of ten MPs named in the Commons as 'fifth columnists' seeking to undermine British society from within the Labour Party. Unabashed, she supported **Tony Benn** for the party leadership, chaired the Campaign Group when it broke away from *Tribune*, and invited Sinn Fein spokespeople to Westminster. Yet even the Tories admired her stalwart work on the Agriculture Select Committee. Maynard served on the party's NEC for fifteen years, with a one-year break when the right engineered her defeat. To her friend **Tam Dalyell**, she was 'politically utterly Utopian, and quite dotty' but she possessed heart and soul and inspired many young people to come into politics. She retired in 1987, bequeathing her seat to the infinitely less principled David Blunkett, and died in 1998 in her native Yorkshire.

MICHAEL MEACHER had a virtually blemish-free record as a Leftie until he was blown out of the water by Richard Hartley QC in a libel trial against the *Observer*. In 1990, he took on the oldest-established left-of-centre newspaper, which had pointed out a slight discrepancy between his hard-Left political views and his impeccable middle-class credentials and lifestyle. He lost the action, and much face, but he clung grimly on and survived to become a long-serving minister under New Labour. Meacher was a member of the Shadow Cabinet, and should have been appointed to the real thing. Instead, he was offered environment protection outside the Cabinet. It was a deliberate slight, as

Meacher recognised in a phone call to this author at the *Independent on Sunday* on 3 May 1997. But he rode over the snub, and became a useful pair of hands in awkward public arguments on issues as wide as GM foods and refrigerator destruction.

Meacher was a scholar at Berkhamsted School, followed by New College, Oxford, and lecturing posts at York University and the LSE. His socialism was cerebral rather than gut, though his concern for the poor and the elderly was genuine. He has been MP for Oldham West since 1970, and stood as left-wing candidate for the deputy leadership of the party in 1983, and came a respectable second to **Roy Hattersley**. Thereafter, he became known as '**Benn**'s vicar on earth' and although consistently elected to the Shadow Cabinet, was shifted from pillar to post. Meacher was thought too close to the unions while shadowing Employment, and elbowed aside in favour of **Blair**. He has been described as a thinking and quite private man, not without warmth and humour, who can be 'charmingly indiscreet, even about colleagues'. This latter quality has probably held him back as much as his determination not to abandon socialism with the same gusto as New Labour politicos. He was not offered a post in Blair's first Cabinet, as party convention demanded, but accepted the role of Environment Minister, which he kept until the botched reshuffle of June 2003. Freed from ministerial responsibilities, he identified the overweening power of the United States as the world's greatest problem.

IAN MIKARDO combined a steadfast public commitment to nationalisation with a considerable private entrepreneurial flair that would have attracted charges of hypocrisy in a man of less charm. Even so, it was often noticed that he did not practise what he preached. In that respect, 'Mik', as he was universally known, had a great deal in common with the rich Jewish businessmen in the East End who secretly funded the Communist Party for decades. He was also the most skilful excavator of money from delegates' pockets in the annual appeal for funds at Labour Party conferences.

Mikardo was born in Portsmouth in 1907, the son of Jewish migrants from the Tsarist empire. His father Moshe, a tailor from Poland, and his mother, Bluma, spoke Yiddish at home and put their son into a rabbinical school. He transferred to the local grammar, and as a young man joined the Labour Party and its affiliated Zionist arm, Poale Zion. He became Labour candidate for Reading in 1944, and at conference that year moved the radical motion demanding wide-scale post-war nation-alisation of industry. Herbert Morrison, noting his skill, remarked: 'Young man, that was a good speech, but you do realise, don't you, that you've lost us the general election?' Mik won his Tory marginal, and kept it for fifteen years. In 1964, he returned as MP for Stepney, and remained there as the seat went through various guises for more than twenty years. Yet he never held ministerial office, having been ruled out by Attlee on racial grounds (he didn't want any more of 'the Chosen People' in government). Apart from his very long stint – three decades – on the national executive, Mikardo is best remembered for his co-authorship of the influential pamphlet *Keep Left* in 1947. A sequel, *Keeping Left*, in 1950, had less impact.

Accused of being a 'fellow traveller', not least because of his flourishing East–West trade interests, he was kept out in the cold by Harold Wilson, a 'profound mistake' according to **Tam Dalyell**. His reward was Mikardo's powerful opposition from the backbenches on unilateral nuclear disarmament, Vietnam, incomes policy and the reform of trade union law. Mikardo also discovered that right-wing officials at Labour HQ were keeping intelligence files on party candidates, using internal informants and MI5. Mik figured on a list of fifteen 'crypto-Communists' drawn up by the Campaign for Democratic Socialism. But his enemies failed to evict him from the party, and Mikardo formed an alliance with **Clive Jenkins**'s union ASTMS, which was instrumental in propelling his old Bevanite chum **Michael Foot** into the leadership over **Denis Healey** in 1980. Mik was the house bookie at Westminster, always willing to take a bet on elections and invariably collecting. His beetle-browed mildly conspiratorial image was a godsend to cartoonists, and Winston Churchill once remarked: 'I'm told he's not as nice as he looks.' On retirement in 1987, he wrote an elegant memoir, *Back-Bencher*. He died in 1993.

ALAN MILBURN came to Westminster trailing clouds of Leftiousness. They soon dissipated, leaving only rampant ambition. He is spoken of by Labour MPs who cannot stomach **Gordon Brown** as a possible New Labour successor to **Tony Blair**, but there is scant evidence of Milburnism or Milburnites. Indeed, his original affiliations lay with the ultra-Left. In the early 1980s, he ran a radical bookshop in Newcastle with the politically correct name, Days of Hope. Inevitably, given the cannabis culture of the time, it was better known as Haze of Dope. Milburn's friends have denied that he was a dopehead, and *Independent* profile writer Sean O'Grady acidly observed that smoking cannabis might have weakened the ideological drive of the Newcastle cadre. Milburn was deeply involved in the International Marxist Group, the British Section of Trotsky's Fourth International, and shared a flat with a group of young revolutionaries. He was rather old to be a Trot, well into his twenties and armed with a BA in history from the University of Lancaster, but he took his turn selling Marxist literature and far-out magazines like *Black Dwarf*. He was also co-founder of Trade Union CND.

The wannabe premier now says he has grown up. 'There is nothing to hide. Like many people in the early 1980s I had very left-wing views. The Labour Party and myself have done a lot of growing up since then.' Nothing to hide? All this is glossed over in the *Dictionary of Labour Biography* entry on Milburn, though it was written by Richard Elsen, one-time deputy head of Labour's notorious Rebuttal Unit. Milburn has now joined the **John Reid** 'take no prisoners' style of political management. It is a far cry from his origins as the son of a single mother who worked in the NHS as a secretary. He never knew his father, and was brought up in Tow Law, a Durham pit village. He shone academically at the local comprehensive, and after Lancaster University returned to Newcastle to do a Ph.D., which remains unfinished. One thing that did finish during his conversion to Blairism was his marriage to Barbara 'Mo' O'Toole. They wed in his Trot days in 1982, and divorced seven years later. Milburn moved on to a relationship with Dr Ruth Briel, a consultant psychiatrist and Labour activist whom he met on the campaign trail in 1987. They have two sons but remain 'happily unmarried'.

Milburn, originally a Brownite, was elected to Westminster from Darlington in 1992. He served as a junior Treasury minister after the 1997 general election, but gradually shifted to the Blair camp. That is where the jobs are, and in due course he was rewarded with Health Secretary after **Frank Dobson** was eased out. He likes rap music, but will now never have to take the rap for the débâcle of foundation hospitals and the Private Finance Initiative NHS. In June 2003 he dramatically quit Cabinet, pleading the customary argument that he wanted to spend more time with his family. On this occasion, it appeared to have more justification than most others, but some commentators observed that by distancing himself from an increasingly unpopular Blair, Milburn would be well positioned to take on Gordon Brown in a future leadership contest.

JIM MORTIMER can fairly claim to have been the only Marxist thinker of modern times to become general secretary of the Labour Party, but he is chiefly remembered at present for his appalling gaffe in the 1983 general election. **Michael Foot**, the Labour leader, was under intense pressure for his lacklustre campaign. Emerging from a meeting of the Campaign Committee, Mortimer announced: 'At the committee this morning we were all insistent that Michael Foot is the leader of the Labour Party and speaks for the party and we support the manifesto of the Party.' That Labour should be reduced to a virtual vote of confidence in its disastrous standard-bearer in the heat of an election campaign spoke volumes for its unity – or lack of it. Mortimer's father, a devout socialist raised in Bradford where the ILP was strong, had syndicalist and militant views, and never joined the Labour Party. Young Jim chose books on Marxism as prizes when he attended Portsmouth Technical School, and as a teenager attended meetings of the Labour League of Youth, though he remained a committed Methodist.

While an engineering apprentice in Portsmouth dockyard, he joined the Socialist League, and publicly spoke in favour of a united front with the Communist Party and the ILP, particularly on the issue of arms for the Spanish government and support for striking apprentices on Clydeside. A workmate denounced him to the authorities as a 'subversive', and Mortimer decided to seek his future in London. When war came, he volunteered for flying duties in the Fleet Air Arm, and was turned down on political grounds. The recruiting officer asked if he would 'subvert the constitution' and was plainly not satisfied with the answer. Mortimer returned to the tools, and joined the Young Communist League, becoming Hounslow branch secretary. He quit and joined the Labour Party, not as a result of some great political conversion, or recognition of 'the God that failed', but over post-war strategy. Mortimer went to Ruskin College, Oxford, on a TUC scholarship, leaving the shop floor for good. He worked in the TUC's Economic Department and as national official of the Draughtsmen's Union, without abandoning his Leftist credentials. Indeed, in 1953, at the height of the Cold War, he was expelled from the Labour Party for refusing to resign from the British-China Friendship Association, of which he was vice chairman.

He was readmitted in 1958, and ten years later was asked by **Barbara Castle** to join the Prices and Incomes Board, a statutory body charged with implementing Labour's pay policy. The PIB was wound up by the Tories in 1971, and Mortimer claimed it was 'not a futile experiment' even though it had not worked. Soon after, he was granted a visa to visit the USA only after protracted 'security' inquiries. Mortimer moved on to London Transport as board member for industrial relations, and later to the chairmanship of ACAS, the conciliation service but quit in January 1980 after the Thatcher government embarked on anti-union legislation. He became general secretary of the Labour Party in 1981 by a one-vote majority vote of the NEC. In his autobiography, *Life on the Left*, he had no regrets for his 'own goal' over Foot, and was proud of being made an honorary member of the NUM after the great strike of 1984/5. His final verdict was: 'The record of the Communist trend within the world labour movement has been more spectacular, both in achievements and failings, than that of the social-democratic trend. The Russian Revolution, despite the ultimate collapse of Soviet power, is likely to be seen in the future as one of the turning points of world history. For the first time an attempt was made to construct a new kind of society based upon the social ownership of industry and co-operative farming. It had many achievements to its credit' ... But then his free copies of *Trud*, the Soviet trade union newspaper, stopped.

N

DAVE NELLIST was memorably described as 'prolier than thou' for his ability to combine a hard-line proletarian attitude with a religious angst about all things socialist. He was the only Labour MP who almost survived Neil Kinnock's witch-hunt against the Militant Tendency, but in the end even this lanky, bearded, slightly scruffy (why are the ultra-Left always so badly dressed?) prophet from Coventry was expelled from the party. Born in Saltburn, Teesside, in 1952, the son of a fitter, he worked in various manual jobs and endured a three-year spell of unemployment before being elected MP for the safe seat of Coventry South East in 1983.

To the usual range of Leftie causes, he added the treatment of Tamils by the Sri Lankan government, the plight of Palestinian trade unionists, strikes by school children and vagrant British youth, though he would not have used that expression. Nellist was expelled on the eve of the 1992 election, an act described by **Tony Benn** as 'the grossest miscarriage of justice'. He had been reselected by his local party and the NEC, but the Labour leader wanted no Militant candidates in the poll he might win. **Terry Field**s, MP for Liverpool Broad Green, met the same fate. Their departure diminished Parliament, where the 'Millies' could always be relied upon for an exotic quote or theatrical event. When the Tory government cut benefit to striking miners' families by £1 a week in November 1984, a number of Labour backbenchers protested by standing in front of the Mace. Characteristically, Nellist went one further, tearing up the speech notes of Social Services Secretary Norman Fowler. In 1990, he had to apologise to the Speaker for crossing the floor to give some tongue pie to Education Minister Angela Rumbold. They just don't make them like that any more, and if they do, none make it to Westminster.

EDITH NESBIT is known foremost as a children's writer, particularly *The Railway Children*. But she was also a Leftie, indeed a founder of the Fabian Society. She was born in 1858, the son of a schoolmaster, and educated by her mother in France after her father died when she was only six. While still only nineteen, she defied Victorian morality by becoming the partner of Hubert Bland, a writer of reformist views. When their daughter was well on the way, they married, and in 1883 joined with other radicals, including the philosopher Havelock Ellis and the Quaker Edward Pease to set up a debating society. They called themselves the Fabians, numbering about thirty individuals. Its aim was to popularise ways of improving the social system. Edith and her husband edited the society's journal, and within months other radicals flocked to their cause, including **Annie Besant**, the **Webbs**, and George Bernard Shaw, whom Nesbit described as 'the grossest flatterer I ever met, horribly untrustworthy, very plain like a long corpse with a dead white face . . . one of the most interesting men I ever met.' The Fabians prospered, as did Edith's writing career, which drew her away from political campaigning, though in 1908 she published *Ballads and Lyrics of Socialism*. She died in 1924.

MELITA NORWOOD was unmasked in 1999 at the ripe old age of eighty-seven as Agent Hola, the 'granny traitor'. A lifelong Communist, she admitted passing secrets about the atomic bomb project to the Russians in the immediate post-war years, but claims that she was the KGB's top female agent up there with **Fuchs** and **Philby** were derided by espionage experts. Norwood was personal assistant to the director of the Non-Ferrous Metals Research Association, which was involved in the Tube Alloys Project, code-name for the British A-bomb. She handed over confidential documents to her Soviet handlers, and never regretted it. 'I did what I did, not to make money but to help prevent the defeat of a new system, which had, at great cost, given ordinary people food and fares which they could afford, given them education and a health service … In general, I do not agree with spying against one's country.' Nor do the intelligence services like to be made to look like monkeys by an elderly lady living out her last days in Bexleyheath. They decided not to prosecute her, a view upheld by New Labour Attorney General Sir John Morris. Norwood was named as a Soviet agent by KGB defector Vasili Mitrokhin in 1992. Seven years later, the security allowed Mitrokhin to go public on her, causing a brief Philby-style furore. But Norwood admitted that she was 'not technically minded' and even ex-KGB spymaster Yuri Modin described her as 'unimportant'. She carried on with her *Morning Star* round .

ALAN NUNN MAY, the nuclear physicist jailed for passing atomic secrets to the Russians during the Second World War, discovered to his cost the limits of Communist comradeship. When he emerged from a six-year sentence in Parkhurst prison, Nunn May expected to be cut by most of his friends, and he was not disappointed. 'But,' he told Conor Cruise O'Brien, 'I was bewildered to find that *all* my Communist colleagues and acquaintances cut me dead.' His offence, in their eyes, was to have pleaded guilty to the espionage charges, which embarrassed the Soviet Union. 'I should have pleaded *not* guilty, thereby enabling the Soviet Union to accuse the British government of having framed me, while plausibly asserting their own innocence,' he said. Innocence played a large part in Nunn May's life. Born in 1911, the son of a Birmingham brass founder, he shone academically from childhood. He took a first in physics at Trinity College, Cambridge, then researched his Ph.D. under Rutherford, Cavendish Professor of Experimental Physics. He joined the Communist Party at Cambridge during the 1930s, but was neither showy about his politics nor a member of the clandestine group of apprentice Soviet agents. His occasional pilgrimages to Moscow did not attract attention, and the outbreak of war found him lecturing at King's College, London, while working on top-secret radar research. Later, he joined the anonymously titled Tube Alloys Project, Britain's bid to build an A-bomb.

When the work was transferred to Canada in 1943, Nunn May went with the British team, and it was there that he was contacted by Soviet intelligence, in the shape of Colonel Nikolai Zabotin, military attaché at the Russian embassy in Ottawa. Nunn May, who knew that the Germans were also working on a nuclear device that could be dropped on the USSR, readily agreed to supply information. Under Zabotin's guidance, he paid a number of visits to nuclear establishments in the USA, prompting American suspicions. His Soviet handlers insisted on his acceptance of a $200 payment, plus two bottles of whisky, the receipts for which helped unmask him when a Soviet intelligence officer, Igor Gouzenko, defected. He always claimed to have destroyed the money. In 1945, Nunn May passed to the Russians a full scientific description of the first atomic bomb, detonated in New Mexico in July 1945. At the end of the war, he returned to his academic post in London, and had clearly decided to break with Soviet intelligence, failing to keep an appointment with his controller. Gouzenko's evidence pointed conclusively to Nunn May, and he admitted the whole 'extremely painful affair', which he had embarked upon solely as 'a contribution to the safety of mankind'.

He was sentenced to ten years, and on his release returned to Cambridge where he was blacklisted for the next decade. In 1952, he married Viennese-born Dr Hildegarde Broda, deputy medical officer of health for the city. Local councillors rejected a bid to dismiss her. In 1959, Nunn May applied for the post of physics professor at the University of Ghana, where Conon Cruise O'Brien was vice-chancellor. He was easily the best qualified applicant, but the university authorities were in two minds about appointing a 'traitor'. His case was supported by the professor of religion, who observed: 'I think Nunn May's decision was gravely mistaken, but I have no doubt it was sincerely motivated on a high moral plane. I can only hope that if I thought as he did I would have had the courage to act as he did.' With such praise ringing in his ears, Nunn May got the job, and eventually became dean of the university. He retired to Cambridge in 1978, and died aged ninety-one in January 2002.

O

GEORGE ORWELL is the nearest thing the Left has to a saint. He is prayed in aid by every politician and polemicist seeking evidence of integrity. A prestigious prize for political writing is named after him, which annually attracts the great and the good to London's clubland.

Yet Orwell, or Eric Blair as he was born, used his unique vantage-point as a rebel old Etonian with impeccable socialist credentials to spy on his fellow Lefties. He did not flinch from using the tactics of the police state that he so graphically (and profitably) exposed, most effectively in his later novels, *Animal Farm* and *Nineteen Eighty-four*. In the 1930s, Orwell employed the brilliance of his reportage in *Down and Out in Paris and London* and *The Road to Wigan Pier* (a Left Book Club best-seller) to reveal the misery of life at the bottom. In the late 1940s, he compiled a 'Big Brother' dossier of 130 'probably unreliable' people he considered to be a threat to the British state. He gave the names of thirty-five Communists, fellow travellers and presumed Soviet sympathisers to the Information Research Department, a section of the Foreign Office controlled by, or at least linked to, MI6, where a close friend Celia Kirwan (to whom Orwell once proposed) worked. Orwell was dying of tuberculosis in a Gloucestershire sanatorium when he was approached in 1949, and admirers have explained his political treachery as a last act of patriotic piety.

The blacklist list of 'crypto-communists' included Richard Crossman, later a Labour Cabinet minister, whom he dismissed contemptibly as 'too dishonest to be an outright FT [fellow traveller]'; the writer J. B. Priestley, named for his anti-Americanism; the poet C. Day Lewis was 'probably now not completely reliable'; playwright George Bernard

Shaw, then in his nineties, was 'reliably pro-Russian on all major issues'. When the list was disclosed in 1996, his IRD contact said: 'If George said these people were what he said they were, I bet he knew. He wouldn't have said it otherwise.' People on the blacklist would not have been shot at dawn, she insisted, merely excluded from working as propagandists for Britain.

This was a neat way of sidestepping Orwell's role as an informer, whose inside information could be (and no doubt was) put to many uses. Unfortunately, Orwell, socialist hero of the Spanish Civil War who achieved his central ambition to turn political writing into an art form, never lived to see the basic thrust of *Animal Farm* come true. He died in 1950, aged forty-six.

BILL OWEN is best remembered as Compo, the lovable rogue in the woolly hat and torn jacket in the BBC sitcom *Last of the Summer Wine*. But he had a distinguished left-wing pedigree, and when he died at the age of eighty-five in 1999, Labour politicians queued up to pay tribute. He was much in demand as a producer for the Unity Theatre and the Red Flag was played by a silver band at his funeral.

Born William Rowbotham in London in 1914, the son of a tram driver married to a laundry worker, he always wanted to go on the stage but his parents could not afford the training. Instead, he became a printer's devil, which he hated. He paid his way through an acting course by singing and playing the drums in London nightclubs, before getting a start in touring rep. During the Second World War he joined the Royal Army Ordnance Corps, rising to lieutenant before injuries sustained during an exercise made him return to Civvy Street. He return to acting, and changed his name after signing with the J. Arthur Rank Organisation. He appeared in forty-six films, and many plays. He also wrote many popular songs for top artists such as Cliff Richard, and appeared in political pantomimes and reviews including *Babes in the*

Wood and *What's Left?* His adaptation of the socialist classic *The Ragged Trousered Philanthropists* was staged.

But the big time came in 1973, when he took on the role of Compo, a Yorkshire pensioner enjoying a second childhood and an unlikely passion for Nora Batty, the wrinkle-stockinged object of his unrequited affections. Though a Cockney, he grew to love Holmfirth, the Pennine mill town where the show was set, and he is buried there. Roy Clarke, writer of *Summer Wine*, observed: 'If there are any other Londoners buried in Holmfirth, I think you can safely assume they died of culture shock. For me, it ranks as one of Bill's finest achievements that he won the respect, trust and even love of that independent, self-reliant community.'

ROBERT OWEN pioneered the concept of a model industrial community, with decent housing, good working conditions, schools for the children of workers and non-profit-making stores. It seemed too good to be true, and it was. Owen, the son of a saddler born in Newtown, Powys, in 1771, was a flourishing cotton manufacturer in Manchester by his early twenties, but spurred by idealism (and the prospect of marriage) he moved to in 1800 New Lanark in Scotland to rebuild the town's mill industry after his own social ideals. Initially, the experiment was successful, and was even exported to the USA where the community of New Harmony was established in Indiana. Owen pioneered co-operative ventures, and was instrumental in the passage of the 1819 Factory Act, which greatly improved conditions at work. Owen returned from America in 1829, and turned his reformist intentions to the trade unions, but finding that workers reacted violently against government repression, he gradually withdrew into a life of writing and teaching his theories of what might now be called communitarianism. He embraced spiritualism before dying in 1858, but his innovative efforts are still revered among co-operators and socialists.

P

SYLVIA PANKHURST was thrown out of the Communist Party for being too left-wing, a more common occurrence than many might believe. As a feminist and suffragette, she far outpaced her sister Christabel and mother Emmeline in drive and commitment, yet they are commemorated in the Women's Social and Political Union memorial in Victoria Gardens, Westminster, and she is not.

She was born in Manchester in 1882, the daughter of a socialist lawyer. As a child, she walked the dingy working-class streets with her father. 'The misery of the poor, as I heard my father plead for it, and saw it revealed in the pinched faces of his audiences, awoke in me a maddening sense of impotence,' she later recalled. He suffered an untimely death when she was only sixteen, and she vowed to pick up his political torch. After Manchester High School, Pankhurst went to the Royal College of Art on a scholarship, but quit in 1906 to work for the WSPU, which he mother had founded three years previously. She served the first of many jail sentences that year, and began the writing that culminated in *The History of the Women's Suffrage Movement* in 1911. In 1912 Pankhurst repudiated the WSPU, charging it with desertion from socialism and sucking up to the middle class with a policy of limited franchise for women.

She turned to the infant Labour Party and its paper for working-class women, *The Women's Dreadnought*. A contemporary described her as 'a plain little Queen Victoria-sized woman with plenty of long, unruly bronze-like hair. There was no distinction about her clothes, and on the whole she was very undistinguished. But her eyes were fiery, even a little fanatic, with a glint of shrewdness.' Her path diverged further from that of Emmeline and Christabel in 1914, when the WSPU supported war and Sylvia was a pacifist. She also pioneered mother and baby clinics in London, citing the death rate of infants as six times higher than that in the trenches. She espoused the Russian Revolution in 1917, but lectured Lenin when she met him on the issue of censorship. Back home, the authorities jailed her for five months for 'seditious' articles in her newspapers. Pankhurst lived openly with an Italian socialist, Silvio Curio, bearing a son Richard in 1927. Emmeline was dismayed that she refused to marry, rejecting the marriage contract, bu took a man's name. In the 1930s Pankhurst campaigned for the Spanish republicans, for Jewish refugees from Nazi Germany and against Mussolini's occupation of Ethiopia (then Abyssinia) and moved there after the war, dying in 1960

WILL PAYNTER was a less flamboyant but more successful

version of A. J. Cook as general secretary of the National Union of Mineworkers. He was a lifelong Communist, who took a career break from the party to work for the Commission on Industrial Relations, set up by a Labour government in the 1980s. Born in a village near Cardiff in 1903, the son of a farm labourer who migrated to the Rhondda pits, he left school at thirteen and was largely self-educated in the fine old South Wales tradition. He followed his father into the mines, and was blacklisted for his part in the 1926 strike. The colliers elected him checkweighman at Cymmer pit in 1929, the year he joined the CP.

A short, wiry man with a canny look, he advanced rapidly through the party echelons and for five years, from 1931, worked full time for the party and the Communist-organised National Unemployed Workers' Movement, receiving further political education at the Lenin School in Moscow. He undertook clandestine work in Nazi Germany, helping Communists and socialist to flee. In 1937, 'not over-enthusiastic' as he had just married, Paynter was sent by the party to Spain as a political commissar to the British Battalion. He was allowed to return home in the autumn, to take up a full-time job as NUM agent in the Valleys.

Despite his well-known political affiliations, Paynter was elected general secretary of the union in 1959, at a time when rank-and-file resentment against poor wages and pit closures was building up. Paynter revived *The Miner*, the NUM's journal, under a professional Fleet Street journalist, Bob Houston, to knit the coalfields into a single force.

However, he left the union (and the party) in 1968 when invited to join the CIR. He quit the Commission when the Tories were elected in 1970, and rejoined the party in 1977. Fortunately, he did not live to see its demise, dying at the age of eighty-one in 1984, the year of the miners' Great Strike. Paynter married twice and had seven children, including two sets of twins.

KIM PHILBY is rightly celebrated as the super-spy of the twentieth century, a traitor to the English upper class and a supreme loyalist to the Communist cause. He forced people to question the nature of patriotism, and his life, chronicled many times over, continues to exercise fascination a quarter of a century after his death as a fugitive from British justice in Moscow.

Born in the Punjab in 1912 as Harold Russell John Philby, the first son of Sir John Philby, the polymath and Arabian explorer, he spent much of his childhood among Indians, prompting his father to call him Kim after the famous Rudyard Kipling character. A King's Scholar to Westminster School, Philby began his journey to the Left at Trinity College, Cambridge. He came under the influence of Maurice Dobb, the Communist don, who recruited him – not to the CPGB, of which he was never a member – but to the revolutionary underground, in Paris and then Vienna, where he married his first wife Litzi, an Austrian Communist. On his return, he was approached by a Soviet contact who offered him work for the KGB. He said later: 'One does not look twice at the offer of enrolment in an elite force.' But he was then obliged to deny his left-wing beliefs, first as a *Times* correspondent on the side of the Fascist Francoists in the Spanish civil war and then to enrol in the wartime Secret Intelligence Service (MI6), the goal of his Soviet controllers.

He rose rapidly through the ranks to become head of Section Nine, the anti-Communist department and then, in 1949, SIS liaison man in Washington with the SIS and the FBI. There, he was of inestimable value to the Russians, and he was spoken of as a likely 'C' – head of MI6. However, his security was compromised by the impending exposure of fellow diplomat–spy **Donald Maclean**, who fled to Moscow with Philby's friend and flatmate in America, **Guy Burgess**. Philby was suspected of being 'the third man' who helped in the escape, but he brazened out an MI5 investigation, including interrogation by the feared William Skardon who broke **Fuchs**. However, Philby had to resign, and spent the next eleven years in a twilight world of occasional work for SIS, the Russians, and journalism, chiefly in the Middle East for the *Observer*, getting divorced and remarrying. When the net finally closed in at the beginning of 1963, Philby was spirited out of Beirut on the Soviet freighter *Dolmatova*, greeted by a fellow KGB officer with the words: 'Kim, your mission has been concluded.'

What was that mission? Reviled by the British establishment, the media and many of his former colleagues in the security services, Philby told Philip Knightley, his masterly biographer: 'It's simplistic to ask why I felt no patriotism for Britain. Which Britain? I'm intrigued when Mrs Thatcher says: "I passionately love my country." Which country is she talking about? Finchley and Dulwich? Or Glasgow and Liverpool? I don't believe that anything that I did harmed my own Britain at all. In fact, I think my work for the KGB served the bulk of the British people.' That was his own epitaph. He died in Moscow in 1988, and on his gravestone in the Kuntsevo military cemetery is a simple red star.

WOGAN PHILIPPS, the 2nd Baron Milford, took political eccentricity seriously, proclaiming in his maiden speech, in the House of

Lords that he was a Communist. Milford, educated at Eton and Oxford, made his startling announcement in 1963, when their lordships were debating the Peerage Bill, the measure permitting reluctant peers like **Tony Benn** to disclaim their titles. He opposed the Bill, but not, to the dismay of fellow barons, earls and viscounts, because he favoured the old regime, but because he could 'never' support any legislation to perpetuate the unelected House of Lords. As a maiden speech could not be interrupted, he was able to declare 'My party and I are for complete abolition of this Chamber, which is such a bulwark against progress.' Earl Attlee noted amusingly that, with no Communists in the Commons, the party's voice could only be heard in the Lords. 'That is the advantage of the hereditary principle.'

Milford's conversion to the Left followed his marriage to the progressive novelist Rosamund Lehmann in the late 1920s, and he was severely wounded while driving an ambulance on the republican side in the Spanish civil war. After a spell in the Land Army during the war, he married again, Cristina, Countess of Huntingdon, a Communist. In 1945, he abandoned his position as prospective Labour candidate for Henley and joined the CP, causing his wealthy father to disinherit him. He persevered, however, and was elected the first Communist member of Cirencester Rural District Council. He was less successful in his bid to become Communist MP for Cirencester in 1950, winning only 423 votes.

During the war (and I am indebted to Neil Hamilton's *Great Political Eccentrics* for this story), Milford's telephone was tapped, albeit amateurishly, by the security services. In his irritation, he was in the habit of commanding: 'Oh, come on, Constable, do get off the line!' PC Plod would apologise profusely and do as he was told. Extraordinarily, Milford's godson, the right-wing Tory Nicholas Ridley, eventually became the MP for Cirencester, after offering his godfather £150 to pay for the deposit to fight against him in the general election of 1959, thereby splitting the Labour vote (but not by much). Milford declined the bribe, and remained true to his cause, insisting on his ninetieth birthday in 1992, 'Even though the Communist Party no longer exists, I am still a Communist.'

HAROLD PINTER is first and foremost the nation's greatest living playwright, but he has also penned some of the most excoriating Leftie criticisms of New Labour and **Tony Blair**, particularly on the war against Iraq. On his website, he describes himself as 'playwright, director, actor, poet and political activist'. His hostility and bitterness are a joy. He argued that Bush and Blair should stand trial as war criminals, and rejected the patronising (and peculiarly British) notion that artists should not have political views – or, at any rate, should not be taken seriously. 'I don't intend to go away and write my plays and be a good boy. I intend to remain an independent political intelligence in my own right,' he said in 2001, the year before he was diagnosed with life-threatening throat cancer.

Born in 1930 in Hackney, the only child of a Jewish tailor, he was brutalised by being evacuated with other boys to Cornwall, and then endured the Blitz. Evacuated with his mother a second time, to Yorkshire, he began a lifelong love affair with cricket and the county club in particular. After Hackney Downs Grammar School, Pinter refused to do his National Service, and was fined as a conscientious objector. He walked out of RADA after only one term, and earned a living as a jobbing actor, while writing poetry (under the name 'Pinta') and beginning his plays that were to revolutionise theatre from the late 1950s. In 1956, he married Vivien Merchant, a union that proved to be deeply unhappy. She died in 1982 of alcohol-related problems, two years after their divorce, and Pinter married the writer Lady Antonia Fraser.

His plays, notably *The Birthday Party*, *The Caretaker*, *The Collection*, *The Lover* and *The Homecoming*, made him an international star, but he never forgot the sometimes difficult left-wing causes that moved him: Cuba, Nicaragua, the Kurds, opposition to the NATO war on Yugoslavia and the ban on atheist contributors to the Radio 4 'Thought for the Day' slot.

PHIL PIRATIN won notoriety as the Communist councillor who, during a heavy blitz, had marched the people down Aldgate to the London Underground station for shelter from the Nazi bombs. The authorities tried to halt this impromptu movement, but it rapidly spread to other boroughs, and provision had to be made for Londoners to sleep and wash on the Tube platforms. Piratin, born in 1907, was the first Communist member of Stepney Borough Council on which he became a 'one-man opposition' to the Labour Party. He entered Parliament in 1945 as the member for Mile End. He and **Willie Gallacher** formed a Communist Party of two on the backbenches. The pair made a point of meeting strikers' leaders whenever they appeared at Westminster. Piratin's constituency disappeared in post-war boundary changes, and he was defeated at Stepney in 1950 by a Labour ex-Mayor of the borough, Bill Edwards, a naval stoker who was the first to go from 'the lower deck' to the Commons in 1942. Piratin collected almost six thousand votes, only a couple of hundred fewer than the Conservative candidate, but his defeat marked the end of Communist parliamentary representation in England.

JOHN PLATTS-MILLS was destined to be a Leftie. His earliest memories of a childhood in New Zealand are of helping his mother on the picket line at the age of seven during a general strike in 1913. His mother Daisy, a doctor, was his political mentor. His father Jack was a Conservative, though his Australian grandfather, Fred, a parson, had tried to save the souls of the Ned Kelly gang, punching on the nose a bishop who protested.

A Rhodes scholarship took Platts-Mills to Oxford, where he was a rowing blue. As a pupil lawyer in London, he was courted by the Duke of Devonshire, no less, to become MP (Tory, naturally) for Eastbourne, but he was moving to the left-wing of the Labour Party. His defence of anti-Fascist demonstrators in the 1930s soon brought him to the attention of the authorities – the Special Branch opened a file on him in 1932. He was also active in the Haldane Society, the nascent NCCL, the Unity Theatre and the support movement for Spanish war volunteers. His best friend, Clive Lewis, a Communist, was killed in Spain, prompting Platts-Mills to say years later: 'Ever since 1938 I have suffered from a tendency to treat members of the Communist Party not as potential traitors and enemies of the working class, as well-behaved Labour Party members seem expected to do, but as slightly over-eager fellow workers.'

On the strength of one big fee, Platts-Mills bought a fifty-acre farm in Essex, which became home to dozens of adults and children – some German and Czech – seeking refuge from the Blitz. The authorities raided his bucolic retreat, but found nothing and then, after rejecting him for the RAF, approached him to work for MI5, spying on progressive governments in exile in London, and on his fellow socialists. His reward was a posting in 1944 to Askern Colliery, Doncaster, to work down the pit as a 'Bevin Boy', hoisting ten tons of coal every shift on to a conveyor belt just like (and to the great amusement of) the miners.

In 1945 he was elected Labour MP for Finsbury, north London, but his unease with the Attlee administration, particularly on foreign policy, was both early and profound. He quickly fell out with 'the great buffoon' Bevin over Greece, Yugoslavia, the USSR, Czechoslovakia and finally Italy (Platts-Mills organised a telegram of congratulation to Pietro Nenni, Socialist victor). In 1948 he was expelled from the Labour Party. With a few other Leftie strops – **D. N. Pritt, Konni Zilliacus** and Leslie Solley – he set up a Labour Independent Group in the Commons, but lost his seat to Labour in 1950. Platts-Mills went back to the bar, remaining active in the peace movement and left-wing politics, and naïve to the point of self-delusion. 'I must have been World Stalin Lover No. 1,' he confessed, incapable of accepting Khrushchev's denunciation of the old rogue in 1956, though his gullibility did not stand in the way of readmission to the Labour Party in 1964. Platts-Mills defended in some of the most notorious cases of the 1980s, including the Kray and Richardson gangster trials, and the trial of the Shrewsbury Two pickets in 1972.

He was a fan of **Arthur Scargill**, and during the miners' strike of 1984 acted as a go-between soliciting funds from the Soviet Union and Libya. He saw 'nothing shameful' about his conduct, and was arguably correct. However, his belief in 'Arthur's vision' of a strong NUM proved as credulous as his faith in Uncle Joe. In later years, Platts-Mills wrote a brutally-frank 655-page autobiography, *Muck, Silk and Socialism*, which represented the last word (and quite a few more) about his odyssey on the Left, before he died in 2001.

HARRY POLLITT deviated from the party line over war against Nazi Germany, and survived to be proved correct. That he could do so was a tribute to his towering presence in British Communism. Pollitt was one of the founding trio appointed by Lenin's Comintern to set up the CPGB on the lines of the Soviet party: run by an iron hand from the centre.

He was born in 1890, into grinding poverty in Droylsden, a manufacturing area of Manchester. His mother Polly, a textile worker, worked a ten-hour shift in the local mill, lost children to sickness, as so many did. But young Harry was different. After watching his sister Winifred die, he vowed: 'I would pay God out. I would pay everybody out for making my sister suffer.' He became a skilled boilermaker, then plunged into organisational work for the unions and Communism. A short, squat man, with an improbably mocking sense of humour, he joined with **Rajani Palme Dutt** to provide a unique intellectual-proletarian leadership of the party. He was the first of a long line of national industrial organisers, and one of the first to see the inside of a British jail for his political beliefs, serving a one-year sentence in 1925. Pollitt organised the flow of young fighters to the Spanish civil war, and paid five visits to the front. His pleas for freedom to pursue a more British line paid off in the thirties, when the CP became for many in the unions and the universities the front line against unemployment and the rise of Fascism.

This period also brought tragedy. Rose Cohen, the woman he loved had married the Comintern's man in Britain then followed him to Moscow. They were both arrested in the Stalin purges of 1937, and shot. In 1939, Pollitt defied Moscow and urged full British participation in the war. He was removed from his post as general secretary, using the unexpected spare time to write an autobiography and cultivate new friends, like the young **Michael Foot**. Pollitt was rehabilitated when Hitler invaded the USSR, returning a more adroit politician than before, able to meet and talk on equal terms with government ministers. In its new guise as a wartime partner of Churchill, the CP flourished. Membership bounded well over 50,000. This was the high-water mark of its political fortunes.

But in the Labour landslide of 1945, he failed to be elected for Rhondda. In 1951, with Stalin's approval, he published *The British Road to Socialism*, the CP's new, non-revolutionary blueprint for political change. Although it sold 150,000 copies in six weeks, Communisim it never found favour with the electorate. In 1956, in poor health, smoking and drinking too much, unhappy with the denunciation of Stalin, Pollitt retired. Four years later, he died of a stroke. For years to come, he cast a long shadow over the Communist Party, but he took his secrets of 'Moscow gold' and his knowledge of high-level Soviet policy and practice to the grave. Francis Beckett, historian of the CP, offered this verdict: 'He cared more than anything about people, and that was what made him a socialist. But he never once told what he knew.'

JOHN PRESCOTT has a chip on his shoulder the size of Ben Nevis, and some would say that great, rearing rock is all that is left of his socialism. However, his Leftie credentials have yet to face the final test. So far, **Tony Blair** has merely raised the hoops through which his 'deputy' has to jump, and made them smaller. He has not set fire to them. When he does, we will know. What will a flaming hoop look like? A legal ban on strikes in the public services? Or the promotion of **Peter Mandelson** over his head, perhaps. If Blair holds on to ultimate power for as long as his supporters wish, the day of reckoning will certainly come and Ben Nevis will erupt.

Meanwhile, it is useful to recall Prezza's political odyssey. The grandson of a Wrexham miner, and son of a white-collar railwayman, Prescott was born in 1938 in Prestatyn, north Wales. He failed the 11-plus, and after leaving Ellesmere Port Secondary school at fifteen, went to work as a trainee chef in hotels before joining the Cunard Line as a steward on transatlantic passenger liners. He also joined the Labour Party and opposed the corrupt right-wing regime in the National Union of Seamen. He was active in the 1966 seamen's strike, which blew the Labour government off-course and prompted Harold Wilson to denounce the Communist-influenced 'tightly-knit group of politically motivated men' running the dispute. Prescott, author of the strike pamphlet *Not Wanted On Voyage*, was in the public gallery when a Labour Prime Minister attacked his union. By then he had taken a diploma in politics and economics at Ruskin College, Oxford, an achievement that taught him 'I had no need to feel inferior to anybody.' No need, perhaps, but a strange compulsion to do so.

Elected for Hull East in 1970, he established himself as spokesman on the shipping industry and was PPS to Trade Secretary **Peter Shore** for two years. He was appointed to the European Assembly, and was Labour Group Leader, arguing for direct elections to what became the European Parliament, though there was a strong element of anti-EEC attitude in his makeup. Prescott supported **Tony Benn** for the leadership in 1976, but **Michael Foot** gave him front-bench responsibility for regional affairs and in turn Kinnock (whom he backed for the leadership) made him Shadow Transport Secretary. After a spat over 'one member, one vote' reforms, Kinnock shifted Prescott to Employment, and after further bad blood demoted him to Energy, a dead-end job. Prescott retaliated by standing against **Roy Hattersley** for the deputy leadership in 1988, and though he failed it was a marker for the future. John Smith gave him back Transport, and Prescott nursed his ambition.

After Smith's death, he ran for leader and deputy leader, easily winning the latter. According to the *Dictionary of Labour Biography*, 'Blair likes and respects Prescott.' According to Woodrow Wyatt, the sentiment is not returned. At a *Spectator* party in November 1995, he recorded, Prezza 'got very drunk. He said he hated Blair and the people round him.' They wanted him to speak 'posh' and grammatically, instead of his normal joined-up shouting. What would be the point of change? Everybody knows what he means, even if they don't know what he says. After Labour's landslide, Prescott was rewarded with the largely courtesy title of Deputy Prime Minister and his own giant department covering Transport, the Environment and the Regions. The DETR was disassembled in 2001, and Prescott was shunted into the siding of Minister for the Cabinet Office. There, he growls in impotent rage. The tabloid press, having nicknamed him 'Two Jags' on account of his personal car fleet, was desperate to find evidence of a girlfriend so they could hoist the headline 'Two Shags' – Prezza has been married to the formidable Pauline for more than forty years – and for a time interest centred on a former aide. But nothing came of the investigations.

DENNIS NOWELL PRITT, the Communist lawyer

and writer, was almost as prolific a collector of Eastern bloc gongs as he was an author, which is saying something as his autobiography runs to three volumes. In the fifties and sixties, he was awarded the freedom of the city of Leipzig, honorary law degrees from Prague, Sofia, Berlin (East) and Moscow, as well as the Lenin Peace Prize, the George Dimitrov Medal, the Star of International Friendship and finally the

Gold Medal of the Czech Society for International Relations in 1968, the year of the Soviet invasion. Born in 1887, and educated at Winchester, London University and Oxford, he was called to the Middle Temple in 1909 and took silk in 1927. Pritt, on the hard left of the Labour Party, was elected MP for North Hammersmith in 1935.

In the thirties, he visited Moscow and satisfied himself that stories of show trials were simply not true. Pritt reached the dizzy heights of Labour's national executive, but was expelled from the party in 1940 after writing *Must the War Spread?*, a book urging that Britain should not go to war with Russia over her invasion of Finland. He then became unofficial leader of five 'independent' Labour MPs, and held his seat under this heading until 1950. Pritt wrote many books and pamphlets about the law and international relations, and was celebrated as the greatest civil liberties lawyer of his generation. As well as chairing the Howard League for Penal Reform, he saw no ambiguity in chairing the Society of Cultural Relations with the USSR.

But today he is really only known conversationally among Lefties for one brief courtroom interlude, involving 'Spud' Jones, the master of a British ship that ran a cargo of potatoes into Coruna harbour during the Spanish civil war. Pritt, suspecting the judge of anti-republican bias, observed that one of the men involved had been 'as drunk as a judge'. The judge intervened: 'Don't you mean drunk as a lord, Mr Pritt?' 'Whatever you say, m'lud,' shot back the barrister. Renowned for his 'Pritticisms', he was fined for contempt, as he had expected. He died, still scribbling, in 1972.

R

REG RACE revelled in the strategic side of Leftie politics, but was eventually too tactical for his own good. A former research officer of NUPE, the public service union, he entered Parliament in 1979 as MP for Wood Green, north London, and rapidly established himself as a member of **Tony Benn**'s inner circle of plotters. He resigned from the Tribune Group because it was not Left enough, and accused Labour MPs of 'obsessive cretinism.' He was the first MP to say 'Fuck' in the Commons, during a debate on sex shops in 1982, when he read out a prostitute's advertisement challenging punters to 'Find me and fuck me.'

Dr Race, as he liked to be known, was Benn's bagman in the abortive 1981 coup against **Michael Foot**, and preferred to lose the 1983 election rather than win it with a right-wing Labour leadership.

With **Ken Livingstone** and **Ted Knight**, he founded Socialists for Labour Victory, but success eluded him. His own seat disappeared in boundary redrawing, and he mounted a campaign to oust the veteran Leftie Norman Atkinson, MP for the neighbouring Tottenham constituency for twenty three years. In the words of **Tam Dalyell**, 'the Reg Race faction was stupid enough to tell **Bernie Grant** what they had already done, and expect him to go along with it'. Instead, Grant seized his opportunity and secured the seat for himself. Race moved on to work for Livingstone at County Hall, until the GLC was abolished. Subsequently, he managed to win the nomination at 'safe' Chesterfield, to succeed his mentor Benn, only to lose it to the Liberal Democrats on an 8.5 swing against the government in 2001, proving that the Left is not always right.

BERT RAMELSON was named in the Commons by Harold Wilson as the central figure in among a 'tightly knit group of politically motivated men' running the seamen's strike of 1966. He was that, and much more, though at the time he dismissed the charge as 'the height of impertinence' towards the national industrial organiser of the Communist Party.

Born Bachran Ramilevich Mendelson, the son of a fur merchant, in the Ukraine in 1910, he was taken to Canada at the age of eleven, and graduated with first-class honours in law at Alberta University. He practised as a barrister for only a year, before emigrating to Palestine, from where he was expelled for causing trouble: opposing a strike by the Jewish trade union aimed at sacking Arabs. He then joined the International Brigade in the Spanish civil war, took part in battles on the Aragon and Ebro front and was twice wounded. In the Second World War, Ramelson was a driver in the Royal Tank Corps. Captured at the fall of Tobruk, he escaped from an Italian prisoner-of-war camp in 1943, and wandered round Mussolini's Italy, finding and lecturing to groups of the underground Italian Communist Party. He was then posted to India as a captain in the legal department.

After the war, he joined the CP and settled in Leeds, where he was a full-time party official for two decades. His main achievement there was to begin the transformation of the Yorkshire miners from traditional, right-wing Labour to the Left, a process that culminated in the election of **Arthur Scargill** as president of the NUM. He took charge of the CP's trade union work in 1965, and over the next twelve years presided over a dramatic surge in Communist influence in the unions, the TUC and the Labour Party. He was very active in promoting strikes, regarding industrial peace as 'a deviation from the norm' in capitalist society. Ramelson once boasted, unwisely but correctly, that he only had to float an idea at the spring trade union conferences for it to become official Labour policy in the autumn. He sent out model resolutions on issues ranging from incomes policy to nuclear disarmament, which

Communists and left-wingers worked through Labour's shambolic policy-making process. Ramelson was also a prolific pamphleteer and an ear-piercing public speaker, a habit ascribed to his partial deafness.

An impish sense of humour came occasionally to his aid. Speaking on the steps of Leeds Town Hall, he was challenged by a heckler about 'the Russian brides'. The USSR had forbidden Russian women who married British men to join their husbands. 'On the edge of the crowd,' boomed Ramelson, 'is Sergeant Pickles of the Leeds Special Branch, whose unenviable task it is to follow me around and make notes on what I say and do. He has heard me answer this question on dozens of occasions and is now word perfect. I hand the meeting over to Sergeant Pickles.'

Ramelson's only foray into parliamentary politics, at a by-election in Leeds in 1963, was a wash-out. He won only six hundred votes in his adopted city. He retired in 1977, but kept up his revolutionary activity as British representative on the World Marxism Review in Prague until it was closed down by the 'velvet revolution'. For years after his official retirement, union leaders paid discreet court to him at his flat in south London. Ramelson was the only old-guard Communist with the nerve to advise Scargill to call off the doomed pit strike in 1984. He got an oath for his pains. He died in 1994, lauded by Ken Gill as 'a giant among Communists'.

VANESSA REDGRAVE is reputed to have had an affair with Fidel Castro, and nothing that she is supposed to have done would surprise or dismay her fans. Redgrave's purist Leftie politics – Workers' Revolutionary Party – place her as an archetypal child of the 1980s. Yet she was born in 1937, son of the distinguished actors Michael Redgrave and Rachel Kempson, did not go to Cuba until 1962, and waited until 1973 before joining the Socialist Labour League (forerunner to the WRP). If it was a long time coming, her Leftiousness has not died away with advancing years, as it does with so many on the ultra-Left who become disillusioned that the revolution is so regularly postponed.

While becoming famous in films like *Tom Jones*, and marrying Oscar-winning director Tony Richardson, and having children, Redgrave found time to organise a full-page advertisement in *The Times* in 1967, condemning the American bombing of Vietnam. She lectured on Marxism in Hollywood in 1974, and supported the Palestinian cause with enthusiasm, giving a speech on repression in Israel when she accepted her Oscar for *Julia* in 1977. This made her a target for Zionist militants in the USA, while the Fascist Combat Eighteen group targeted her at home because of her reported relationship with a black actor. Meanwhile Redgrave, who stood as a WRP-supported candidate for Parliament, was also spied on by the British security services and by the hard-Right Economic League.

In 2003 it emerged that, more than twenty years previously, the Home Office intervened to prevent the granting of charitable status to Redgrave's plans for a £100,000 network of youth training centres that would teach Marxism 'as a world science for the overthrow of capitalism'. The Tory government that feared the centres, being set up when youth unemployment and riots blighted the inner cities, would create a political vanguard to challenge the status quo. Naturally the authorities found no contradiction in this policy and the retention of charitable status for public schools, which prop up the system. Redgrave, now well into her sixties, is still searching for controversial causes: most recently, the Chechen rebels against Moscow rule. Her tireless verve is an example to Lefties who weary.

JIMMY REID was the front man of the Upper Clyde Shipbuilders' work-in in 1971, which forced Edward Heath's government to perform a humiliating policy U-turn. An articulate, engaging young Communist, he never quite fulfilled the expectations of the Left. However, neither did he sell out, as his critics predicted.

Reid was born on Clydeside in 1932, attended St Gerard's School, Glasgow, and became an engineering apprentice. He joined the CP when he was sixteen. It was a call to nationhood and Scottish history, he argued later. North of the border, the party stood for home rule. A lean (in those days), intense man, he rose rapidly in the party, winning election as national chairman of the Young Communist League in 1952. Within seven years he was a member of the national executive and the innermost political committee along with old Stalinist warhorses like **R. Palme Dutt**. Reid spent some time in London, but in 1964 returned to Glasgow to become secretary of the Scottish CP.

He contested the safe Labour seat of Dunbartonshire East that year, and in 1966, collecting less than two thousand votes. But he was a rising figure in the engineering union, the AEU, a member of its ruling lay national committee and a name to be reckoned with in the shipyards along the Clyde.

He shot to national prominence in 1971 as leader of the UCS shop stewards, and their spokesman. He handled the intense media interest with panache, while leaving much of the strategic thinking to fellow Communists **Jimmy Airlie** and Sam Barr. The victory of that campaign, though limited in nature, made Reid a household name in Scotland. He left the CP in 1976, and joined the Labour Party, beginning a new career as a columnist, first with the *Herald*, Scotland's dominant broadsheet, and then Rupert Murdoch's *Scottish Sun*, which initially supported the SNP. His attempts at 'intellectualisation' were derided by some, but he proved a controversial writer.

In the early 1990s Reid sought to break into fresh territory with a Scottish news and current affairs magazine, *Seven Days*, but it folded (after seven issues, according to publishing myth).

Reid was never the kind of man to be bamboozled by New Labour, and little more than a year after **Blair**'s accession to power switched support to the Scottish Socialist Party, inheritors of the Militant Tendency mantle. He left Glasgow to live with his wife on the island of Rothesay, off the west coast of Scotland, but suffered a stroke in 2002.

JOHN REID revels in his hard-man, ex-Communist image. When asked a labyrinthine question on the Common Room corridor in Westminster, he snapped: 'I'm the chairman of the Labour Party – not the fucking Wizard of Oz.' No. And New Labour is not over the rainbow, either. But he behaves as though it is. Under the thankful reign of **Tony Blair**, Reid's rise has been meteoric. After a stint as army minister after the 1997 election, he was promoted to the Cabinet as Scottish secretary in 2001, then to Northern Ireland after the (second) demise of Peter Mandelson, then as chairman of the party and finally to leader of the House in 2003, following the resignation of Robin Cook over the war against Iraq. Reid is regarded as the safest Blairite pair of hands in the Cabinet, and had no qualms about the war, slagging off the million-plus protesters as morally responsible for murder, torture, death and starvation. It was not always so.

Reid was born in a Lanarkshire pit village in 1947, the son of a postman with a classic belief in education as the saviour of the working class. He led a 'strike' by children to win access on cold mornings to the Catholic secondary school he attended in Coatbridge, where he also lost his prefect's badge for smoking – a habit he never lost, claiming to have smoked 110 Embassy Tipped in a single meeting with shipbuilding trade unionists. Reid worked variously as an oil industry labourer and insurance representative before deciding to go to Stirling University, where he was rector of the students' union and took a Ph.D. in African economic history, specifically on how Dahomey coped with the shift from slave trading to palm oil production. While at university, he joined the Communist Party for two years, a step that might have cost him the post of NATO secretary-general, before returning to Labour in 1976. He worked for the party as research officer in Scotland before becoming Neil Kinnock's gatekeeper in 1983.

He entered Parliament in 1987 as MP for Hamilton and Bellshill, and served as defence spokesman for seven years before the New Labour landslide. Reid was a heavy drinker and not always a polite one ('I didn't have a drink problem: I loved the stuff'), until the death of John Smith. He has not been seen with a drink in his hand since, perhaps because he is too busy holding hands with his second wife, Karine Adler. She won a best independent film award in 1998 with *Under the Skin*, her study of a young woman driven to promiscuity by grief. Reid also hit the headlines for the wrong reason when the Commons Commissioner of Standards, Elizabeth Filkin, investigated claims that taxpayers' money had been used to pay political researchers, including his son Kevin. She produced evidence that Reid had put undue political pressure on witnesses. The Labour dominated committee on standards threw out the case.

Where next for the combative postie's son? Assuming that a seat can be found (in England, if necessary) before the next election, some argue that he would be a perfect rival to challenge his one-time ally **Gordon Brown** for the leadership. But is the electorate ready for the only MP to have apologised to this author (no stranger to the sherbet) for drunken boorishness?

RUTH RENDELL, the brilliantly successful crime writer and inventor of Chief Inspector Reg Wexford, describes herself as 'a very bad Christian' and 'very much of the Left'. She gets indignant about issues like racism, and treats them as thematic material for her books, while not wanting to preach at the reader. Her outlook was clearly formed during childhood, when her Swedish mother, a teacher, faced exclusion during wartime north London because neighbours thought she was German.

Born Ruth Grasemann in 1930, she worked for local newspapers, notably the *Chigwell Times* where she met her future husband, Don Rendell. They married in 1950, divorced in 1975 and remarried in 1977, because he was the only person she felt completely relaxed with. He died in 1999. Her string of more than forty award-winning crime stories, written under her name and the *nom de plume* Barbara

Vine, brought her riches and a life peerage as Baroness Rendell of Babergh. But she was active in CND during the eighties, and backed the launch in 1994 of *Red Pepper*, the left-wing magazine edited by Hilary Wainwright. She is a staunch Labour supporter, and advocate of Emily's List, the pressure group set up to get more women into Parliament.

JO RICHARDSON was described by a *Daily Telegraph* obituary writer as the godmother of Bevanism, which seems a compliment too far until the record is scrutinised. She joined the Labour Party in 1945, the year of the Attlee landslide, and became secretary to the left-wing MP **Ian Mikardo**. For the next thirty years, she was the organisational genius behind the left-wing in Parliament as it shifted gears through the Keep Left Group, founded in 1946, then the Bevanites, formed five years later by **Aneurin Bevan** and Harold Wilson before transforming itself into the Tribune group.

Throughout these years, Richardson operated the levers behind the scenes while desperately trying to get into Parliament herself, fighting Monmouth (twice), Hornchurch, and Harrow East before finally securing the succession to **Tom Driberg** at Barking, which duly sent her to Westminster in 1974. Her backstage efforts were rewarded not with ministerial office but the chairmanship of the Tribune Group and a seat on Labour's National Executive in 1979, which she held until 1991. Richardson, who noticed that her mother 'seemed to come into her own after my father died', was a passionate advocate of women's rights, eventually becoming Neil Kinnock's Shadow Minister for Women despite moving her allegiance from Tribune to the Campaign Group.

Richardson was born in Newcastle-upon-Tyne in 1923, the daughter of a Methodist commercial traveller who once contested Darlington for the Liberals. Educated at Southend High School, she confessed to being 'very shy', and never married, nor, so far as is recorded, had a relationship with a man. Her strongest friend in the Commons, who stood at the other end of the Labour spectrum, was Betty Boothroyd, with whom she was a member of Hammersmith borough council in the sixties. While still searching for a seat, she became, in 1960, export sales manager, and a director and shareholder of Ian Mikardo Limited, her first boss's firm specialising in trade with Communist Eastern Europe. The pair wound up the firm when she became an MP. An inveterate ban-the-bomber, pro-abortionist and nationaliser, Richardson declined her one opportunity to stand as the Left's candidate for deputy leadership in 1983, and saw her influence diminish until she was dumped from the NEC in 1990. Partly crippled by arthritis, she shamed delegates by remarking from the rostrum: 'I though I'd show up in case you all thought I'd died.' Little more than three years later, she had indeed gone.

MICK RIX emerged from the obscurity of a train drivers' union branch in Leeds to occupy a front-ranking place in the TUC. At the age of thirty-five he unhorsed Law Adams, who was seeking re-election as general secretary of the footplatemen's union ASLEF. The poll result, in May 1998, sent shock waves through the labour movement, but with hindsight it was merely the beginning of trade union disillusion with **Tony Blair**'s New Labour. Adams, very much of the Old Labour school, was no great admirer of Blair, but he was a party member, unlike Dave Rix (as he then liked to be known), who belonged to **Arthur Scargill**'s 'barmy army', the Socialist Labour Party. He stood for Leeds Central at the 1997 election, and lost his deposit, in common with all the SLP's other would-be MPs. Within two years, however, Mick Rix (as he had now become) disengaged from the SLP and joined the Labour Party. ASLEF, a rich craft union with palatial offices in Hampstead, became home to a number of Leftie causes under Rix, and strikes multiplied. His natural bonhomie and sharp brain assured him of a place centre stage in the councils of the TUC, which by this period was sorely lacking in both.

RED ROBBO was the trademark name of Derek Robinson, the Communist engineering union shop steward in British Leyland's Birmingham plants during the 1960s. Reviled by the tabloid press and hero-worshipped by the Left, in 1980 he was betrayed and abandoned by his union leaders and his members. BL's boss Sir Michael Edwardes decided to take on shop steward power, and sacked the most prominent, Red Robbo, who was convener at the firm's giant Longbridge works. Unofficial strikes for his reinstatement broke out, but after seeing an effigy of Robinson hanging from a mock gallows at a mass meeting, the AEU hierarchy decided that he could be sacrificed.

He never worked in the car industry again, and for many years was the circulation representative, i.e. ambassador for, the *Morning Star* in the west Midlands. He also played a less well-known, but critical, role in the battle of Saltley Gate in 1972, when strikers forced the closure of a vital coke depot during the first national miners' strike. **Arthur Scargill** claimed a strategic victory, but much of the organisation was done by Red Robbo, whose work brought thousands of striking engineering workers into the narrow streets of Saltley. In later years, he was chairman of the Birmingham Union Club and in 2000, at the age of seventy-two, turned out for the 'Great March for Rover' that helped secure the future of the Longbridge plant he had so frequently brought to a standstill in his heyday.

ERNIE ROBERTS pulled off a feat that is never likely to be repeated. He lived a full, long career as a left-wing leader of the engineering workers' union, and after retiring he became a Labour MP at the age of sixty-seven, the oldest new entry to Parliament since 1945.

Born in Shrewsbury in 1912, he won a scholarship to the local school of art but could not afford to take it up. He went down the pit instead at the age of thirteen to help feed his nine brothers and sisters. He moved into engineering, and became a militant shop steward, blacklisted in many Midlands manufacturing plants for his pains. Roberts, a dapper, thoughtful man with a smile playing round his lips, joined the Communist Party, but was expelled in 1941 when he refused to accept that the class war should be put into abeyance while the nation fought a world war. He accused employers of using the war to exploit workers. He was such an indomitable troublemaker that on one occasion a manager, who dare not sack him for fear of a walk-out by the entire workforce, built a wire cage for Roberts on the shop floor as the only way to separate him from the men.

After the war, he joined the Labour Party, and in 1957 he was elected assistant general secretary of the AEU, a post he held for the next twenty years. In that time he espoused every left-wing cause from CND to Workers' Control, the Anti-Nazi League, and the Campaign for Labour Party Democracy. No fringe meeting was complete without him. In 1979, against the odds, he was selected for the safe seat of Hackney North and Islington, remaining an MP until 1987. All his political life, Roberts argued, perhaps naïvely, for the supremacy of the Labour Party conference over the personal whims of its leaders, but he was clear about the political duty of socialists. 'None of the so-called "revolutionary parties" contains the miracle ingredient which is in the hands of the Labour Party: the confidence of an average twelve million voters, most of them working class. What's the point of starting again from scratch?'

Roberts died in 1994, just as his sixth book, *Strike Back*, an autobiography, was being published.

WILLIAM RUST is perpetually remembered wherever the *Morning Star* calls home, currently in Bow, east London. A Young Communist organiser at twenty-two, he became first known as one of the twelve party members jailed in 1925 for seditious libel and incitement to mutiny. Rust was the first editor of its predecessor, the *Daily*

Worker, when it was founded on the instructions of the Comintern in 1930. A tall, portly man, he was 'by nature cold . . . all but incapable of warmth, even though he could generate great heat', according to his news editor. Rust was an unhesitating supporter of the Moscow line, and took a Russian woman as his second wife. During the Spanish civil war, he operated from Barcelona as a British commissar under cover of reporting for the *Worker*.

He resumed the reins of editor in the early days of the Second World War, when the party leadership was split over the Hitler–Stalin pact, and ran an underground news operation when Home Secretary Herbert Morrison banned the paper in 1941. Rust survived the *volte-face* in the USSR's war strategy, and is credited with turning the *Daily Worker* into a popular mass newspaper with office premises in central London and a readership abroad, particularly in the Soviet Union. However, he never lost sight of fundamentals. His staff were 'not journalists, but Communists', he maintained. Nonetheless, in 1948 his vigorous editorship took the paper's circulation to 120,000 a day.

The following year, he was 'branched' by the National Union of Journalists for an intemperate attack on Fleet Street. Planning a robust counter-attack at the union hearing, Rust went to party HQ to gather his evidence and died there from a massive heart-attack, aged forty-six. **Douglas Hyde** said he was 'well informed, but had little culture'. His daughter by his first wife, called Rosa after Rosa Luxembourg, the German revolutionary, survived the horror of Stalin's wartime camps to return to England, an ordeal that Rust preferred to forget. She was largely forgotten. He is commemorated on a plaque at the offices of the *Morning Star*.

S

SHAPURJI SAKLATVALA was the first Communist Party member to be elected to the British parliament, in 1922. He was also a member of the Labour Party, and for good measure the ILP. He became MP for North Battersea, London, then a radical hotbed rather than the gentrified 'south Chelsea' of today. At that time, Labour did not operate a ban on joint membership with the CP, which he joined in 1921, soon after it was established.

Yet Saklatava was born into wealth, in India in 1874. He came to England in 1905 to work for the family firm, and rapidly became involved in the movement for Indian independence. Anti-colonial activity took him into the Social Democratic Federation, forerunner of the CP. He was chosen as candidate in 1921, and though Communists played a significant role in his adoption, Saklatvala was endorsed nationally by the Labour Party.

He won the seat with a majority of more than two thousand votes, but lost it again a year later. He was returned to Westminster after the 1924 election, but in the mid-1920s Labour leaders moved decisively against Communist 'infiltrators'. Membership of the CP was deemed incompatible with the parliamentary road to socialism, and in February 1926 the Battersea Labour Party was expelled. On the eve of the General Strike in that year, Saklatvala was arrested because of a speech he made in support of the coal miners. George Lansbury stood bail, but the MP was jailed for two months.

At the 1929 election, he stood openly as a Communist and was defeated, taking only 18 per cent of the votes cast. He now became openly hostile to Labour, but CP hopes that he could mobilise support for the party in pursuit of this strategy proved groundless. He failed at Glasgow Shettleston in 1930, and again at Battersea North in 1931 when he lost his deposit. Saklatvala was 'a dedicated socialist' who showed that a left-wing militant could win influence within the broad stream of the labour movement,' wrote **Jim Mortimer** in 2002. 'But once he was opposed by Labour or stood in opposition to Labour his support declined.' These reasons deserved discussion, said Labour's former general secretary. 'They are of contemporary relevance.'

ARTHUR SCARGILL led the National Union of Mineworkers down a primrose path of self-indulgent Leftiousness, which destroyed not only his union but the industry that gave it strength. He was recruited into the Communist Party while still a teenage miner in Barnsley in the 1950s, and schooled as the brightest of his generation to supplant the old right-wing regime in the Yorkshire NUM. However, his CP mentors (chiefly **Bert Ramelson** and Frank Watters) underestimated 'King' Arthur's ego, which soon took him out of the party. He sought to retain secret membership, but a meeting of party members at the home of a Communist pit deputy in Darton ruled that he had to remain publicly committed or quit, and he was duly 'de-carded', the quaint CPGB term for expulsion.

Thereafter, his career took off at great velocity: pit delegate, compensation agent, Yorkshire president and national president in succession to Joe Gormley in 1981. His role in the infamous battle of Saltley Gate during the 1972 pit strike, in which secondary pickets closed down a vital coke works in Birmingham, sent shivers down the spine of the establishment and triggered massive legal retaliation when the Tories returned to power. In fact, while Scargill took most of the credit, the spade work for Saltley was done by Communists in the city, mainly engineering and transport workers. But in the Scargill myth, it simply became 'the greatest day in my life'. It also spawned a semi-literate left-wing syndicalism, lionised in *New Left Review*, quite unlike anything in the British political tradition.

His fusion of trade union and political militancy finally came to grief in the Great Strike of 1984–5, which defeated and split the union, and decimated the coal industry. Scargill, however, emerged with his self-esteem intact and able to buy Treetops the second largest house in his home village of Woolley. Disillusioned with Blairism, he also founded his own political party, the Socialist Labour Party, which contested (without winning) many parliamentary seats and kept him briefly in the headlines. Scargill, an inveterate fan of the opposite sex, divorced his loyal wife Anne and finally 'retired' in 2002. However, he maintained a £1,000 a month paid consultancy with the 5,000-member rump of the NUM. To the end he insisted, 'I was right.' His tragedy was that he believed his mantra; the miners' tragedy was that they could not see through it.

SID SCHOFIELD was an unassuming vice-president of the National Union of Mineworkers in the 1960s with a great deal to be unassuming about. He would often wail to journalists that 'There is a third national officer of this union – me.' However, he rescued himself from total obscurity in 1972 with a brilliant lie told during negotiations to end the first great pit strike. The government-appointed Wilberforce Inquiry, charged with finding a solution to the dispute that had brought the nation to its knees, proposed wage rises of 18 per cent. The NUM executive sensed there was more to be had, and rejected the package. National officials were asked how the vote had gone. Before Joe Gormley (president) or Lawrence Daly (general secretary) could speak, Schofield swore that it was 14–11. Ministers at the Employment Department despaired, and the miners were invited to 10 Downing Street where they played havoc with Edward Heath's whisky stocks, while negotiating many millions more. Too late, ministers discovered that canny Sid had lied. The vote had been 13–12. 'If we'd known that,' mused one later, 'we'd have locked them in a room at the Department with the beer until one of the bastards wilted.'

SIR STEPHEN SEDLEY is regarded as one of the most left-wing members of the judiciary, and fellow lawyers believe his progress at the bar was held back by political objections from the establishment. A member of the Haldane Society of socialist lawyers and the National Council for Civil Liberties, his appointment as a High Court judge in 1992 caused a frisson in legal circles. His elevation was interpreted as a signal that politics is no bar to judicial advancement, and *The Times* reported that 'He is the most left-wing Queen's Counsel to reach the senior ranks of the judiciary.' His record of appearances, in the Blair Peach case, the Carl Bridgewater murder trial, the Helen Smith inquest and the appeal of Stefan Kisko, is cited in support of his Left credentials. In the 1960s, he was a tutor at the Communist University of London, which attracted more than a thousand students, teaching a critical approach to the conventional university tuition.

Thirty years later, he is still a pedagogic progressive. As the first chairman of the Bar Council's sex discrimination committee Sir Stephen pleaded in 2001 for more of a judicial mix on the bench to bring 'a fresh dimension of experience and understanding', a face that was not white, male or elderly and personal lifestyles 'which are not necessarily orthodox'. He is, of course, white, male, aged sixty-four, and married with three children. But that's not the point.

TOMMY SHERIDAN languished on the lunatic Left fringes of Scottish politics until Margaret Thatcher brought him inside the fold by jailing him. Sheridan won a Glasgow city council seat in 1992 while serving four months in Saughton prison for defiance of the poll tax laws. He came out of jail penniless but a working-class hero, and went on to found the Scottish Socialist Party, winning a seat in the first Scottish Parliament for four hundred years.

A charismatic figure, known variously as the Peter Pan or Robin Hood of politics, Sheridan was born into a strong Labour family in Glasgow in 1963. He joined the party, but at the age of seventeen he also joined the Militant Tendency, then at the height of its entryist campaign. Along with more well-known figures, Sheridan was expelled in the Kinnock purge of 1989, but instead of disappearing back into the woodwork he refashioned 'the Millies' with a tartan stripe. His heroes were the Red Clydesiders of the 1920s, particularly John MacLean, whose goal was a Scottish Socialist Republic. His Marxist hectoring is subtly reworked through underdog nationalist themes, like: '**Tony Blair**'s cool Britannia still means freezing Scotland.' His party has scored as high as 20 per cent in opinion polls across Scotland, not merely in Glasgow. Sheridan takes votes from disaffected Labour and SNP electors, and there are many of those.

As a latter-day Braveheart, he plays the media like a violin. Asked why he married his wife Gail in a Catholic Church in 2000, when he disapproves of both marriage and religion, he disarmed critics by saying: 'Because I love her.' His charismatic style has taken him far, but the sharp suits, the sunbed-tan, and the swish house in Cardonald prompt unfavourable comparisons with **Derek Hatton**. He may have soared too high already.

EMMANUEL SHINWELL called his autobiography –

published in 1955 when he was over seventy but with another thirty years to live – *Conflict Without Malice*. Friends and enemies alike must have relished his attempt at irony, for few political careers have been marked with such ill-will and spite. Even in a party known for its consuming personal loathing, Manny stood out as the greatest hater of his generation. He needed enemies, and they were never in short supply. As a self-confessed thug on 'Red Clydeside' in his early days, he counted himself 'one of the most humble' social reformers of the twentieth century, while Attlee was 'a nonentity'. Harold Wilson praised his tenacity and raw ability, but noted his many political failings, which prevented him ever reaching the top.

Shinwell's beginnings were inauspicious. Born in 1884 in Spitalfields, east London, the eldest of a tailor's thirteen children, he was sent to work at the family sailor's outfitters in South Shields at the age of eight. He learned life the hard way in the rough port, and when his father took him to Glasgow in 1894, he had a strong boy's pair of fists. At the age of fourteen he was briefly a prize-fighter, and his physical courage came in useful when he became an official of the Seamen's Union. Perched on his father's shoulder, Manny had seen John Burns speak in the great London dock strike of 1889, but his political awakening came on Glasgow Green when he preached science and Darwinism at the turn of the nineteenth century before espousing socialism via the ILP. He was prominent in the Glasgow Trades Council, and in November 1918 stood at the head of 'the greatest strike that has ever taken place'. Lloyd George's government feared Bolshevism, and despatched 12,000 troops and tanks to the city. The 'uprising' ended with the brutal suppression of a riot in George Square on Bloody Friday in January 1919, and Shinwell was jailed for five months for incitement to riot. At his trial, the police quoted passages from Manny's notebook, which spoke of the Commons as an illegal assembly. 'Workers' and Soldiers' Councils, Soviets, are needed as the first stage in the establishment of a true democracy,' he wrote. 'We must use every ounce of energy to smash the government.' Prison made Shinwell a better socialist, according to his biographer Peter Slowe 'at one and the same time conniving with the establishment and seeking to destroy or radically alter it'.

In the years that followed, conniving got the upper hand over destruction. In 1922 he was elected Labour MP for Linlithgow, and served briefly as a minister in Ramsay MacDonald's government. In and out of Parliament in the turbulent twenties, Shinwell formed a violent antipathy towards his one-time hero Ramsay Mac over the betrayal of 1931 and defeated him at Seaham in 1935. His only real claim to fame in the locust years that followed was a physical assault in the chamber on a Tory MP. During the wartime coalition, he refused to serve as a junior food minister telling Attlee he would 'do very well outside the government.' He was a fool to reject office out of a misplaced *amour propre*, and his attacks on Churchill did not lift his political profile. After the Labour landslide of 1945, Attlee called Shinwell into the Cabinet to nationalise the mines, which he did successfully, though his handling of the 1947 fuel crisis was inept. Hugh Gaitskell recorded that Manny's presence in the Cabinet spoilt the atmosphere. 'He throws apples of discord the whole time.' Shinwell became a hard-line Minister of Defence in 1950, and even proposed sending 'a platoon or two' of British soldiers to fight in America's Vietnam War. In 1970, he became a life peer, only to resign the party whip in 1982 in protest at the 'left-wing drift' in Labour policy. Shinwell had come a long way from Red Clydeside, but he was still offering to hit his political opponents in his eighties. He died aged 101 in 1986, having published his third volume of memoirs, pugnaciously entitled *Lead with the Left: My First Ninety-Six Years*.

PETER SHORE fancied himself mightily as a left-wing leader of the Labour Party, an illusion from which he was rescued by what a *Times* obituarist called 'a clique of ageing Bevanites.' Shore was the archetypal backroom boy, the Transport House researcher who believed he could jump the counter and do a better job than the landlord. He loathed Hugh Gaitskell, and sided subsequently with the Bennite Left. The association did him no good. Nor did his failure to make friends on the Westminster social circuit.

Shore, a tall, stooping, donnish figure, was born in Great Yarmouth in 1924, the son of a banana boat captain. He won an exhibition to King's College, Cambridge, and took a second in history while chairing the university Labour Club. He did national service in the RAF, and toyed with the idea of working for the Foreign Office or the United Nations before following his socialist convictions into the service of Labour as a policy wonk. He was elected to the safe seat of Stepney in 1965, and swiftly became Harold Wilson's PPS. Two years later, he was in the Cabinet as Economic Affairs Secretary, but he was demoted to Minister without Portfolio in 1970 for opposing Barbara Castle's *In Place of Strife* union curbs.

When Labour returned in 1974, Shore was successively Trade, then Environment Secretary, but missed out on Foreign Secretary (to David Owen) because of his long-standing hostility to the EEC. He moved away from CND and the Left, and made enemies in the unions over the electoral college for choosing the party leader – steps that vitiated his own leadership ambitions in 1980 when James Callaghan stood down. **Clive Jenkins** and **Ian Mikardo** led an unholy alliance of union barons and left-wingers to drive through the candidature of **Michael Foot**, squeezing out Shore in the first ballot. Shore swung his support behind Foot against what he saw as an opportunist **Denis Healey**, thereby ensuring the validity of his own prediction that Labour would lose the next two elections. Shore was a virtually forgotten figure in Neil Kinnock's Shadow Cabinet, and even more so when John Major sent him to the Lords in 1997. In 2001, he collapsed while speaking in the Chamber, and died two months later. Essentially, Shore was a man of the Left who was left behind.

CLARE SHORT has played eloquently to the strengths of her Leftie-persona, finding herself able to rock the New Labour boat while never really having to rebel until the war against Iraq was over. Willing to wound but afraid to strike, she loyally supported **Tony Blair** through all his foreign military adventures, becoming in the process the longest-serving Minister for Overseas Development. It is a formidable achievement, though it is possible to ponder what it has been for. Uniquely, while despising the black arts of spin doctors, she also pulled off a brilliant news management of the ghost-like emergence of a son from a past life. None of this would have been guessed at from her Bennite political origins, when she was the spotless Leftie who put principle before preferment, quitting Labour's front bench twice rather than support the Prevention of Terrorism Act or the first Gulf War.

Clare Short was a bright child, the second of seven, born in 1946. Her Irish Catholic father was a teacher, her mother a bookkeeper. After St Paul's Grammar School, Birmingham, where she was remembered as the most confident girl in her class, she studied political science at the universities of Keele and Leeds. But instead of following her father as expected to the chalk face, she passed the civil service exams and worked at the Home Office as private secretary to Tory minister Mark Carlisle. Short continued this role with his Labour successor, Alex Lyon, when Harold Wilson returned to power in 1974. At the age of twenty-eight, she began an affair with Lyon while they were on a ministerial visit to India. Lyon was fifteen years older, married with two children. Short had been married at university, when she was eighteen, and had a son, Benjamin, who was given up for adoption; the marriage ended in divorce six years later. Short's working relationship with Lyon ended soon after the affair began, but they lived together and eventually married in 1982. However, their time together was not endless bliss. Lyon lost his seat in 1983, in the general election that returned Short as MP for Birmingham Ladywood. He fell victim to Alzheimer's disease, and died a lingering death in 1993.

Short's political career began with a bang when she accused Alan Clark, the playboy Tory minister for employment, of being 'incapable' at the Despatch Box. To describe an MP as drunk in the Chamber is not permitted, and Short performed verbal convolutions to escape suspension. Years later, Clark admitted that she was right. She had also made her mark, and continued to make it with controversy over page-three pin-up girls, the Irish question, the national minimum wage, black sections in the Labour Party, American imperialism, feminism, quotas for women MPs, nuclear arms and a host of other issues. Appointed junior defence spokesman in 1985, she quit over the Prevention of Terrorism Act three years later, arguing that it drove young people into terrorism. Returning to the front bench in 1989 as social security spokesman, she resigned again in 1991 after refusing to be silent on the Gulf War.

Her real rise to prominence came after the election of Tony Blair (for whom she did not vote) as party leader. He took her into the Shadow Cabinet as Shadow Transport Secretary, and she delivered support for the abolition of Clause IV and other contentious anti-Left issues such as the ban on Liz Davies standing as Labour candidate in Leeds North East. Short blotted her copybook with a refusal to condemn strikes by London Underground workers, and Blair moved her to Overseas Aid. She got the job in 1997, and called it 'undoubtedly the best job in government…by definition noble'. She finally quit in May 2003, several weeks after the resignation of Robin Cook and her own threat to go if the UK did not have UN authority to invade Baghdad, which it did not. Her departure was tarnished by its tardiness, but she did level sharp shafts of criticism at Blair's dictatorial style, accusing him of misleading the nation over a secret deal with President Bush to go to war.

Ever since her tirades against page-three girls, the tabloid press has taken an obsessive interest in Clare Short's private life. And it has been interesting. In 1996, the son she had given up for adoption – now a thirty-something called Toby – had set out to find his natural mother, and a Sunday newspaper got wind of it . To forestall bad publicity, Short pre-emptively broke the story through a friendly female columnist. 'My son is a beauty,' she raved. Her possessive joy did not go down well with Toby's wife Annie.

The story does not end there. In 1997, Short was accused of being a marriage wrecker after having an affair with her dead husband's friend Labour MP Jim Marshall. He left his wife for Short, but she did not live with him and the affair ended. The story has a happy ending. Son Toby, a Tory when she was reunited with him, joined the Labour Party. Aaaaaaaah!

RENEE SHORT did her best to live up to the soubriquet 'Red Renee' bestowed on her by the tabloid press. While a Labour MP and a member of the party's National Executive Committee, she also served as secretary to the Anglo-Soviet Parliamentary Group, treasurer of the British-German Democratic Republic group, ditto of the British-Romanian Friendship Association during the time of Ceascescu, and vice-chairman of the East-West Trade Group. She was also a zealous visitor to socialist countries, more diligent in this direction (as *The Times* noted drily at the time of her death in January 2003) than in visiting her Black Country constituency, an oversight that ended her political career. By then, she had mellowed, moving into the soft-Left camp in support of Neil Kinnock.

Born in 1919, the daughter of a Romanian–Hungarian engineer and Jewish mother, Short was brought up by her Church of England grandparents. Educated at Nottingham High School and Manchester University, she became a journalist but her real passion was politics. She was a councillor in Hertfordshire and fought hopeless seats in 1955 and 1959 before landing Wolverhampton North East in 1964. She was an ardent campaigner on women's rights, drug abuse and sexual health, but showed an ambivalent attitude towards immigration, which her political neighbour Enoch Powell exploited with his 1968 'rivers of blood' speech. Short condemned the speech, but argued for dispersal of new migrants away from Wolverhampton.

However, her unrelenting hostility to Harold Wilson, and after him James Callaghan, on the NEC, and her patent lack of interest in her constituency (particularly when contrasted with her passion for breeding poodles) marked out Short for deselection. She just avoided this fate in 1983, but stood down voluntarily in 1987 when it was clear that she would not survive a second vote. In retirement, she was honoured for her medical campaigning, and became president of the Nursery Schools Association.

JIM SILLARS announced in 1994 that he had 'retired from the political scene', which was the Scottish nation's loss rather than his own. Scotland had produced too few genuine Lefties in the last quarter of the twentieth century to mislay another. Variously described as the eternal rebel of Scottish politics and the Idi Amin of Scotland, Sillars pursued a wayward path across three decades of political life. The son of an Ayrshire train driver, he began life as a railway fireman, before a stint in the Royal Navy as a radio operator. He joined the Labour Party in 1960 while working in the fire service (and incidentally a member of the FBU executive), and was a full-time election agent before winning South Ayrshire in a 1970 by-election.

Sillars was an early advocate of Scottish independence, and split from the Callaghan government in 1975 over Labour's 'weak' devolution bill. He formed and led the short-lived Scottish Labour Party, and was defeated on his home ground by Labour in the 1979 election. He then joined the SNP, as one of the radical '79 group (later suppressed), later proclaiming that he was 'not a Marxist, although that is through choice, not anxiety'. Sillars became the deputy leader and intellectual power-house of his adopted party, formulating the policy of Independence in Europe. In 1988, he staged a remarkable parliamentary comeback, taking the rock-solid Labour seat of Govan, Glasgow, in a 33 per cent by-election swing to the SNP. He proved to be just as much a thorn in the Tories' side as he had been in Labour's, leading opposition to the poll tax and taking issue with the 1991 Gulf War. He lost his seat in 1992 to Labour left-winger Ian Davidson. Sillars had an equally colourful private life. His marriage to Agnes Sproat ended in 1980, and the following year he married the charismatic nationalist Margo MacDonald, who had earlier matched his feat in winning Govan for the SNP. He quit the 'absurd and childish game' of politics, and wrote a column for the *Scottish Sun* while working for the Arab-British Chamber of Commerce in London. The new generation of SNP leaders regarded him as 'an extinct volcano', but for the Blairite generation, he became 'an icon of Scottish politics'.

ALAN SIMPSON is a leading figure of the left-wing Campaign Group of MPs at Westminster but he will never be truly the leader of the parliamentary Left in the way that, for instance, **Aneurin Bevan** unquestionably was. A diffident style and an unaggressive nature hold him back from being the natural standard bearer of the dwindling band of socialists in the Parliamentary Labour Party.

Born the eldest of seven, in Bootle, Liverpool in 1948, he attended the local grammar school and Trent Polytechnic in Nottingham, where he graduated with a degree in economics. He worked in the city as a community officer and on anti-vandalism projects before joining the Racial Equality Council as a research officer. Political progress has been…well, measured. Simpson joined the Labour Party in 1973, and became a Nottinghamshire county councillor fourteen years later before taking Nottingham South from the Tories in 1992.

He opposed the war against Afghanistan, and he is crazy about sport, playing in goal for the House of Commons football team and for tennis and cricket teams. He claims to be 'slightly embarrassed' at being dubbed the Michael Owen of the Green Benches, because he is an Everton fan, while Owen plays for Liverpool. He puts this modest challenge to **Blair** on his website, along with the fact that he proposed to his partner Lizzie over the public address system at Goodison Park when Everton were playing West Ham. Simpson likes to be thought of a 'good-humoured, imaginative and iconoclastic' and his aim is to put 'colour and excitement into the politics of the 21st century'. He could have fooled me, but he hasn't.

DEREK SIMPSON resigned his job as a local official to take on the might of the right-wing machine of the engineering union, Amicus. The union's rulebook, drawn up by the ruling 'moderates' compelled him to quit before he could stand for general secretary, while the incumbent, Sir Ken Jackson, stayed in office despite being over retirement age. This interesting state of affairs marked the culmination, and downfall, of the arrogant old regime that had held power for four decades. To the chagrin of Downing Street, Simpson, the 'man from nowhere', won the election by 400 votes in 2002. In fact, he came from somewhere – Sheffield, where the AEEU was still in good left-wing heart.

After leaving school at fifteen, he was apprenticed to a local engineering firm, and was soon a shop steward, then works convenor before being appointed Sheffield district secretary in 1981. This post had earlier been held by the legendary Communist George Caborn, whose son Dick became a government minister. Simpson took after the father, joining the CP. He moved to Derby as district official there, before taking the momentous decision to challenge the Right's assertion that no election was required. Simpson took legal advice, ironically under Thatcherite labour laws, which compelled Jackson to hold a ballot. Despite considerable and inept attempts at ballot-rigging by the Right, he triumphed and consternation gripped the old brigade. The shredders worked overtime at union headquarters in Bromley, prompting comparisons with the panic in the Stasi building when the Berlin Wall came down.

Simpson, fifty-eight at the time of writing in 2003, has almost a decade to turn round the ossified structures of Amicus, and New Labour is still coming to terms with the man who promised to give **Tony Blair** 'a fucking migraine.' He is a keen chess player, who took an Open University degree in mathematics and computer studies. During the leadership campaign, Simpson was reunited with his former wife Frieda. They divorced thirty years ago and both married other partners, then each divorced again and they are now reunited.

DENNIS SKINNER made himself into a political legend while never sitting on a parliamentary committee or holding any form of government office. He does it by sitting on Labour's left-wing 'awkward squad' front bench for hour after hour, rising at regular intervals to aim a shaft of wit at his opponents. That his repartee owes more to the pit cage than the drawing room does not matter. He is capable of brilliantly wrong-footing the most elevated of speakers, with a disconcerting, earthy jibe.

Skinner comes from a Leftie miners' family in Derbyshire. His father was sacked after the 1926 strike, and his brothers were 'Clay Cross martyrs' in the row over local government funding. Skinner, born in 1932, was a collier and part-time singer in working-men's clubs, imitating Al Jolson and Johnny Ray. He did not join the Labour Party until he was twenty-four, and became MP for the safe seat of Bolsover in 1970. He then began a career, which endures to this day, of espousing every left-wing cause that came across his field of vision, including the bid to halt expulsion of the Militant Tendency. He emerged as the most trusted lieutenant of **Tony Benn** and **Arthur Scargill**, for which he still shows no public repentance. But it is as the 'abrasively proletarian conscience of the hard Left' that he has made his name. Skinner's flint-like integrity does not permit him to drink with Tories, or journalists.

He is teetotal, anyway, and in the agreeable political village that is Westminster he shuns company as if it might compromise his socialist principles. The same goes for staying in 'posh' hotels during Labour Party conference week, and for Commons 'freebies' abroad. He does not possess a passport, which perhaps makes his thoroughgoing contempt for the European Union easier to bear. A keen cyclist, he suffered a skull fracture falling off his bike in 1980. But his rugged righteousness availed him nought when the newspapers discovered that the long-married Skinner was living with his American researcher Lois Blasenheim and he became the butt of the newspaper cartoonists' jokes.

JIM SLATER was named by Harold Wilson as one of a 'tightly knit politically motivated men' responsible for the first all-out seamen's strike in 1966, which blew the Labour government off course. The six were made scapegoats for Labour's loss of office in 1970, although the reality was much more complex. Slater, a hard-drinking, amiable Geordie, was a member of the executive of the National Union of Seamen.

Born in South Shields, he went to sea as a deckhand on collier ships carrying coal to London. In the Second World War he was torpedoed twice during the battle of the Atlantic and once spent several days at sea in an open boat. His employer took him off pay as soon as he got into the lifeboat. He also served on the Arctic convoys to Murmansk. In post-war years, Slater was sharply critical of the collaborative relationship of the NUS with the shipping employers, and led an unofficial strike in Liverpool. He was struck off the seamen's register for more than a year, which effectively made him unemployable.

But the union leaders could see the writing on the wall, and relented. Slater was elected north-east secretary of the NUS in the early 1960s, and to the national executive in 1964. Following the eight-week strike, Slater was a marked man, classified with Communist Party industrial organiser **Bert Ramelson** as a wrecker. There is no doubt that Ramelson played a key advisory role in the 1966 dispute, but even he could not magic up discontent. The strike was supported right round the world. Slater became assistant general secretary in 1970, and general secretary four years later. He raised the profile of the NUS within the TUC, and confronted the shipping employers for a second time in 1976 when he won pay rises substantially above the Labour government's ceiling. In 1984, he went to the aid of striking miners, imposing a blockade of coal imports and secretly funding the NUM campaign. The employers reacted to NUS militancy by 'flagging out' much of the British merchant fleet to cheap foreign labour, but Slater did not abandon his political position.

His union boycotted VE Day anniversary celebrations in 1985, when Slater argued that it would be 'grossly hypocritical' to join Thatcher at a service when she had halved the merchant fleet in six years, a feat unrivalled by the U-boats. He was ousted from power the following year by the 'moderate' Sam McLuskie, but he was never silenced. Slater dropped dead from a heart-attack in Liverpool Cathedral during Battle of the Atlantic celebrations in May 1993.

DONALD, LORD SOPER was the nearest thing to a Methodist saint, and his all-encompassing bag of progressive attitudes gave him an iconic status among the forces of Leftiousness. To his fellow peer, Lord (Norman) Tebbit with whom he clashed on the BBC Radio programme *Today*, he 'always appeared the epitome of sanctimonious ill-judgement'. For decades, he was a familiar figure at Speaker's Corner and at Tower Bridge, where he dispensed Bevanite wisdom on every issue of the day from vivisection to nuclear war. His sermons also appeared in *Tribune* for two decades during **Michael Foot**'s editorship. Soper was the first Methodist minister to be appointed a life peer, and among the many unofficial titles bestowed on him was National Chaplain to the Labour Party. **Tony Benn** found it 'very sweet' when the venerable cleric told him: 'I'm a Bennite.' It is surprising that Soper did not sink under the weight of so much adulation, but fortunately he did not have to put his politics to the test in an election because, as Harold Wilson observed, such ideals are most unlikely to survive the rough-and-tumble of politics.

Donald Soper was born in south London in 1902, the son of God-fearing, teetotal, non-smoking parents who thought the theatre was the work of the devil. His mother was a teacher, and his father a claims adjuster in the City, a very stern puritanical man for whom everything was black or white. 'Black was anything he considered wrong,' recalled his daughter. It is easy to see where the young Soper's moral universe was formed. In less austere times, his grandfather was the model for one of the *Three Men in a Boat* by Jerome K. Jerome. Soper was a lifelong pacifist, though at Haberdasher's Aske's School he was a sergeant-major instructor in the School Cadet Corps 'teaching men old enough to be my father to stick bayonets into one another'. At Cambridge, he took a first in theology, and then a doctorate at the LSE. His induction into the ministry in the Old Kent Road in 1926 was a profound shock. He had only experienced poverty and deprivation at second hand, as issues. Now he saw the real thing. He also made his mark in the early days of Christian broadcasting, and for more than forty years was superintendent of the West London Mission at Kingsway Hall.

His preaching knew no bounds, however, and as an enthusiastic member of the Peace Pledge Union he was considered so dangerous a pacifist that he was banned from the airwaves. In the post-war world, he turned more to politics, arguing that 'Socialism is the economic and political expression, in time, of what I believe to be the Kingdom of God.' For good measure, Labour's nationalising Clause IV expressed 'the ultimate principle that emerges from our Lord's teaching'. A Labour Party that was not Socialist, he opined 'is a contradiction in terms, and more or less a waste of time'. With **Tom Driberg** and R. H. Tawney, Soper founded the Christian Socialist Movement and, when it came soon after, he was a natural for CND, in which he took a leading role. Towards the end – he died in 1998 – he confessed that 'the more I think about the next world, the more perplexed I get.' What endures is his public speaker's sense of humour. Asked by an American reporter what he thought of the death of God, Soper shot back: 'I hadn't heard he was unwell.'

DAVE SPRINGHALL unwisely took it upon himself to bring the Soviet Union up to date with British war plans in 1943, and was sentenced to seven years' penal servitude for his pains. A former sailor thrown out of the Royal Navy in 1920 for communist activities, he became a leading figure in the Young Communist League, and an unlikely go-between linking the Cambridge University Communists and King Street. He graduated to the CP central committee and was sent to Spain as a political commissar during the civil war. Heavily built, and prone to break into a hornpipe when excited by drink, Springhall was deeply loyal to Moscow. Party chiefs warned about 'Springie', a national organiser during wartime, about his over-enthusiastic relations with Soviet Embassy diplomats, guessing that he might be passing on secrets. He denied the suggestion, but police raided his house and his office, finding incriminating documentary evidence in both. Springhall had been acquiring information from army and RAF contacts for his Russian friends. He was immediately expelled from the party. As CP historian Francis Beckett points out, they caught a working-class lad engaged in a spot of low-grade spying, but complete missed the Cambridge ring. They followed Springhall everywhere, yet never asked why he spent so much time in Cambridge. **Kim Philby**, passing on similar information, went undetected.

JOHN STRACHEY had more political homes than most successful players of the system have in the country. Jennie Lee complained that he 'had no compass on his ship and was all over the place'. Strachey started in the ILP, then moved to Oswald Mosley's New Party, forerunner of the British Union of Fascists, before veering sharply back towards Communism under the guidance of **R. Palme Dutt**. In the 1930s he became a regular columnist on the *Daily Worker* and wrote two key works of the decade: *The Menace of Fascism* and *The Theory and Practice of Socialism*. In 1936, with Harold Laski and Victor Gollancz, he formed the influential Left Book Club to further the spread of socialist ideas and combat Fascism. In 1945 he returned to Westminster as a Labour MP, finding preferment under Attlee as Air Minister, Minister for Food and finally as War Secretary in 1950 at the height of the Cold War, completing a political odyssey as strenuous as anything performed by Odysseus.

Born in 1901 into high society, John Strachey was the son of the owner–editor of the *Spectator*, then (as now) a Right-wing magazine. He was educated at Eton and Oxford before joining Papa on the paper. Like others of his generation, Strachey could not resist the siren call of socialism, and in the 1920 edited the ILP journal *Socialist Review*, promulgating a more aggressive economic strategy than Labour leaders including nationalisation of the Bank of England. His search took him towards Marxism (while not ruling out marriage to an American heiress, whom he soon ditched for an English vicar's daughter), but the CP rejected his membership application. Undaunted, Strachey became the leading Communist commentator of his day before joining the RAF for service in the Second World War.

In his ministerial years, Strachey is remembered for two things: his passionate advocacy of the scheme to promote the farming of groundnuts in colonial Africa, which was a disaster, and his equally strong enthusiasm for higher defence spending to restrain the spread of Communism for which he had so ardently campaigned in the thirties. His final rejection of Communism in *Contemporary Socialism* (1956) confirmed his position as a leading Right-winger in the Labour Party. Dr Philip Larkin has suggested that Strachey could have expected a senior job in the Wilson government of 1964, but he died suddenly in 1963. His only other claim to fame was the caustic advice offered by Attlee when Strachey asked for approval for publication of a small 'non controversial' collection of poems. Attlee refused permission, and when asked why, said: 'Don't rhyme, don't scan.' He could have been talking about Strachey's life.

JOE STRUMMER was the intelligent, anarcho-Leftie face of punk rock who never compromised with the establishment, musical or media. As front man of The Clash, he was the creative genius of sixteen top-forty hits, including 'Rock the Casbah', 'Bankrobber' and 'I Fought The Law'. Billy Bragg said he gave punk its political edge, and Strummer was always to be found at the forefront of workpeople in struggle.

When he died of a heart attack in 2002, the firefighters were in dispute with New Labour, and a fire tender headed his funeral cortège. But Strummer – real name John Graham Mellor – was born in Ankara, Turkey, the son of a British diplomat posted variously to Cairo, Mexico City and Bonn. He was sent home to board at City of London Freemen's School at Ashtead and was later expelled from the Central School of Art, London. He took up busking and changed his name after a companion was charged with assaulting a policeman with a violin, forming his first band the 101'ers, named after the address of the west London squat where they lived. His real fame came after the collapse of the Sex Pistols, when Strummer's angry lyrics, fulminating against capitalism and all its works, found a resonance in Europe and America in the late seventies and early eighties.

He railed against the Vietnam War, unemployment and racial violence, and despised James Callaghan as much as Margaret Thatcher. 'It was us against the world . . . touching the audience,' he argued. 'You really think you are doing something and maybe for that moment in that hall you are.' An American critic agreed, uttering 'disbelief that mere humans could create such a sound, and disbelief that the world could remain the same when it's over'. However, the world showed itself obstinately capable of getting down from Strummer's punk highs. The Clash eventually split up, and Strummer fronted the Irish band, The Pogues, before forming his own Mescaleros.

To the end, he refused to perform on the 'manipulative' *Top of the Pops*, rejected huge offers of money to re-form The Clash in America, and insisted on low cover prices at the expense of royalties. An avid reader of the *Daily Telegraph*, Strummer was rewarded with a full page on his death plus a half-page editorial describing him as the conscience of punk rock. The paper's rock critic called him 'a lovely bloke, a man of the people, still angry with the world's injustices, but gentle, humble and heroic to the last'. Few Lefties ever gained such an accolade.

SCREAMING LORD SUTCH, leader of the Monster
Raving Loony Party, was a borderline Leftie, qualifying largely on the
basis of his role in the death of the centre-right Social Democratic Party.
He contested forty elections in thirty years, losing thousands of pounds
in deposits, but gaining much in public affection. His crazy top hat, gold
lamé suits and an electioneering style more suited to his rock'n'roll background than traditional politics were a breath of fresh air in the 1980s.
And some of his policies – votes at eighteen, all-day opening for pubs,
abolition of the 11-plus – are now part of everyday life.

Born David Edward Sutch, he changed his name by deed poll to the
3rd Baron of Harrow, his native suburb of London. He entered politics
at the Stratford by-election in 1963 after the resignation of John
Profumo, the War Secretary who lied to Parliament over his relationship
with call girl Christine Keeler. In that poll, Sutch received only 208 votes.
But in a by-election in Bootle many years later he despatched David
Owen to oblivion by taking three times more votes than the SDP. He
became the longest-serving political leader in the country, and wrote an
autobiography, *Life as Sutch*. However, the clown concealed a depressive
figure, and Sutch hanged himself at the age of fifty-eight in June 1999.
Orthodox politicians could not praise him enough, but his obituary is
surely in his own words: 'Why is there only one Monopolies
Commission?'

T

PETER TAAFFE 'undoubtedly sees himself as the modern British Lenin, who will take over at the moment of crisis and lead us to socialism', according to the writer Michael Crick. His train to the Finland station has obviously been severely delayed. As leader of the Socialist Party, the successor to Militant, he has, at most, five thousand adherents, and his influence is a far cry from the heady days of the late seventies and early eighties before he was expelled from the Labour Party in **Michael Foot**'s purge of 1983. Taaffe, born in Birkenhead in 1942, the son of a sheet metal worker, proudly wears a small scar on his forehead, the result of a ceiling falling on to his bed during childhood. Armed with a handful of GCEs, he climbed out of poverty by studying for accountancy and then working for Liverpool City Council's housing department. He arrived in the Labour Party in his teens, via listening to Richard Crossman, canvassing with a Marxist comrade and reading social realist novels. He wrote articles for *Socialist Fight*, and in 1964 became editor of *Militant*, moving to London to await the call to power. He is still waiting.

PETER TATCHELL is one of those infuriatingly necessary people in whom the Left has, fortunately, abounded down the century of socialism. He takes enormous physical risks to confront tyrants, and still comes back for more. He was grievously let down by the Labour Party in the nauseating Bermondsey by-election of 1983, yet he never lost faith in direct action. Tatchell was born in Melbourne, perhaps the most European of Australian cities, in 1952, the son of evangelical Christians.

He taught in Sunday school as a teenager, before his first job as a window dresser.

He quit his native country in 1971 to avoid the Vietnam draft, and came to Britain where he took a sociology degree at North London Polytechnic, a hotbed of Leftiousness in the 1960s. He also became active in the gay rights movement, and joined the Labour Party in 1978. Tatchell recruited so many new members into the moribund Bermondsey Labour Party that Walworth Road bosses feared that he was an 'entryist'. When the local MP, Bob Mellish, a right-wing former Chief Whip, announced his intention of standing down, Tatchell was adopted as candidate and then bounced into a by-election. Initially, party leader **Michael Foot** said he would 'never' stand for Labour. The ubiquitous friends insisted that Foot, being deaf, thought that Peter Taaffe, the arch-Trotskyist, was under discussion. Whatever, party bosses failed to halt the tide of anti-gay prejudice that inundated Labour's campaign and handed the hitherto safe seat to SDP-Liberal Simon Hughes.

Tatchell became a full-time campaigner on human, and specifically gay, rights, forming groups like OutRage!, dedicated to 'outing' secretive homosexuals in public life. He also makes 'about £6,000' a year from freelance journalism, and lives like a monk in a Southwark council flat just off the Elephant and Castle. He was badly beaten up by Robert Mugabe's thugs in the Brussels Hilton in 2001, when trying to 'arrest' the Zimbabwean tyrant for human rights crimes. 'I love other people and I hate injustice,' he admits. 'I've probably got an exaggerated sense of empathy.' He also confesses to 'five great love affairs'.

MARK THOMAS, the stand-up comedian with a conscience, once described himself as 'a libertarian anarchist'. He was a member of the Labour Party for only a year, and is now actively hostile to the **Blair** project. He stood as an independent in the Hemsworth by-election of 1996, dismissing New Labour as 'right wing fucks who haven't got a clue.'

He also rejected an invitation to write jokes for **Robin Cook**, who can write his own anyway. Given his origins Thomas is a classic rebel. His father, 'a Thatcherite before Thatcher', was a builder during the week and a lay preacher on Sundays. His grandfather was a member of Mosley's Blackshirts. A Londoner by birth, he went to Christ's Hospital School, Sussex, on a scholarship, and then to Bretton Drama College, Wakefield. Early stints on *The Mary Whitehouse Experience* and *Friday Night Live* brought him his own show, *The Mark Thomas Product*. His relentless harassment of the DTI's funding of big projects such as the Kurdish dam, prompted Trade Minister Dick Caborn to seek 'information/dirt in order to rubbish him'. The minister insisted it was 'a purely procedural request for background'. Thomas, originally known for hilarious stunts like reading **Alastair Campbell**'s erotic fiction outside Westminster, these days applies a harder, more investigative edge to his shows. His opposition to Blair reached its zenith in the war against Iraq, when he lambasted anyone other than family and friends who shouted, 'Support our boys' as either a fool or a callous cynic of the worst kind.

WILL THORNE gave the world the GMB union, a distinction of which he would be proud but one that has proved dubious at various points. His mass union, originally of gas workers and general labourers, developed into an ossified bureaucracy that hindered rather than encouraged the forces of Leftiousness.

Thorne was born in Birmingham in 1857, the son of a brickmaker who died in a fight with a horse-dealer soon after Will had been put to work at the age of six in a ropemaker's business. He absconded when his employer cut his wages, and did various manual jobs, including a period 'on the tramp'. At eighteen, he went into the gas industry, moving to London with his wife and two children in 1882. This was a time of social and political ferment in the capital, and Thorne became active in the Social Democratic Federation, meeting the leading socialists of the day.

Eleanor Marx, Karl's daughter, taught the illiterate gasworker to read and write, and he swiftly became a powerful public speaker. Thorne thought of himself as a Communist at the time, and Engels gave him an autographed copy of *Das Kapital*. In 1889, he was a leading figure in the formation of the National Union of Gasworkers and General Labourers, defeating **Ben Tillett** in the election for general secretary. The new union won an eight-hour day – the first in industrial history – and aroused the wrath of employers round the country to little effect.

Thorne remained general secretary of the union for the next forty-five years, surely a record. During his time, membership rose dramatically, to almost half a million. This was the 'new' unionism, organising unskilled trades though to be beyond the reach of labour organisation. Thorne went into politics, first as a councillor in West Ham and then as MP for the borough in 1906, holding on to the constituency (redrawn as Plaistow) until he quit before the 1945 election, aged eighty-eight. As a parliamentarian, Thorne was out of his depth. Philip Snowden mocked him for his inadequate grasp of language, more suited to mass meetings than the Commons, though he did pay tribute to his skills as 'a very good sharp-shooter' at question times. Thorne also moved to the right, as did his union, and as do so many firebrand politicians when they succumb to the lethal embrace of Westminster.

But nothing can take away his battle for the eight-hour week, memorably described in his autobiography *My Life's Battles* as a means of reducing 'the inhuman competition that was making men more like beasts than civilised persons', a nineteenth-century ideal still applicable in a twenty-first-century cursed with 'presenteeism'. Thorne died in 1946.

BEN TILLETT is most often mentioned as the man who won the London dock strike of 1889, and this he did. But he left a greater legacy in the Independent Labour Party and then the modern Labour Party, in the formation of both of which he was powerfully instrumental.

Yet he had little to guide him, other than natural drive and a passionate commitment to the cause of a better life for working people. He was born in Bristol in 1860, the son of a stevedore. His 'brave, gentle, Irish' mother died when he was a year old, and he endured abuse at the hands of stepmothers, which left him with a nervous stammer. He ran away with the circus, as an acrobat, and worked as a shoemaker before joining the Royal Navy and then the Merchant Marine. He travelled the world before being wounded and invalided out in 1876. He moved to London, married, and found work in the London docks and became active first in the Tea Operatives' Association and then the Dock, Wharf, Riverside and General Labourers' Union of which he was general secretary from 1889 until it merged into the nascent TGWU in 1921.

Tillett overcame his speech impediment so successfully that he became the great mob orator of his day, a skill that he used to great advantage in the successful 'dockers' tanner' strike of 1889. Philip Snowden observed that he offered workers 'the vision of the new Earth'. He was also a brilliant organiser of industrial action and public support. Tillett's sense of social responsibility was founded in Christian socialism. He was a self-taught Congregationalist and adherent of temperance, and a member of the Fabian Society. He almost succeeded in becoming an MP in 1892. However, he quarrelled with **Keir Hardie** (for whom he was 'a dirty little hypocrite') and Ramsay MacDonald, and in 1908 attacked them in a pamphlet *Is the Parliamentary Party a Failure?*, a question that begged only one answer. He quit to join the Social Democratic Party, and as an anti-pacifist had no difficulty winning a seat at Salford as an Independent Labour candidate in a by-election in 1917. Tillett was adopted as Labour candidate in 1918, and, though he described himself as 'the rottenest politician in the world', held the seat, with a five-year break, until 1931 when he quit.

Tillett took up drink, and the quasi-religious right-wing sect, the Moral Rearmament League, but took no further part in orthodox politics before dying in 1943. Tom Mann left this description: 'He was short in stature, but tough; pallid, but dauntless; affected with a stammer at this time, but the real orator of the group . . . he would reach the heart's core of the dockers.'

RICKY TOMLINSON found fame in the 1990s as the irascible, couch-potato head of the *Royle Family* television sitcom. But he had been in the headlines thirty years previously, when he was a flying picket during the 1972 building workers' strike. Tomlinson was jailed for two years for conspiracy, unlawful assembly and affray, after a trial that he has always insisted (with some justice) was political. Scouser Tomlinson was an unlikely Leftie.

Trained as a plasterer, his introduction was by way of the National Front, some of whom were 'really nice guys', he later insisted, 'worried about their kids and their country – not skinheads or thugs'. Life on the building sites of Merseyside, where he saw appalling conditions and regular injuries, converted Tomlinson to the Left. He became a shop steward in the building workers' union, UCATT, and when its leaders launched a national pay strike after the successful miners' strike, he was in the front line. Flying pickets sought to bring out men still working in the Chester/North Wales area, and on one of these raids, violence was alleged at a site in Shrewsbury. No arrests were made that day, and the strike was called off after big pay rises were conceded. But public – and political – concern had been roused by the use of flying pickets. Tory MPs were appalled that **Arthur Scargill**'s tactics could transfer to other industries. In February 1973, five months after the strike, police began making arrests. The trial of six pickets, including Tomlinson, took place before Mr Justice Mais at Shrewsbury in October. The judge reproved the defence QC, **John Platts-Mills**, ruling that 'for conspiracy, they never have to meet and they never have to know each other'. Tomlinson and his fellow Leftie Des Warren were found guilty. In the dock, Tomlinson delivered a long tirade against the political nature of the trial, and looked forward to the day when 'another charade as this' would never happen.

He was deceiving himself. Many such prosecutions took place in the pit strike a decade later. Tomlinson served his time, but like the IRA prisoners in the H-Blocks, he refused to wear prison clothing and was put into solitary confinement. Years later, a rich and famous actor, he was 'gobsmacked' to discover that Special Branch officers regarded him as a political thug and kept files on him. He should have known that no serious Leftie was safe then, and probably not now.

DAVID TRIESMAN was appointed general secretary of the Labour Party in 2001, but he was not exactly at pains to disclose his full political pedigree. Triesman joined the Labour Party before his seventeenth birthday, he assured members who were quitting in droves three years later. True, but he also joined it again when he was thirty-four, having quit in 1970, the year of Wilson's defeat, to join the Communist Party. He remained in the CP until 1976, before returning to the fold. Triesman first came to public notice in 1968, when he was suspended from Essex University for breaking up a meeting addressed by a defence industry scientist. His fellow students went on strike and forced the university to reinstate him.

After a stint as a youth footballer with Spurs (of whom he remains a passionate fan, like Iain Duncan Smith), Triesman made a career in education trade unionism, becoming general secretary of the Association of University Teachers, from which obscurity he was plucked by Tony Blair to succeed the failing Margaret McDonagh after the general election. He steered the move from Millbank (which was 'a response to a particular historical phase') to Old Queen Street, but could do nothing to stem the haemorrhaging of membership, down from a 1997 high of 400,000 to an estimated 180,000. He also inherited a £6 million debt and a profoundly suspicious trade union movement. The debt is being whittled away at about the rate of membership losses, though not as quickly as trade union disillusion mounts.

VIC TURNER was one, and probably the most politically motivated, member of the Pentonville Five, jailed in July 1972 for defying the orders of the Tory-appointed, but short-lived, National Industrial Relations Court (NIRC). The five – Turner, Derek Watkins, Bernie Steer, Con Clancy and Tony Merrick – were all London dockers. They were active in the long-running battle to sustain the National Docks Labour Scheme, which reserved port work for registered dockers, and was criticised as a 'jobs for life' scheme. A haulage firm, Midland Cold Storage, successfully sought an injunction from the NIRC forbidding the picketing of their container-handling premises in the capital in pursuit of this campaign. Dockers defied the court order, and warrants for contempt were issued in the name of Turner and his four fellow-workers. They were arrested and taken to Pentonville prison. The port of London was immediately paralysed by a strike of 40,000 dock workers. National newspapers were closed by printers striking in support. Sympathy action spread to London buses, and other industries. French dockers promised to 'black' cargoes for the UK. Faced with such an unprecedented wave of anger, the normally pusillanimous TUC General Council called a one-day national (i.e. general) strike in protest at the jailings, and the wider issue of the hated Industrial Relations Act. The stoppage would have been illegal, but in view of the likely widespread support, the Official Solicitor, a little-known figure who looks after the rights of minors and contemnors, moved to have the men released. To tumultuous scenes of welcome from thousands of demonstrators, the Pentonville Five were let out of jail on 26 July.

The fight against the 1971 Industrial Relations Act went on, and was successful. But under Thatcher, the Tories had their revenge, abolishing the dock labour scheme, sacking thousands of men, and tying down the trade unions with repressive legislation that made the 1971 Act look like a charter for civil rights. Vic Turner, a Communist since 1953, was well known in the East End, where he led rent strikes. With the demise of the CP, he joined the Labour Party, became a Newham councillor in 1994 and eventually Mayor of the borough. In 1997, he was awarded the TUC's Gold Badge of Congress, the highest honour it can bestow. That did not stop him supporting the reborn Leninist CPGB. He told the party's *Weekly Worker* that the liquidation of the old Communist Party left him 'with a sense of personal loss as well as a loss for the whole working class movement'.

WAT TYLER is remembered by every schoolboy of my genera-tion as the leader of the peasants' revolt in 1381. He can also be legitimately dubbed the first true British Leftie, and certainly the first to pay with his life. Richard II decided to go after his subjects who were not paying their taxes, levied on every subject aged fifteen or more. A tax collector sought to prove that Tyler's daughter was of taxable age by stripping her naked and assaulting her. Walter Tyler, a man of Kent living in Maidstone, reacted furiously, dashing in the fellow's brains with a hammer. Peasants congratulated him, and elected him leader of a revolt that first took Rochester Castle, then moved to Canterbury, Blackheath and London, where Tyler met Richard II at Smithfield. Tyler approached the fourteen-year-old monarch 'with great confidence, on a little horse, that the commons might see him'. The king asked why he did not disperse his raggle-taggle army of 100,000 men, but in his best shop steward manner Tyler read out a list of demands including complete equality among all people (save only the King), an end to serfdom, and stripping the Church of its wealth.

The king promised concessions, and Tyler got back on his horse calling for beer of which he drank 'a great draught'. An argument arose with a king's valet who accused Tyler of being the greatest thief and robber in Kent. Wat tried to stab him, and in the resulting mêleé, William Walworth, the Mayor of London, slashed him with his cutlass. He was taken to St Bartholomew's hospital, but Walworth had him brought out and beheaded. Tyler's head was taken to the king on a pole. The revolt collapsed. The peasants 'fell to the ground there among the wheat'. Richard promised the rebels a pardon and free passage home, but as with the way with kings, reneged on his pledge and hanged 1,500 presumed ringleaders after trials in which Judge Tresilian warned the jurors that they would hang if they failed to convict. So ended the first big strike against the establishment.

U

HARRY URWIN was the quiet one with the white hair who stood just a little way behind **Jack Jones** when the TGWU was in the news. He was the union's deputy general secretary, destined always to be the bridegroom to his charismatic chief. Urwin, the son of a Durham miner, worked briefly in the pits before heading for the burgeoning manufacturing centre of the Midlands in wartime. He followed Jones up the union's promotional ladder, concentrating on industrial law and shop-floor organisation. His dry sense of humour could be heard in derisive remarks about the 'gold-plated six' – TUC leaders (including Jones) who sat on the National Economic Development Council. Urwin was TUC negotiator with Employment Secretary James Prior on the Tories' first tranche of union reforms in 1979, and scorned government assurances of flexibility with this story: police who caught a boy writing 'All coppers are bastards' on a wall merely ticked him off and then took him for a ride in their squad car. Next day, they caught him again, this time writing, 'All coppers are cunning bastards.' Urwin died in 1996, aged eighty.

W

BOB WAREING is the Charlie Drake from hell, in the eyes of the Blairites. He was suspended from Parliament in 1997, for failing to register a Serbian business interest, and joined virtually every anti-government rebellion of New Labour's two parliaments. The son of a Scouse lorry driver, Robert Nelson Wareing was educated at a council school in Liverpool and the local high school, Bolton College of Education, before taking an economics degree extramurally at London University. He became a college lecturer, and was elected to Merseyside County Council, becoming Labour chief whip and chairman of economic development, and at his third attempt entered Parliament as MP for West Derby in 1983. In his maiden speech, he claimed that the media were trying to destroy the Labour Party, and then proceeded to give the newspapers as much ammunition as they might wish over the next twenty years, from CND to the Serbs. Few now remember Charlie Drake, the comedian for whom he is a lookalike, and this ballet-loving, Everton-supporting Leftie has given more entertainment than offence.

PETER WATKINS deserves a place in any compilation of Lefties for his stunning film *The War Game*, which exposed the consummate lie of civil preparedness for nuclear attack on Britain. Harold Wilson's first government and Watkins's bosses at the BBC shamelessly colluded in suppressing the documentary. The furore drove him out of the country to make films in Scandinavia, the USA and France, but his radical edge was never blunted. Decades later, the BBC finally plucked up the courage to show *The War Game*, and it was published on video in

2003. *The Media War*, made after the Gulf conflict in 1991, was his verdict on the manipulation of the media by the military. Before going into semi-retirement in Canada, he made a five-hour reconstruction of the 1871 Paris Commune uprising. At the age of sixty-seven, he had not lost his critical candour, telling Peter Lennon: 'The crisis in television is immense.'

SIDNEY and BEATRICE WEBB are always spoken of in that order, but she was unquestionably the more original and creative of this famous Fabian partnership.

Beatrice Potter was born in 1858, the eighth daughter of a wealthy railway magnate. Her mother had radical political connections, and Herbert Spencer, the philosopher of individualism, was a regular visitor to the family home. Bound by the conventions of the day, 'Bee' longed for an epic life, like St Theresa. Educated at home by a progressive graduate of Newnham College, Cambridge, she smoked and talked philosophy late into the night. Her passionate sense of engagement first found an outlet in the East End of London, as a social investigator. The poor had different names for her: busybody being the kindest. She took over the management of Katherine Buildings, dockland tenements for the casual labourers, campaigning against dirt, laziness and 'immorality'. Loose women were unhesitatingly evicted. Beatrice herself was desperately in love with Joseph Chamberlain, the twice-married Liberal politician, but believed that marriage would be 'intellectual suicide'.

She was well launched on her career as a social engineer when she met Sidney Webb, a clerk, the son of a woman hairdresser, who wore shiny suits and spoke with a Cockney accent. George Bernard Shaw thought him the ablest man in England, but Sidney was also ugly and unattractive to women. A broken heart in Brussels prompted thoughts of suicide, but Beatrice was a revelation: a handsome, rich, well-connected woman with intellectual instincts like his own. He wooed her with radical promises, insisting 'together we could move the world', Quite where to was not clear. She helped him with his book on the co-operative movement, while 'the loving comrade' worked on her *History of Trade Unionism*. The marriage of fellow workers followed in 1892, soon after Sidney was elected as a progressive councillor on the London County Council. But that was far enough for Beatrice. She discouraged him from seeking a parliamentary constituency, and they settled in Millbank with two maids, far away from the 'barbarians' of Katherine Buildings.

Beatrice was slow to quit her anti-suffragist, anti-ILP attitudes. The politics were all in her head. She found the miners 'dense' – as well she might, given their different educational fortunes. But she and Sidney forged ahead, with the creation of the Fabian Society and then of the London School of Economics, their 'child'. There were no real ones. In 1905, she was appointed to a Royal Commission on the Poor, where her reformist ideas met strong opposition. She had been appointed by the Tory leader, Arthur Balfour, with whom there was a mutual attraction. Her biographer Caroline Seymour-Smith suggests that Beatrice fantasised about sex with powerful men. But there is no evidence that it came to anything. She was shocked even by sexually explicit statuary on a tour of India with Sidney, and appears to have given up sex after the age of fifty. While Sidney was active in forming the Labour Party, Beatrice did not join until her sixtieth year, and even then was unsure if it was ready to form an opposition, much less a government.

Sidney finally entered Parliament for the 'dense' miners of Seaham, County Durham, in 1922. Naturally, the Webbs wrote a book about the miners. After Ramsay MacDonald's famous victory in 1923, Webb went into the Cabinet as President of the Board of Trade. In the second Labour administration of 1929, Webb took the Colonial Office and became Lord Passfield. Meanwhile, Beatrice wrote her autobiography, before turning to what she saw as her vision of the future: the Soviet Union. The Russian ambassador, Sokolnikov, graced her dinner table, and in 1932, after Sidney had abandoned the treacherous MacDonald and his national government, the Webbs went to the USSR. It was not quite what Beatrice expected. There were no chamber-pots on the boat, prompting an irate latter to the captain, but once in Moscow, she fell 'hopelessly in love' with Communism, noting with approval that there was 'singularly little spooning' in public parks. Back home, Stalin's portrait dominated the staircase. At the age of eighty-three she was still writing pamphlets with catchy titles like 'The Truth About Soviet Russia'. She did not live to see her ideas about the welfare state enacted by the Attlee government, dying in 1943, but 'the goat' Sidney did, living until 1947. They are the only couple whose ashes are interred in Westminster Abbey. The jury is still out on their philosophy of 'the inevitability of gradualness'.

SID WEIGHELL liked to be called a Yorkshire terrier, a working class-hero battling on behalf of underpaid railwaymen. In fact, he was more of a poodle to successive generations of Labour leaders, a loyalty that proved fatal when he finally overplayed his hand.

The son of a railwayman from Northallerton, Yorkshire, he was a semi-professional footballer while working on the LNER footplate. He was also active in the Labour Party, acting as agent in his native constituency. But his first love was the union through whose ranks he rose swiftly to become general secretary in 1972, in succession to Sir Sidney Greene. Weighell energetically support the Wilson government's Social Contract, deriding wage militancy as 'snouts in the trough'. In defiance of his delegation's wishes, Weighell secretly cast the NUR block vote for a 'moderate' of his own stripe, rather than the left-wing candidate of the NUM. His treachery came to light when the votes were recounted for quite another reason. Weighell realised that the game was up, and offered his resignation. He then appealed to the NUR delegate conference that had mandated him, hoping for a reprieve. But his resignation was accepted by a clear margin, and he fell on the sword of his own forging. Weighell died in 2002. He married twice, his first wife and daughter dying in a road accident in 1956 while he was at the wheel.

CHARLIE WHELAN climbed to success on the back of New Labour, and then spectacularly repudiated it after conceiving a visceral hatred of **Tony Blair** and **Peter Mandelson**. Best known as the man who made, or at least promoted, government policy on the Euro from his mobile phone outside the Red Lion pub in Whitehall, he was a great deal more integral to the success of **Gordon Brown** than superficial observers have grasped.

Whelan is a somewhat contradictory figure. He was born in 1954, the son of a Tory-voting civil servant, and went to a minor public school in Surrey after failing his 11-plus. He became a Communist while taking a degree in politics at the City of London Polytechnic. Whelan was a fixer in the National Union of Students when future Labour Cabinet ministers such as **John Reid** (another CP member at the time) and Charles Clarke were finding their way to power. He worked for a time as a foreign exchange dealer in the City, before the Leftie urge took him to work, at very modest pay, as a dogsbody for the Amalgamated Union of Engineering Workers. There he met and formed a lifelong political associ-ation with **Jimmy Airlie**, hero of the UCS work-in on Clydeside and latterly the union's national secretary for the motor industry and a member of its executive council. Airlie was a Leftie legend, and it is no exaggeration to say that Whelan worshipped him.

By degrees, Whelan moved up the promotion ladder at the AUEW, becoming head of media relations and simultaneously reviving his old skills as a fixer behind the scenes in relations with other unions. His casual, jaunty style, coupled with an ability to hold his drink as well as the most hardened industrial or political correspondents, belied the serious nature of his political mission. But in the aftermath of the One Member, One Vote battle in the Labour Party, in which he played a prominent role, he came to the eyes of the Labour leadership. After the 1992 general election he was approached by Peter Mandelson to come and work for the party. Whelan, who had left the CP in 1990, agonised briefly and then agreed to go, but only if he could work directly either for Tony Blair or Gordon Brown.

He was taken on in 1993, joining the Shadow Chancellor's team at about the same time as Ed Balls, his economics adviser recruited from the *Financial Times*. This formidable trio set about killing off Labour's traditional 'tax and spend' image and fashioning a new trust for the party among voters. Brown, a former television journalist, had been the most profuse feeder of newspaper offices' fax machines, but Whelan slashed his output, severely rationed his interviews and made him a remote, austere figure more befitting the public's idea of a chancellor. The makeover worked, but his sedulous promotion campaign took an Exocet hit when John Smith died and Blair (covertly backed by Mandelson) immediately thrust himself into pole position to succeed as leader – despite a long-standing understanding between him and the Shadow Chancellor that Brown, much his senior in every respect, would have first crack at the leadership.

From this point can be dated Whelan's loathing of Blair and Mandelson, for what he (rightly) saw as their treachery. When New Labour triumphed at the polls in 1997, Blair spent two hours in the rose garden of Number 10 begging Brown to get rid of Whelan, whom he saw as the dangerous co-architect of a 'government within a government' at the Treasury. Brown refused, and the three musketeers entered government together. For almost two years, Whelan enjoyed the high life of a top government spin doctor: travel, a raffish relationship with the media, but also grinding hard work to achieve brilliant exposure for 'his' Gordon. Blair made repeated attempts to get rid of him, but Brown defended Whelan. However, tensions at the highest levels of government finally exploded when this author, having written a life of Gordon Brown, published *Mandy*, an unauthorised biography of Peter Mandelson. It revealed the secret £373,000 loan made to Mandelson to buy a luxury flat in fashionable Notting Hill.

In the furore that followed, Mandelson was forced to resign as a minister. Whelan, wrongly accused of being the source of the leak, came under intense pressure to quit. The newspapers treated his role as a splash story, and tabloid editors despatched reporters to find him in northern Scotland in the New Year of 1999. Under the influence of Airlie (now dead), Whelan had conceived an abiding passion for the Highlands. Taking as his maxim 'spin doctors must go when they – not the politician for whom they work – become the story', Whelan resigned. Unlike Mandelson, who was given compensation for loss of ministerial office, he received nothing. He was joined on his walk into the wilderness by Geoffrey Robinson, Paymaster General, who had loaned the money to Mandelson: the first recorded case of a politician sacked for being on the give, not the take.

But this was not the end. Whelan found himself strongly in demand for newspaper and television interviews, appearances that soon translated into real work as a columnist and commentator in publications as various as the *New Statesman* and the *Mail on Sunday*. He turned down a £200,000 publishing contract to write a book on his years inside the Brown camp, pleading loyalty to his old boss. He continues to write and broadcast, spending much time with his partner Philippa Clarke in the home on Speyside he bought from his earnings as a journalist. He remains a member of the Labour Party, still optimistic that Brown will succeed Blair. His language might have been unduly colourful – his favourite description of a story he wished to kill was 'absolute parcel of bollocks' – but at least he offered a human face to New Labour, something sadly lacking in the hostile, vindictive years that followed. He was Gary Lineker to Alastair Campbell, Blair's Vinnie Jones.

ELLEN WILKINSON ended her controversial life at the age of fifty-six in 1947 with an overdose of barbiturates. She was the only woman member of the Attlee cabinet, and as Education Minister introduced free school milk (a privilege withdrawn by Margaret Thatcher).

But she was best known as 'Red Ellen', the firebrand socialist with red hair to match, who walked at the head of the Jarrow March against unemployment in 1935. She was then Labour MP for Jarrow, where eight out of ten were jobless. Her own long march began in Manchester where she was born in 1891, the daughter of a textile worker who voted Conservative. Her mother, of course, did not have a vote, and Wilkinson was an early suffragette. She read history at Manchester University and became deeply involved in left-wing movements: for peace, for jobs, trade unionism and feminism. In 1920, while an official of the Co-op workers' union, she was a founding member of the Communist Party and attended the Red International in Moscow a year later. By 1924, however, she quit and was elected MP for Middlesbrough.

She became PPS to Health Minister Arthur Greenwood, the notorious drunk, but lost her seat in 1931, but returned to Jarrow four years later, a constituency she represented to her death. Harold Nicolson confided to his diary: 'I do so like that little spitfire.' Others shared his admiration, and more. **John Platts-Mills** has described Ellen entertaining guests in black trousers like pyjamas, in her ill-lit flat, which was partly coloured black, including the 'seductive boudoir'. It was common knowledge, he added, that she was 'in extremely close relations' with Herbert Morrison. In Parliament, though she was 'rather homely', her flaming red hair and 'jolly good figure' proved attractive. 'She could, and did, get on with everybody, and she was into everything,' recollected Platts-Mills. He also lays her disillusion with the Labour government's achievements directly at the door of Ernest Bevin. Her achievements were real, however.

She raised the school leaving age to fifteen, and as a backbencher reformed the hire purchase laws to stop unscrupulous traders battening upon the poor.

EMLYN WILLIAMS, the miners' leader not the playwright, was a short, wiry, sharp-witted, chain-smoking man who had a way with the girls on the mountainside in South Wales. Known affectionately as 'Swanny' after the Swan Hotel in Aberdare kept by his grandfather, Williams was the architect of the disciplined return to work that ended the great pit strike for jobs of 1984/5. As president of the Welsh NUM, he led a solid walkout in his coalfield that lasted almost a year. By contrast, miners elsewhere had 'scabbed' to such a degree that half the industry's workforce had gone back. The solidarity in his area gave Williams the moral authority to demand that the union call off the dispute with an orderly march back, brass bands blowing and heads held high.

When **Arthur Scargill**, refused to use his presidential casting vote on the NUM executive to grasp this exit strategy, Williams called him a coward to his face and won the backing of a special delegate conference to end the greatest dispute since 1926. Williams followed his father down the pit, and after war service in a tank regiment, he returned to the coal face but eventually became full-time official in the Valleys. He was part of the NUM Left Forum, which, in the 1960s, gradually wrested control of this once-powerful union from the 'moderates', but Williams was always a Labour man, not a Communist, and he shared the Welsh scepticism about Scargill. He served on the party's national executive for a couple of years, before falling victim to the general disapproval of 'Scargillism'. He could be a stern father-figure in public, rounding on some – very much younger and larger – rowdy miners at a conference: 'Call yourselves socialists? Behave yourselves.' They did. Williams died in 1995, ten years after retiring to his pint and game of crib in the British Legion club, Cwm Bach.

AUDREY WISE is not mentioned in the *Dictionary of Labour Biography*, but she is assured of an honoured place here. She infuriated male commentators, who called her a Geordie housewife who could not tell Stork from butter and spoke like a Dalek. But she was an undeviating Leftie of the kind who would now never be allowed near Westminster by the Labour Party. Born in Newcastle in 1935, the daughter of a shop worker who sat on the city council, she went to the local high school before becoming a shop assistant, receptionist, shorthand typist and researcher.

Aged twenty-one, she was elected to Tottenham Borough Council, and won Coventry South-West in the 1974 'who rules?' election while the miners were on strike – with her total support. She immediately plunged into every left-wing controversy available, from nuclear weapons to workers' control, and was to be found on the Grunwick picket lines. But her stridency did not pay off electorally. In 1979, Wise lost her seat, not returning until 1987 when her high profile as a constituency member of Labour's national executive helped her secure the nomination for safe Preston South. Wise promptly resumed hostilities against the Labour leadership from within the Campaign and Tribune groups, opposing the bombing of Iraq and Yugoslavia and the expulsion of Militant. **Tony Benn** asked her to be his running mate in a challenge to Kinnock. She refused.

Wise was proud to be the first elected woman president of her (and her father's) union, USDAW. She was a long-standing member of the Health Select Committee, and an indefatigable disciple of Leftiousness until her death from a brain tumour in 2000. Benn said: 'If half the Labour MPs were of the kind that Audrey Wise was Parliament would be transformed, because she wasn't frightened by anybody.'

DEIRDRE WOOD, a perfectly harmless Leftie, was destroyed by the right-wing tabloid press in the critical by-election at Greenwich, south London in 1987. Her defeat at the hands of the long-defunct SDP prompted a major rethink in Labour strategy, designed to rule out any repeat of that political débâcle. Wood, a rotund, 'forty-ish' lady with few claims to the intellectual high ground, was a member of the Inner London Education Authority (also defunct). After the death of the sitting right-wing Labour MP, Guy Barnett, she was chosen to fight the seat a few months ahead of Neil Kinnock's first general election contest. She promised the leader 'not to drop him in it', then proceeded to do so.

The *Daily Mail* exposed her 'big fat lie' – that she was forty-four. It was also disclosed that she was living in some style with a man who had been a militant shop steward in the 1979 winter of discontent, and now ran a newsagent's shop that sold porn videos. Her father was exposed as a violent drunkard thrown out by her mother. She had also supported the ultra-Left on the GLC in their defiance of the law by not setting a rate. When her media minders tried to turn the tables, the operation turned into a fiasco, in which 'a lachrymose Deirdre Wood relived her grim working-class childhood', according to Andy McSmith, then a Labour Party press officer. For her minders, it was the by-election from hell, and Labour went down to a dramatic defeat. Perversely, the local party chose her to fight the general election, with exactly the same result, after which Ms Wood disappeared into obscurity.

TONY WOODLEY emerged from the woodwork as the Leftie who took on the Transport and General Workers' Union establishment, and won. In May 2003 he secured the general secretaryship easily against Jack Dromey, promising to 'put Labour back into the party' and to take a tougher line against employers.

One telephone call to ex-Rover chief John Towers, begging him to head the Phoenix venture to save the Longbridge car-making plant, brought him fame. The ploy worked, saving the jobs of tens of thousands of workers in Birmingham from the clutches of venture capitalists Alchemy. Woodley was then automotive group secretary of the TGWU.

Within a year the members had rewarded him with the union's number two job.

It was a dizzy upward climb for an 11-plus failure, born in 1948 in Wallasey, who left school at fifteen with no qualifications. 'Our primary school teachers looked at us, decided who would be able to afford a grammar school uniform and gave them special attention,' he recalled. 'The system failed people like me.' Woodley went into the merchant navy, but returned to land and a job at Vauxhall's Ellesmere Port works. Like his father, a convenor at the plant, he also became a shop steward and then full-time officer based in Birkenhead *en route* to national office. He made no bones of his Leftie credo, telling voters in the 2003 leadership election: 'I am not a supporter of New Labour. It has been too concerned with doing favours for business, too wedded to privatisation, too dismissive of trade union concerns to merit the unconditional support every trade union would like to give a Labour government. If the interests of T&G members clash with government policy, so be it.'

Woodley has a long scar across the right-hand side of his face, a childhood injury inflicted when he was knocked down by a car. Some of his supporters hope he will leave the scars on **Blair**'s back that he once figuratively boasted about, but he is likely to prove more pragmatic than polemic.

Z

KONNI ZILLIACUS is the political list compiler's dream, being the only Leftie (apart from Zinoviev, who does not qualify) whose name begins with the last letter of the alphabet. After his death in 1967, he was exposed as a Soviet agent by spy writer Chapman Pincher, but his ambiguous loyalties had long been known to Labour Party leaders. Pincher claims that Zilliacus appeared on a secret list of 'underground' CP members procured by MI5 in 1955. He had been a Labour MP for a decade at that stage, and influential in the shaping of the party's foreign policy in pre-war years. We have it on the authority of the Communist defector **Douglas Hyde** that such figures did indeed exist. In 1945, he recollected, a man telephoned him at the *Daily Worker* and announced he was the new Labour MP for his constituency. 'He followed it with a loud guffaw and rang off. I had known him as a Communist Party man for years.' When the full election results were published, the CP had 'at least eight or nine cryptos' in the Commons in addition to its two publicly acknowledged MPs.

Zilliacus was born in Kobe, Japan, in 1894, the son of mixed Finnish-Scots parentage, and educated partly in Britain. In the First World War, he served in the Royal Flying Corps, but more significantly as an intelligence officer in the British Military Mission in Siberia where his sympathies lay with the revolution rather than his military superiors.

He joined the Labour Party in 1919, and worked for the League of Nations Secretariat in the inter-war years. Zilliacus's strongly anti-fascist memorandum on war and peace was adopted by the party conference in 1934, but he quit the League over Munich and returned to Britain to work for the Ministry of Information. He was an open advocate of closer relations with the USSR and co-operation between socialists and Communists at home.

That was acceptable in wartime, but after 1945, when he was elected MP for Gateshead, very much less so. 'Zilli' accused the Attlee government of risking war with the USSR by slavishly following US foreign policy, and in 1949 he was expelled from the party. The Russians were not so keen on him, because of his links with breakaway Yugoslav President Tito. According to Andy McSmith, Stalin's police 'tortured Hungarian and Czechoslovak Communists into confessing that Zilliacus was a British spymaster'. Readmitted to the party in 1952, he was elected MP for Manchester Gorton. Zilliacus was active in the Victory for Socialism campaign, prompting Labour leaders to draw up secret files on his activities. They denounced the 'crypto-Communists' group of MPs in 1961, and Zilliacus was suspended for two years. Briefed by the garrulous right-wing George Brown, Pincher claimed that Zilliacus used his parliamentary position to associate overtly with KGB agents. He lingered on in Parliament for five more years, before taking his secrets to the grave.